Introductory Certificate in Marketing

Introductory Certificate in Marketing

David R. Harris and Neil Botten

Routledge
Taylor & Francis Group

LONDON AND NEW YORK

First published by Butterworth-Heinemann

This edition published 2011 by Routledge

2 Park Square, Milton Park, Abingdon, Oxon OX14 4RN
Simultaneously published in the USA and Canada by Routledge
711 Third Ave, New York, NY 10017

First edition 2008

Notice
No responsibility is assumed by the publisher for any injury and/or damage to persons
or property as a matter of products liability, negligence or otherwise, or from any use
or operation of any methods, products, instructions or ideas contained in the material
herein.

British Library Cataloguing in Publication Data
A catalogue record for this book is available from the British Library.

Library of Congress Cataloguing in Publication Data
A catalogue record for this book is available from the Library of Congress.

ISBN: 978 1 85617 524 1

Designed and typeset by P.K. McBride

Printed and bound in India by Replika Press Pvt. Ltd.

Contents

Part 2: Understanding customer relations 87

Part 1
What is marketing?

Overview

The first half of this book covers Unit 1 of the Introductory Certificate in Marketing syllabus.

This part of the syllabus seeks to provide the backdrop to the importance of marketing in terms of what marketing is and how it is defined. It focuses on the role of marketing, its cross-functional importance and its contribution to business success. It also looks at the role of marketing as a service provider within the organisation.

It provides a basic understanding of the internal and external marketing environment and the marketing mix, with consideration of how these factors differ from one sector to another.

It also provides the foundations needed for the functional and aspirational goals of the Level 3 market, whilst giving explanation to the language and terminology of marketing.

After working through this half of the book, students should be able to demonstrate a sound knowledge and understanding of marketing and its contribution to organisational success.

Overarching learning outcomes

By the end of this unit, students should be able to:

◆ Define marketing in the context of an exchange process.

◆ Determine the importance of marketing as a cross-functional activity contributing towards business success.

◆ Explain the importance of understanding the organisation's marketing environment and the impact it has upon an organisation's ability to satisfy customer needs and wants.

◆ Identify each element of the marketing mix in the context of customer needs and achieving customer satisfaction.

◆ Apply the marketing mix to a range of different organisational sectors and contexts.

Learning outcomes and syllabus content

Chapter 1

Understanding the role and function of marketing (weighting 15%)

1.1 Define marketing as an exchange process

1.2 Explain the role of marketing in achieving customer satisfaction

1.3 Determine the importance of the role of marketing as a cross-functional activity within the organisation. The links with marketing and other functions

1.4 Explain the key differences between internal and external marketing and the role of marketing as an internal service provider within the organisation.

Chapter 2

Understanding the marketing environment (weighting 30%)

2.1 Explain the importance of understanding the organisation's marketing environment in order to effectively manage the marketing process, and satisfy customer needs.

2.2 Explain the concept of the PESTEL model and show how each of these factors impact upon the organisation, its ability to undertake marketing activities successfully, cost-effectively and competitively.

2.3 Identify the key characteristics of the micro-marketing environment.

2.4 Explain the processes that can be used for monitoring the marketing environment.

Chapter 3

The marketing mix (7 Ps) (weighting 40%)

3.1 Explain the importance of the 7 Ps of the marketing mix as a series of tools co-ordinated to develop and delivered to meet customer needs and wants

Chapter 4

How marketing is applied in different organisational contexts (weighting 15%)

4.1 Explain the different ways in which customers (Business to Business) and consumers (Business to Consumer) make their buying decisions.

4.2 Explain the different ways in which the marketing mix is used in different organisations to influence the buying-decision making units.

Unit 1
The role and function of marketing

Marketing as an exchange process

Definitions of marketing

Newspapers and other media tend to use 'marketing' as an alternative to selling, advertising, or retailing. Marketing is, however, a much broader concept embracing all these areas plus many others besides. Marketing is in evidence all around us, from the packaging on the products we buy, to our recognition of companies through their logos and symbols, or the television advertisements we watch. The choices we make as consumers are likely to be shaped in some way by marketing. So what exactly is marketing?

The Chartered Institute of Marketing (CIM), when answering this question, suggests that all organisations either knowingly or unknowingly engage in marketing to some degree:

> *Think about what you do. You probably make a particular effort to know your customers well. Your instincts tell you that getting to know what your customers want on an individual basis and giving it to them is what will keep you in business. You know that you can't stand still, and that you need to improve and extend existing products and sometimes develop new ones. (CIM)*

If this description rings true, then your marketing activity closely fits the classical definition of marketing.

> **Marketing is –** the management process responsible for identifying, anticipating and satisfying customer requirements profitably. (CIM)

This definition acknowledges the importance of the customer, their requirements and the careful planning processes needed to achieve the organisation's goals. It follows that marketing is a business activity that should be at the core of any organisation. Marketing is relevant to any business irrespective of its size or nature of operation. Kotler (2003) is not alone in believing it is key to achieving organisational goals.

> *It is all about getting the right product or service to the customer at the right price, in the right place, at the right time. Business history and current practice both remind us that without proper marketing, companies cannot get close to customers and satisfy their needs. And if they don't, a competitor surely will.*

The exchange process

The process of marketing is said by Michael Baker, University of Strathclyde, to be:

> *concerned with the establishment and maintenance of mutually satisfying exchange relationships.*

In order that this process can actually embed itself within the organisational culture, we must ensure that our customers become aware of the products and services that have been developed to meet their needs. Communication is, therefore, key to the continuance of the marketing process and continuous evolution of the products and services offered.

Figure 1.1: Exchange relationships

Baker's definition also encompasses the communication between the organisation and its immediate environment (Figure 1.1). It is essential that relationships with other stakeholders such as suppliers, distributors and the internal audience are fully developed to ensure mutually beneficial communication will result in sustainable competitive advantage for all involved in the process.

Marketing and customer satisfaction

Marketing, analysis and planning

When we looked at definitions earlier, the first definition of marketing was based on 'identifying, anticipating and satisfying customer requirements'. This definition clearly shows that the marketing process has a close relationship with various stages of the strategic planning process, as follows.

◆ During the analysis of the organisational environment, marketing can perform marketing research to help the organisation understand the nature of customers, markets and competitors. It is important that any such analysis is not just static (i.e. looking at current customer requirements), but also dynamic (in terms of forecasting changing customer requirements over the planning period).

◆ During the analysis of the organisation's position, marketing research can focus on the effectiveness (or otherwise) of the current marketing activity.

◆ During the setting of objectives, marketing should ensure that customer satisfaction is at the centre of the organisation's aims (see below).

◆ When identifying and evaluating alternative strategies, marketing can evaluate the likely impact of strategic options, both on the organisation's marketing function and on customers.

Making customer satisfaction a business objective

Satisfying customers is at the heart of marketing. Who then assumes responsibility for this important function? Possibly the marketing department or the sales force? True, such personnel can have an influence on customer satisfaction, but marketing as a philosophy is wider than this narrow group of employees. Employees outside the marketing department or sales force can also play an important role in determining customer satisfaction.

Marketing is more than just a range of techniques that enables the company to determine customer requirements; rather it is a shared business ethos. The marketing concept is a philosophy that places customers central to all organisational activities. The long-term strategies of an organisation might be centred on profit maximisation, market share growth, or growth in real terms but none of this can be achieved without satisfying customers. Without customers there would be no business.

Organisations who put customer needs first and provide products and services that meet these needs in this way are said to be 'market orientated'. Some organisations however still reject or ignore such a philosophy. For these organisations making products assumes prime concern followed by an attempt to 'get customers'.

Boddy and Paton (2002) summarised alternative organisational philosophies into four categories. Business may have a number of orientations:

◆ With a **production orientation**, the managers consider the priority is making products affordable and available. Customers are considered to be only concerned with price. The management's energy is directed to lowering the costs of both production and physical distribution.

◆ The **product orientation** assumes that the product itself is the primary driver for the consumer. The assumption is that customers want supreme quality and functionality. In the new product design process, this orientation can result in products with features (involving additional production costs) that consumers simply do not want or use. This orientation can occur when senior management have a technical orientation and are more concerned with the product, than the consumer. 'Build a better mouse trap and the world will beat a path to your door' is not marketing reality.

◆ **Sales orientation** assumes that consumers are reluctant to buy products and all that is needed is heavy promotion and sales. In the past, telesales in the area of home improvements (e.g. double glazing) focused on this type of orientation. It can develop out of a product orientation when the 'product' does not sell itself.

◆ **Marketing orientation** starts with the philosophy that only if the organisation understands the benefit needs and wants of the consumer can it devise products and services that satisfy the marketplace.

The word 'marketing' can be used to describe a function (the Marketing Department) or an activity. However, it also describes a culture and orientation where all the people in the organisation appreciate their role in delivering ultimate customer satisfaction. In new product development, there is no debate as to if the process should be 'market-led' or

7

'technology-driven'. Products that do not satisfy consumer benefit needs will not succeed. Products that are poorly designed and poorly manufactured will not succeed. In the market-orientated organisation, the satisfaction of customers is seen as central to the development and maintenance of long-term profitability. This implies the integration of all the business functions to arrive at customer-centred marketing performance.

Question 1.1

Under what market conditions could product orientated organisations best succeed?

Activity 1.1

Re-read the descriptions of the different orientations and identify organisations, with which you are familiar, that seem to fit each orientation.

The evolution of marketing

Stages in the evolution of marketing can be identified within the UK, linked to periods in history:

◆   **The production era** – The rapid growth in production from factories towards the end of the Industrial Revolution gave rise to this thinking. Rising standards of living fuelled demand, but customer preferences were not accounted for, instead output was maximised wherever possible.

◆   **The sales era** – 'The depression' due to the downturn in the world economy through to the immediate post Second World War period provided a background. In order to stay competitive firms needed to sell goods rather than just produce them. A growing expertise in sales techniques developed including more attention being paid to advertising.

◆   **The marketing era** – When in the early 1960s demand for goods was matched by supply, organisations began to try to better understand their customer base, and the use of segmentation and differentiation strategies heralded a new era.

◆   **The relationship era** – Towards the very end of the twentieth century, organisations began to realise that transactional marketing was a risky approach, as customers were far less loyal than previously. This led to the development of relationship marketing, where far greater emphasis is placed on customer loyalty.

Ensuring marketing practices secure customer retention

Everyone wants to retain their existing customers. Few companies, however, are implementing positive strategies aimed at retention. Most companies are organised for customer acquisition. Their advertising and sales programmes are designed to find and promote their products and services to new customers. The companies are organised on a product or brand basis, not on a customer segment basis. While they all have customer service departments, and most have a customer service free-phone number, they lack an integrated marketing strategy that is directed at retention, and that defines retention as the measurement of success.

You have probably heard it said that 'It's ten times cheaper to keep a customer than it is to get a new one.' Most people would agree with this statement, even though they have no way of proving it. Indeed, the majority of large organisations today are experimenting with database marketing programmes aimed, in large part, at retention. Most of these companies are not yet sure whether their experiments will be successful.

Question 1.2

Think back to the old corner grocer. Prior to 1960, most groceries in the UK and US were sold in small grocery stores. The proprietor would meet you at the door. He knew you by name. He knew your preferences. He would put things aside for you. He built his business through recognising his customers and doing favours for them. How has the growth in supermarkets changed this situation?

Marketing as a cross-functional activity

Marketing and the organisation

The modern view is that marketing activity does not just happen within the marketing department. For such activity to be effective, the marketing function needs to interact with other functions throughout the organisation (as shown in Figure 1.2).

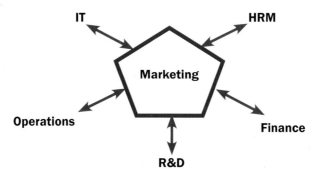

Figure 1.2: Marketing as an integrated activity

For this integrated approach to work, there needs to be a dialogue between marketing and each of the other functions. Marketing is both customer and supplier to each function (as discussed in the next section on internal customers), and there is an assumption implicit in any customer relationship that information will be complete, accurate and on time. Some of the main information exchanges are identified in tables 1.1 to 1.6.

Question 1.3

What are the marketing-related information exchanges between the other functions, shown on Figure 1.1, that do not directly involve marketing?

What might the benefits of an 'integrated approach' be, to the organisation and to the customer?

Table 1.1: Information exchanges with research and development

Topic	Information from marketing	Information to marketing
Customer	Ideas for new or changed products, to meet new or changing customer needs	Products in development, their features and benefits
Timings	When best to launch products, bearing in the state of the market, or competitor activity	Lead-times, and forecasts of new product development schedules

Table 1.2: Information exchanges with human resource management

Topic	Information from marketing	Information to marketing
Planned activity levels and financial implications	The nature and timing of planned activity, to ensure appropriate human resources are available	Resource availability and constraints
Organisational design	The future size and shape of the marketing department	Organisational policy and procedure relating to staff levels, recruitment, selection, redundancy, etc.

Table 1.3: Information exchanges with finance

Topic	Information from marketing	Information to marketing
Budget	Planned activity levels and likely financial implications	Budget allocation
Activity and performance	Actual activity levels and expenditure	Variances from budget, key areas for attention
New projects	Timings, costs, resource usage	Evaluation of the financial feasibility of the project

Table 1.4: Information exchanges with operations

Topic	Information from marketing	Information to marketing
Demand	The likely impact of planned marketing activity on the mix and demand level for products and services	Capacity constraints, and any issues relating to the organisation's ability to meet projected demand levels
Quality	Customer perceptions of product/service quality, and any need to improve	Any likely quality issues, so marketing activity (particularly PR) can be planned
Stock	Levels required to satisfy any likely demand level changes	Availability, and details of any slow-moving items that could be cleared by short-term promotions

Table 1.5: Information exchanges with information technology

Topic	Information from marketing	Information to marketing
Content	Advertising and promotional content to be added to the website/intranet/extranet	New technologies available for communicating marketing messages
Customer service	Answers to queries/FAQs	Queries/FAQs
Design	User requirements for IS functionality	Performance capabilities, technical specifications

Table 1.6: Information exchanges with customer services		
Topic	**Information from marketing**	**Information to marketing**
Feedback	Action taken following customer feedback	Customer comments
Product/service features and benefits	Selling messages	Customer reactions, customer needs/requirements

Internal marketing

Internal and external customers

Customers fall into two main categories, external and internal – each having very different needs and expectations of the organisation.

External customers

These are individuals who have no connection with an organisation, other than that they may have purchased goods or services in the past, or are purchasing at present. They can be either the traditional customer/consumer who buys a multitude of goods and services for their own use or that of their family. This category is referred to as Business-to-Consumer market (or B2C), the business consumer who is buying on behalf of their organisation, known as Business-to-Business (B2B), or individuals selling to one another (C2C).

Internal customers

Internal customers are those people and departments, within your organisation, with whom you exchange the products and services (often information) you create. Consider your internal customers, and how important it is that there is good internal communication in an organisation. Consider also how the roles might sometimes be reversed, with you as the internal customer.

For example when you, as an employee, receive your pay slip from the finance department, you are the customer and expect it to be correct, to be delivered on time and the salary payment actually credited into your bank account. If there is a problem, you expect to be dealt with courteously and promptly. You do not expect to have to engage in lengthy correspondence to rectify a mistake. If you do receive information from the finance department – say, for example, about a new profit-related pay scheme – you expect it to be clearly written and well presented.

At other times, you could be the service provider to your colleagues or line manager; for instance, when you are asked to cost the production of a sales promotion item as part of a future promotional campaign. Your internal customers will expect you to have completed the task on time, accurately, and to present it clearly at the next planning meeting.

Internal marketing

So internal marketing is about working together with colleagues and providing them with a good service so that, as a team, your organisation achieves its goals.

Activity 1.2

Draw a network diagram that shows the customer/supplier relationships between yourself and others in your organisation.

Extranet services for supply chain support

Extranet – a collaborative network that uses intranet technology to link businesses with their suppliers, customers, and other businesses that share common goals. (CIMA)

An extranet can be viewed as a part of a company's intranet that is made accessible to other companies or that is a collaboration with other companies.

Many organisations use this tool as a means to obtain competitive advantage. For example, a computer manufacturer may allow customers to access the support database providing details of parts used in each computer along with known problems or errors with those parts.

This will allow the customer to diagnose faults with their computers more quickly, and also help the manufacturer provide an additional useful service, at effectively zero cost.

The current competitive business climate often requires a team of separate business partners to work together to meet the diverse, complicated, demands of today's markets. This team of partners has been referred to as a 'business ecosystem'. It has been suggested that only a truly cooperative system is suited to assemble the creative ideas necessary to develop complex new products, achieve manufacturing agility, and attain a long-term customer focus. Much of this cooperation can be achieved by applying Internet technology. The fairly recent emergence of extranets may bridge the gap between intranet and Internet applications.

Case study: Tesco

Twelve years ago Tesco, the UK's largest supermarket, and a global operator, hired a company called Dunnhumby to help with the loyalty card that Tesco operated with its customers. In every four-week period nearly two-thirds of UK households shop at Tesco and approximately 15 per cent of all expenditure in shops is taken by Tesco. In part that success is due to the effectiveness of the Clubcard. On behalf of Tesco, Dunnhumby tracked the shopping habits of 13 million households in the UK. A retail analyst at Cazenove recently wrote that the advantage of Tesco was not scale, contrary to popular belief, but the Clubcard. He stated that the card gave an array of tangible benefits across virtually every aspect of the business.

The purchasing behaviour of customers is used to create a picture of the kind of person the cardholder actually is – effectively the same as an observer standing at the checkout counter. Unlike a market researcher, the Clubcard records everything, doesn't forget and does it for virtually every customer rather than a 'representative' sample – it doesn't take long on the analysis either. Judgements can be made about the changing make-up of the family – there are new babies or children have left home – and they can decide whether you are a good cook, or time poor, and make an good estimate of social class.

Approximately 5 billion pieces of data are captured every week. Each separate product has its own set of attributes and these values build a composite picture of the purchasers. The information is stored in an enormous search engine that can be accessed, at a price, by more than 200 consumer goods companies such as Procter & Gamble, Coca Cola and Unilever. The database at Dunnhumby is 40 terabytes in size and is tied into the electoral roll, the Land Registry and the Office of National Statistics. Shortly after a new product is launched, or a new promotional campaign started, those companies can access information which will tell them not only the effect of the launch but who is actually buying. Brand managers can determine whether their new product is appealing to young singles, empty nesters or any other social lifestyle group.

Dunnhumby claim that it is the best source that a supplier can use since no other source is so representative of the population. For £50,000 a year, suppliers get access to a 10 per cent sample of the data in the system. This may seem expensive but it is the largest customer survey in the country and, increasingly, when Tesco buyers make decisions about new products they like to see the projections based on data with which they are familiar. It isn't an industry standard – but Tesco would be very pleased if it were to become so.

For Tesco, the information allows better targeting of customer segments not just by knowing what they do buy but also by what they don't. An example would be meat – which very few families don't buy at some time during a month. Not all families shop exclusively at one supermarket much as Tesco's and others would like them to. By looking at the data for a particular social group Dunnhumby can identify which product categories were missing from the shopping basket – allowing Tesco to make particular offers to try to attract that group to start buying that particular category of product. This would mean that people would come into a store and would spend more each time they visited.

At one store when this approach was first tested the turnover went up by 12 per cent. One of the biggest tests in this direction was wine. Although customers were buying wine in the cheaper varieties they were not buying from the more expensive end of the product range. Mining the data showed that there was insufficient variety at the top end of the range and once choice was offered sales went up significantly. It had been very noticeable that, at Christmas, shoppers were trading up to 'better' wines and these seasonal sales had been lost – until the information became available in such a user friendly form.

Dunnhumby do not use traditional social segments but group people on the basis of what they buy. One category being 'convenience' which is further subdivided into 'time poor, food rich' and 'can't cook, won't cook'. By knowing what customers want, Tesco have been able to make a number of positioning decisions, such as the move into smaller format stores, Tesco Express, the launch of the website, mobile phones, insurance and the Finest Food range. At one early presentation to the board of directors by Dunnhumby, Lord MacLaurin, the former Tesco Chairman, said "you know more about my customers after three months than I know after 10 years'.

Practice objective test questions

A Marketing is a:

1 Communications process

2 Management process

3 Operational process

B According to Boddy and Paton, in what orientation do managers consider the priority to be making products affordable and available?

1 A product orientation

2 A marketing orientation

3 A production orientation

C According to Boddy and Paton, in what orientation does the organisation assume that customers want quality and functionality?

1 A product orientation

2 A marketing orientation

3 A production orientation

D According to Boddy and Paton, what orientation assumes that customers are reluctant to buy goods?

1 A product orientation

2 A marketing orientation

3 A sales orientation

E An exchange where an individual buys on behalf of their organisation is known as:

1 B2C

2 B2B

3 C2C

F An extranet can be viewed as part of a company's:

1 Intranet

2 Supply chain

3 Product portfolio

Further work

Search the Internet for further definitions of marketing.

Look at your organisation's mission statement. Does it appear to imply a marketing orientation? Find mission statements for competitor organisations. Can you see apparently different orientations within your industry?

Re-draw Figure 1.1 from your own point of view. Re-create Tables 1.1 to 1.6 with details of the communications you exchange with your internal customers and suppliers.

Look at the intranet and extranet services provided by your organisation, or one with which you are familiar, and assess their marketing content.

Unit 2 The marketing environment

The importance of the marketing environment

The marketing environment

The environment refers to those things outside any system that have some sort of effect on the way that system operates. As 'marketing' is a sub-system of 'the organisation', we can view the marketing environment as being made up of two component parts (Figure 2.1).

◆ **The internal environment**, consisting of the other parts of the organisation that impact on the operations of the marketing function.

◆ **The external environment**, consisting of those things outside the organisation that affect the way marketing works.

Figure 2.1: The marketing environment

The internal environment

The marketing-orientated organisation is effective and offers goods and services to its customers, which have appropriate market valuation and are affordable. To be profitable, the organisation needs to be efficient and to make and market products and services in the most economic way consistent with the required product quality and standard of service. The value chain provides the marketer with a tool to appraise the internal efficiency and effectiveness of the organisation.

The primary activities are the day-to-day activities that we need to undertake to provide goods and services to the marketplace. However, just as a car will not go forever if it is not refuelled, longer-term support activities are required to ensure that the primary activities can continue successfully. As always with business models, intelligent creative interpretation is required to apply them. The end result of well-tuned, balanced, primary and support activities adds value for the mutual benefit of the organisation and its customers. The value chain model is illustrated (Figure 2.2) and explained below.

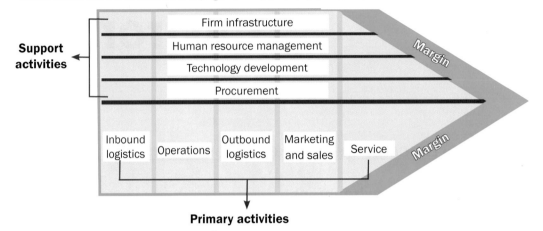

Figure 2.2: The value chain, after M.E. Porter (1980)

Inbound logistics

These are the activities and facilities for receiving raw materials with associated storage and quality procedures for a manufacturing organisation. For a service organisation, this could be ensuring the right number and type of telephone lines, for example, for a telephone-sales insurance company.

Operations

For a manufacturing company, these are the processes used in the manufacture and testing of a product. Typical examples are the manufacture of consumer electronics. Where the product is very expensive and customised, batch assembly might be appropriate. For vast volumes of lower-cost products (e.g. personal stereos), the process may be highly automated. For a service such as insurance, it may be the complex calculations undertaken to evaluate the risk for a new customer and set the appropriate premium, or simply the processing of claims.

Outbound logistics

For the manufacturing organisation, this is the packaging and the physical distribution of the product. This aspect of the value chain clearly links up with the P = Place (physical distribution) of the marketing mix (see Unit 3). Different approaches may be appropriate for the same product under different outlet conditions. In a bar, soft drinks such as cola may be dispensed from a multi-dispenser that uses mains water to dilute concentrated flavoured syrup. This is effective and appropriate as there is a relatively high volume of consumption and the product is consumed immediately on the premises. For home consumption, however, the dilute product is manufactured and packed in non-returnable bottles or cans. For a service such as insurance, the outbound logistics involves the efficient delivery of documentation to the client.

Marketing and sales

For the manufacturing company, the cycle is; customer's order, the product is manufactured or taken out of stock, delivered to the clients and, most importantly, payment is made. Slow payments damage cash flow, which is bad. Non-payment and bad debts are disastrous! The sales cycle involves a number of functions. Sales plans drive the production schedule and stocking requirements. For a supermarket, the sales system can be considered as the checkout. Remember this is not just the laser reader and payment system (electronic point of sale – EPOS), but also involves efficient and friendly operation by a person. The best information and communications systems will not provide a quality experience if run by an unfriendly or poorly trained operator.

Service

Here we have to take care how we define service. This is not the overall efficiency of the value chain but should be taken to cover value-added service for the product or service. As an example, for a car manufacturer this might include maintenance servicing (and spare parts) and financial services such as insurance and a loan to buy the vehicle. For an insurance company, it might involve providing emergency advice (e.g. where to find a plumber at midnight when a pipe bursts). This aspect of the value chain interacts with the service extension of the marketing mix. In a competitive world, one strategy to differentiate a product is to augment its value with added and distinctive service elements.

Firm infrastructure

This covers very general aspects of the business, such as reputation, image and tangible assets. Companies need to ensure they have the relevant approach to their operations and markets. Thus, low-cost airlines are ruthless in cost-cutting with a very basic 'no frills' strategy. Their proposition to the market is that no one will get you there more cheaply and their value chain is tuned to move people at the lowest possible cost to selected low-cost destinations (often at less fashionable or less convenient airports). The leading airlines provide a 'value-for-money service' with a different proposition: to fly people round the world in comfort. This implies a complex interconnecting system of hub and long-haul routes to be operated with comparatively lavish facilities such as 'club' lounges and operating from major airports such as Heathrow. Other issues that need to be considered include whether the organisation wants to be a market leader (implication: heavy investment in research and development) or a market follower.

With customer expectations continually rising, companies have to move beyond ISO 9000 not only to satisfy but also to delight customers. Environmental issues are now so important that they have their own standard, ISO 14000. With strict liability and higher costs of compensation, not only are high standards of safety ethically necessary but also good business sense. Fair treatment of all relevant stakeholders and general corporate behaviour again is not just to make the management and owners feel good, but also to make good business sense. Failure to be considered a good corporate citizen can result in very active disruption of the business by pressure groups (e.g. animal rights campaigners for companies perceived to be conducting unnecessary animal tests). All employees must be committed to safety, quality and environmental issues.

If the organisation's buildings are dilapidated and machinery outdated then poor products and services will be produced, often expensively. The financial structure may affect how the value chain is tuned. In the case of a public company, the shareholders want good share growth and good dividends *now!* Failure to deliver may leave the firm vulnerable to hostile takeover. If an individual wholly owns the business, a longer-term view can be taken, with, say, more investment in research and development resulting in profit further in the future. Similar issues apply to small start-up firms: too often, reliance is placed on bank overdrafts that can be called in at any time, when a different framework of finance requiring longer-term lending would be more appropriate. The wrong financing for an organisation can be just as disruptive as marketing the wrong product or manufacturing using the wrong technology.

Human resource management

No organisation can be better than the people in it. Even with the most effective equipment and the best facilities, customers will not be happy if front-line staff are not well trained and empathetic. Roles and responsibilities must be effectively defined by job descriptions and organisational structures. The nature of people (e.g. recruitment processes and procedures), their skills (e.g. effective training) and motivation (e.g. appropriate reward systems) are key. This aspect also interacts with the marketing mix in the element P = People.

Technology development

To remain a market leader, attention must be paid to developing the product (new product development), the manufacturing operations and logistics (the first three elements of the value chain primary activities), sales (e.g. Internet sales systems) and marketing (e.g. new methods of market research). Any element of the value chain can be improved and needs development for a successful organisation.

Information and communications systems have been added to the traditional value chain model, as an appropriate framework is vital for most companies, and for some e-based organisations it almost is the whole organisation. In knowledge-based industries, the ability to lever knowledge and skills internationally with the Internet, intranets and others is vital. For the modern company, it is just as bad for the computer to crash as for there to be a total power-out. In both cases, all operations can come to a shuddering halt.

Procurement

Procurement, the purchase of the inputs to the value chain, is vital. For a supermarket, the greatest percentage of costs is the price it pays for the items on the shelves. Getting the right products at the right price is vital. Marks and Spencer at one time found that its clothing was perceived to be unfashionable and over-priced. Urgent attention had to be focused on buying products that appealed to customers at prices that were competitive. Procurement not only covers the purchase of the materials for manufacture, but also covers all inputs to the operation. An extra £10,000 of sales may give you £1000 profit. The £10,000 saved in purchasing is £10,000 straight into profit. In marketing, it is vital to get the best prices for printing and media space to get the most out of a limited budget.

Controllable and uncontrollable environmental factors

All organisations will be subject to environmental factors and in many cases these will be uncontrollable. For example any company operating within Europe will be aware of the demographic trends that are leading to an increasingly ageing population. Declining birth rates and longer lives are both contributing to the overall trend, and are not things which companies can influence and, therefore, have no control over the overall effect of more old people. However, if we take the case of a company in the tourism industry they may be able to exercise some control over the factors which are important to them. As the population becomes older and more active in their later years they can modify the holidays they offer and to a small extent influence the nature of holidays that older people take. By marketing holidays specifically for older people they can mitigate the effect of an uncontrollable factor and possibly even capitalise upon it.

The PESTEL model

The PESTEL model – overview

The PESTEL model gives us a framework for analysing the major influences that impact on the marketplace. Major changes in the macro-environment can, at times, take place quickly (for example, 9/11). With rapid changes, it is vital to analyse the impact of the event on the organisation. Slow changes such as shifts in population demographics are also important, since if the organisation is not alert, the change can become so advanced before its impact is detected that major problems arise; even survival may become questionable. For travel agencies, the opening of the Channel Tunnel was a major event, which could be clearly identified. The change in social attitudes to holidays from 'package' to 'à la carte' has been more incremental. However, failure to respond to either would impact on the profitability of the business and service to the customers.

Table 2.1: General overview of selected key PESTEL issues

PESTEL element	Selected key issues
Political	Stability, attitudes to industry, attitudes to competition, climate for 'free trade', attitudes to foreign investors
Economic	Business cycle, inflation rates, interest rates, disposable income, wealth distribution, consumer spending patterns, credit availability, employment levels, exchange rates, taxation
Social/cultural	Demographics, society, culture
Technological	Inventions, discoveries, information technologies
Environmental	Consumer pressure, volatile organic compounds (VOC), Persistent Organic Pollutants (POP), Ozone depletion/CFCs, global warming, genetic engineering issues, environmental fate, laws, sustainable development, life cycle analysis
Legal	Monopolies and mergers, competition, consumer legislation, health and safety, consumer safety (e.g. strict liability), employment law, environmental law, regulations (e.g. labelling), codes of conduct, self-regulation

Political factors

There are a number of facets to 'political' issues. Politics and politicians shape laws, and many organisations see the lobbying of politicians as a key part of their strategic plans. This is not restricted to commercial organisations; social marketing groups have become most active in this area, as seen in the successful campaigning for smoking bans and the current targetting of junk food by the healthy living groups.

Government policy

Government policy is such a broad area and can affect all of the other categories in a PESTEL analysis. Governments will influence the economic factors in a country by deciding taxation rates for individuals and companies, societal factors by education and training policy, technological factors by policies which encourage research and technology transfer, environmental factors by recycling policy and taxation of landfill charges, legal factors by their policy of the sale of goods and credit agreements.

Insight: The downside of smoking bans

As more states pass indoor smoking bans (Illinois and Maryland laws go into effect this year) policymakers are often told there's no downside, says Michael Pakko, an economist at the Federal Reserve Bank of St. Louis. "But I'm sceptical about free lunches," he says. In the January issue of the St. Louis Fed's *Regional Economist* Magazine, Pakko argues that such bans can lead to revenue and job losses. His study of Delaware's three casino-racetracks found a loss of 15% in slot machine revenues in the 2 years after a clean-indoor-air act took effect in 2002. He also cites a 2001-2004 nationwide study by two economists now at the universities of Wisconsin (Milwaukee) and South Carolina. It found smoking bans caused job declines of 4% at bars. "Smoking and drinking go together – they're what we call 'complementary goods,' " says Pakko, who acknowledges that the bans involve "public health as well as economic issues."

Source: Newsweek, 2008

Changing governments

Clearly, a change of government when there are privatisation or nationalisation policies (depending on their political colour) has an impact on the macro-environment.

International politics

There are a number of political bodies that rest above national governments. In Europe this is through the European Union, in North America via the North American Free Trade Agreement (NAFTA), in the Pacific Basin via the Asia-Pacific Economic Forum (AFTA) and through similar pacts in Latin America such as the MERCOSUR customs union. Although these are often considered to be cooperative trade bodies they are, increasingly, political in their outlook and behaviour. Globally, we can add the World Trade Organization to this list of organisations and, as business becomes increasingly more international this body regularly finds itself mediating between the national interests of large companies and industries.

Local government

Organisations also need to consider not only the national political issues but also regional and local ones. Often the expansion plans of a supermarket are dependent on winning a lot of local political debates in order to gain the required planning permissions.

Economic factors

Economics is often seen as a dense and difficult mathematical subject. Certainly, governments employ many statisticians to collect and analyse the figures. However, it is important to realise that economics is at the core of marketing. The Retail Price Index is not a mathematical abstraction. It is an exciting reflection of how people live and how the pattern of spending changes. These reports are excellent sources of secondary data for marketers.

Interest rates

Interest rates will affect the organisation in different ways. As they rise it will impact upon consumers' ability to spend, or borrow to spend, and may reduce demand for products or services on offer. Such a rise will also impact upon the organisation in terms of its own borrowings, this will affect the profitability and may prevent marketing departments obtaining the investment that they need to carry through their plans. However, for companies in the financial services industry a rise in interest rates may encourage potential customers to save rather than spend making it easier to market their services.

Exchange rates

Exchange rates between currencies occur because of the perceived value, or purchasing power, of the currency of a two different countries, or in the case of the EU, groups of countries. The stronger an economy the higher will be the value of its currency against that of a weaker one. Interest rates will also have an effect on exchange rates since, as interest rates rise in one country, those with money to save will tend to deposit in that country since it will earn more interest and is perceived to be safer because of the strength of the currency. At the time of writing, in early 2008, the US dollar is quite weak compared to sterling and the euro and many people are finding it advantageous to fly to America to shop from clothing and other consumer goods. For the marketing manager a currency needs to have value, but that value should not be so high that people prefer to shop in other countries.

Wealth

Economics is much more marketing orientated than some sources would indicate. The value of a house is what people are prepared to pay. This is a consumer issue involving social attitudes and values. When people see that house prices are rising, they can cash in on this (in 2007, the majority of mortgages were not new but re-mortgages) to spend on consumer durables and that longed-for world cruise. When credit is widely available, it is as much how people feel as what they have actually got (disposable income) that drives the high street. If they do not have it they can borrow it.

Taxation and the viability of the business

Taxation affects business in several different ways.

◆ Many goods and services are purchased out of consumer disposable income. An increase in direct taxation (i.e. income tax) will reduce levels of disposable income, and may thus reduce demand.

◆ If goods and services are subjected to indirect taxation (e.g. value added tax) demand may fall as customers perceive price increases.

◆ The level of corporation tax may affect the number of business start-ups, or the growth rates of existing businesses. Higher levels of corporation tax act as a disincentive to earn increased profits.

Social factors

Social influences impact on the consumer decision-making process. Attitudes change quickly; for example, 20 years ago one could smoke on a transatlantic airliner, but now in most countries, the social trend is to have smoking eliminated from public buildings. Social changes can also impact on media habits. The move of the serious daily papers from 'broadsheet' format to 'tabloid' has been in response to commuters wanting something that can be read on crowded public transport.

It should be remembered that elements of the PESTEL model interact. A development in technology (text messaging on mobile phones) can influence social changes in the population (e.g. the development of 'text speak', now being adopted by Scrabble™ players).

Increased mobility

Population shifts can affect the nature of society. Both Europe and North America have become much more multicultural societies, reflecting the global movements of population in the twentieth century. This affects the demand for products and services and this, in turn, generates demand for special communication channels. With broadband technology, TV can now not only be a medium of mass advertising around a soap opera but also become highly targeted for special social groups.

Social marketing

Social marketing was 'born' as a discipline in the 1970s, when Philip Kotler and Gerald Zaltman realized that the same marketing principles that were being used to sell products to consumers could be used to 'sell' ideas, attitudes and behaviours.

Kotler and Andreasen define social marketing as:

> differing from other areas of marketing only with respect to the objectives of the marketer and his or her organization. Social marketing seeks to influence social behaviours not to benefit the marketer, but to benefit the target audience and the general society.

This technique has been used extensively in international health programmes, especially for contraceptives and oral rehydration therapy (ORT), and is being used with more frequency in the United States for such diverse topics as drug abuse, heart disease and organ donation.

Representation of family

The traditional representation of family, as a heterosexual life partnership where the male is the 'breadwinner' and the female is the 'homemaker' is no longer valid. Despite this fact, many marketing campaigns continue the myth that such family units are still the norm. Modern marketing must recognise that there is an increasing diversity in structure of the family unit, and must plan campaigns accordingly. The use of the term 'family' in market segmentation and product targeting is (or should be) obsolete.

International and cultural differences

General cultural knowledge includes implicit theories about the world we live in that are largely shared by the members of our society. But in addition to this shared set of ideas, we also have personal knowledge that can conflict with accepted, culturally derived practices. For example, a boy growing up in China may generally accept the importance of his relationships with others, and therefore seek to keep harmony with family members. But more personal knowledge – such as being exposed to pictures of American cultural icons like Green Day or Madonna – may lead him to wear clothes that his parents don't like.

Notions about cultural differences are often the basis for international marketing communications as well as global brand management strategies. Indeed, the perceived importance of cultural issues has been increasing, fuelled by new technologies that allow marketers to reach consumers across country boundaries. Marketers are spending increasing amounts of time and effort trying to understand subtle cultural differences.

Activity 2.1

Research how organisations such as Nike, IBM, and Google are varying their offerings across national boundaries.

Changing social values

Other changes in the social environment have a direct impact on marketing. Many of these changes are quite gradual, but their effect is significant, for example:

◆ Changing attitudes to debt, consumer credit and financial stability.

◆ Changing attitudes towards 'conspicuous consumption' and waste.

◆ The growing importance of 'fashion' among age groups that were historically not perceived as fashion-conscious.

Activity 2.2

Can you think of other social trends that impact on marketing?

Technological factors

The beginning of the twenty-first century has been interesting for the number of hundredth birthdays including that of the first powered flight and the original development of brands such as Ford. Mass air travel and mass ownership of cars have altered society.

In the twenty-first century, convergent information and computer technologies will transform society. The Internet was originally conceived as a technical solution to a military planning problem: how to maintain communications after a nuclear attack. With commercial and consumer access to broadband, this technology has moved far from the uses originally conceived for it. The Internet is rewriting ways of conducting business in both the B2B and the B2C sectors. The development of digital cameras embedded in mobile telephones is adding yet another dimension to people's ability to communicate.

The marketer needs to interpret these developments creatively and imaginatively. For example, the impact of the Internet on book sales is not uniform. Some directories and reference books have, in effect, ceased to exist as people gain this type of reference information directly from the Internet. We may well be happy to buy the latest blockbuster online from Amazon. However, the book addict is looking for a shopping experience and specialist shops are adapting to this, hence leading to trends such as coffee shops within bookshops to provide the right atmosphere and give shoppers an offline experience, the real joy of book buying.

Production capabilities and techniques

Over the past twenty years a new form of manufacturing has evolved: the computer-aided design and manufacturing operation (CAD/CAM) which is aligned to new methods of production such as cellular manufacture (small divisions within a factory having responsibility for output quality and costs). CAD and CAM are also the keys to flexible manufacturing as they enable computerised machines to perform a variety of functions. When CAD and CAM are integrated it is possible to achieve computer-integrated manufacturing (CIM) whereby a system directs data flow whilst also directing the processing and movements of material.

These IT developments may be allied to production techniques imported from Japan including just-in-time, JIT.

JIT methods of production involves developing:

> a production system which is driven by demand for finished products whereby each component on a production line is produced only when needed for the next stage.
>
> (CIMA Official Terminology)

Product development

The use of large, powerful databases and sophisticated computer modelling packages has radically changed the process of product development. It is now possible to model the appearance and performance of new products without manufacturing models and prototypes. One such impact of this type of technology has been to shorten the lead time on new car models from the 1970s average of 30 months to a current norm of 26 weeks (MIRA).

Enhanced communications

Of all the aspects of the technological environment, none has changed as rapidly as communications technology. Mobile phones, the Internet, cable television and media messaging mean that we can now contact pretty much anyone, pretty much anytime.

This leads to huge challenges for marketers, for example:

◆ Word of mouth on new products can grow exponentially. Viral marketing means that a weak product can be 'found out' in a matter of hours, while a strong product can 'stock out' in the same period.

◆ On the Internet, your nearest rival is only 'one click' away. Customers are now less loyal, to both products and retailers, than they have ever been. Price comparison takes seconds, feature comparison a few seconds more.

Activity 2.3

Ask anyone from your grandparents' generation how people used to communicate with each other in 'the olden days'.

Environmental factors

Environmental issues have become increasingly important as the stark truth confronts society that gross consumption of finite resources cannot continue forever and that, in the long term, sustainable production and distribution is the only way forward for society as a whole. Some of the issues may be rather technical: such as whether genetic engineering is beneficial to society and the economy (largely the view in the United States) or something with too many risks (possibly the majority view in Europe).

Waste and packaging

Consumers are becoming increasingly aware of the issue of waste, both in the production process and as a result of 'excessive' packaging. Domestic waste management systems are reaching breaking point in many countries, and there is a global trade in recyclable waste. The issue of waste management and recyclability is now a major component of packaging design – packaging is no longer just designed to protect and promote the product.

Sustainability

Consider the impact of a product over its total lifespan: raw materials (e.g. steel, wood), manufacture (e.g. pollution issues), distribution (e.g. energy use), consumer use (e.g. energy-efficient deep freezer) and disposal (e.g. recycling targets). This is important, as it is not acceptable to abdicate responsibility. Therefore, a garden centre selling hardwood garden furniture needs to be assured that sustainable and legal logging has produced the wood. A car manufacturer may no longer consider that its environmental responsibilities have ended with the sale of the car, but must build into the vehicle the capacity for it to be recycled, and provide facilities for this.

Climate change

Climate change is the variation in the Earth's global climate or in regional climates over time. It involves changes in the variability or average state of the atmosphere over durations ranging from decades to millions of years. These changes can be caused by dynamic process on Earth, external forces including variations in sunlight intensity, and more recently by human activities.

In recent usage, especially in the context of environmental policy, the term 'climate change' often refers to changes in modern climate (or global warming). Current studies indicate that greenhouse gases are the primary cause of global warming. Greenhouse gases are also important in understanding Earth's climate history. According to these studies, the greenhouse effect, which is the warming produced as greenhouse gases trap heat, plays a key role in regulating Earth's temperature.

The biggest factor of present concern is the increase in CO_2 levels due to emissions from fossil fuel combustion, followed by aerosols (particulate matter in the atmosphere), which exert a cooling effect, and cement manufacture. Other factors, including land use, ozone depletion, animal agriculture and deforestation, also affect climate.

Corporate social responsibility

CSR has been defined as having four dimensions: economic, legal, ethical and philanthropic. As such society can:

◆ require business to discharge its economic and legal duties

◆ expect business to fulfil its ethical duties

◆ desire business to meet its philanthropic responsibilities.

CSR has also been defined as:

> the continuing commitment to business to behave ethically and contribute to economic development while improving the quality of life of the workforce and their families as well as of the local community and society at large

> (World Business Council for Sustainable Development)

From the same source, perceptions of CSR in different societies and cultures were given as:

> CSR is about capacity building for sustainable livelihoods. It respects cultural differences and finds the business opportunities in building the skills of employees, the community and the government (Ghana)

> CSR is about business giving back to society (Philippines)

In America there is more emphasis on the philanthropic approach to CSR, where companies will make charitable donations to society or its representatives. We can contrast the European approach where the emphasis is on business processes which are more socially responsible, complemented by investment in communities for reasons which are supported by good business cases.

Case study: The Body Shop

The Body Shop has become synonymous with ethical trading, proclaiming its beliefs on its packaging and advertising. Its ethical pronouncements have become part of its marketing strategy. Yet this can still lead to problems – whether of your own creation or not.

A decade ago, it emerged that almost every cosmetic the Body Shop sold had almost certainly been tested on animals. According to regulations in the United States, the European Union and Japan, no product could be sold unless it had been certified as safe. To gain such certification it would have to be tested on animals. New methods to gain safe certification had to be found, and the Body Shop now carries a disclaimer on animal testing – it has added 'since 1991' to its publicity.

The issue is not whether the Body Shop intentionally or innocently misled; rather it is that the negative publicity is stronger because of the previous ethical stance.

Hennes and Mauritz (H&M) is a company that has clear moral principles, with strict rules ensuring that no sweatshop workers are used to manufacture its clothes. It also supports Wateraid.

But H&M does not publicize its moral code; it does not advertise itself as an ethical company. It believes that its brand values are fashionable clothing and affordable prices. It focuses on promoting that and nothing else.

When asked, it reveals what it has in place to ensure moral behaviour. But H&M does not want customers to think it is jumping on the ethics and responsibility bandwagon.

Source: The Marketer, January 2005

Legal factors

Law affects everything we do in marketing. Every aspect of the marketing mix has legal issues that need consideration. When researching, we may well have to take account of data protection legislation. Lack of knowledge is no defence. Therefore, it is vital that a marketer is aware of which aspects of a marketing plan may be affected by laws and seeks professional advice where uncertainty prevails. This is particularly important when implementing marketing plans developed for one country in another, where a different legal system prevails. A competition that is an instant hit in one country may simply be illegal elsewhere. Apart from legal constraints, there may be voluntary codes of conduct imposed by the industry. Thus, much of advertising regulation may not be imposed by government law but by industry codes of conduct enforced within the industry by the industry.

Consumer protection

Consumer protection is a form of government regulation that protects the interests of consumers. For example, a government may require businesses to disclose detailed information about products – particularly in areas where safety or public health is an issue, such as food. Consumer protection is linked to the idea of consumer rights (that consumers have various rights as consumers), and to the formation of consumer organisations that help consumers make better choices in the marketplace.

While laws concerning sale of goods date back 100 years, the only phrase you need to memorise is 'The Sale of Goods Act 1979 (as amended)'. The 'as amended' is important because it refers to laws which have extended the basic 1979 Act and using the phrase tells the trader that not only do you know basic consumer law, you know it has been amended too.

The Sale of Goods Act lays down several conditions that all goods sold by a trader must meet. The goods must be:

◆ As described

◆ Of satisfactory quality

◆ Fit for purpose.

As described refers to any advert or verbal description made by the trader. Satisfactory quality covers minor and cosmetic defects as well as substantial problems. It also means that products must last a reasonable time. But it doesn't give you any rights if a fault was obvious or pointed out to you at point of sale. Fit for purpose covers not only the obvious purpose of an item but any purpose you queried and were given assurances about by the trader.

If you buy something which doesn't meet these conditions, you have the potential right to return it, get a full refund, and if it will cost you more to buy similar goods elsewhere, compensation (to cover the extra cost) too.

Consumer interests can also be protected by promoting competition in the markets that directly and indirectly serve consumers, consistent with economic efficiency, but subject to competition law. The United Kingdom is a member state of the European Union and so is bound by the consumer protection directives of the European Union. Domestic (UK) laws originated within the ambit of contract and tort but, with the influence of EU law, it is emerging as an independent area of law.

Consumer Ppotection issues are dealt with when complaints are made to the Director-General of Fair Trade. The Office of Fair Trading will then investigate, impose an injunction or take the matter to litigation. The Office of Fair Trading also acts as the UK's official consumer and competition watchdog, with a remit to make markets work well for consumers. At a local, municipal level complaints by be dealt with by Trading Standards departments.

Data protection

The Data Protection Act 1998 gives individuals the right to know what information is held about them. It provides a framework to ensure that personal data is handled properly.

The Act works in two ways. First it states that anyone who processes personal information must comply with eight principles, which make sure that personal information is:

◆ Fairly and lawfully processed

◆ Processed for limited purposes

◆ Adequate, relevant and not excessive

◆ Accurate and up to date

◆ Not kept for longer than is necessary

◆ Processed in line with your rights

◆ Secure

◆ Not transferred to other countries without adequate protection.

The second area covered by the Act provides individuals with important rights, including the right to find out what personal information is held on computer and most paper records.

Should an individual or organisation feel they're being denied access to personal information they're entitled to, or feel their information has not been handled according to the eight principles, they can contact the Information Commissioner's Office for help. Complaints are usually dealt with informally, but if this isn't possible, enforcement action can be taken.

Activity 2.4

Consider the impact of PESTEL on an advertising campaign for a burger chain.

The micro-marketing environment – overview

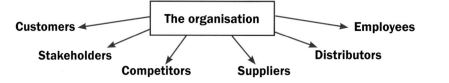

Figure 2.3: The micro-marketing environment

Customers

> **Customer** – a person or company who purchases goods or services (not necessarily the end consumer). (CIM)

The marketplace consists of the buyers and users of the organisation's products and services, and the immediate microenvironment in which the purchase and use take place.

In some circumstances, it is a little difficult to define precisely who the customer is. This may be because the organisation is a not-for-profit or social marketing organisation or the definition of customer is not obvious for the product or service. Students, employers and parents can all be considered as 'customers' of a college in the sense that each of them may be making direct and indirect payments. The key concept is that of stakeholders. We can then accept that customers are a key stakeholder group and that a college has many and complex stakeholder groups.

Buyers can exert power over the organisation. Viewing the situation from the point of view of a hotel in a ski resort, it can be seen that in the high season, rooms are expensive as demand is high (low buyer power). However, out-of-season prices can be lower as customers can shop around (high buyer power). In general, from the viewpoint of the brand manufacturer of consumer goods, the power of the buyers is twofold. If the supermarkets do not stock the product then the customers are not able to buy it. If the customers select another brand as better value for money, the situation is just as bad. To address these two influences, brand manufacturers use marketing strategies directed at both the retail channels (push strategy) and the consumers (pull strategy).

Stakeholders

> **Stakeholder** – a person or organisation that has an interest in the strategy of the organisation. Stakeholders normally include shareholders, customers, staff and the local community. (CIMA)

As such we can consider them to be people and organisations who have a say in:

◆   What you are to do

◆   What resources you have

◆   What you should achieve.

They are affected by, and feel they have a right to benefit or be pleased by, what you do.

It is essential to satisfy or at least manage all the legitimate stakeholder expectations. It is no use marketing a toy to parents only for them to find their child does not play with it. Equally, it does not help if the parents do not buy the toy in the first place.

Most organisations operate within a framework of law and rules, which are enforced by regulators. For a manufacturer of shampoo, safety in manufacture and in consumer use is subject to regulatory control. The marketing claims made for the product (e.g. 'anti-dandruff' shampoo) will fall under the jurisdiction of the Advertising Standards Authority. The activity of a firm will be scrutinised by pressure groups with their own specific agenda. In Europe, animal testing of personal care products has been discontinued; however, international companies who operate under different standards in their home market may also come under pressure in Europe. In the fashion sector of the market, consumer pressure groups may consider marketing claims extravagant and products over-priced. A key PR activity is to lobby regulators and address the issues raised by the pressure groups.

In today's just-in-time (JIT) environment, close relationships are vital with suppliers who are increasingly being viewed as another sphere of 'internal' stakeholders rather than being 'outsiders'. Firms both compete in the marketplace and will also collaborate (e.g. to lobby regulators when all manufacturers are faced with a common threat such as a poorly framed EU draft directive).

Within the industry, there may be associations such as the Article Numbering Association (industry forum for ensuring the effective and efficient use of bar codes to the benefit of both manufacturers and retailers of consumer products).

The media are a significant influence on the brand. Celebrity endorsement in the editorials of the glossy fashion press can be a very positive influence. Adverse reports in the consumer or environmental pages of a paper can have a negative effect. The trade press can be important in maintaining credibility with B2B customers and in attracting the most able staff to join the organisation.

Competitors

Competitors – companies that sell products or services in the same market place as one another. (CIM)

'In-segment' competition is what most people would call 'normal' competition: the battle between close competitors such as Tesco and ASDA. There are other companies that compete but not in such a direct way: Boots competes with ASDA in the personal care sector but not in clothing. However, it should be remembered that a large, distant competitor could have a significant impact on a small organisation. The supermarkets' move into bookselling has become a major threat to independent and specialist bookshops. By creaming off the sales of the latest blockbuster, the remaining sales of specialist books may not provide enough revenue to keep the small outlet above breakeven sales volumes.

Suppliers and distributors

Suppliers – organisations or individuals that provide inputs (materials, labour, services) to the organisation.

Distributors – organisations or individuals that help to get the outputs of the organisation (products, services) to the end customer.

There is also the potential influence of suppliers on the organisation. Again, this may be direct or indirect, further down the supply chain. Therefore, a company may be spoilt for choice for a possible supplier of personal computer hardware, but still have to purchase a Microsoft operating system. It is not by accident that Microsoft is one of the most profitable organisations in the world.

An organisation may be integrated to minimise some of the competition forces. The brand manufacturer may own raw material suppliers and also own the retail outlets (managing both supplier and buyer power). This type of vertical marketing system (VMS) can be achieved by other devices. In the contractual VMS, the same end is achieved not by ownership but by the framework of contractual relationships. The Body Shop developed with the manufacture of its products and many of the outlets working under a franchise system. Here, the outlets are owned by individuals who then operate them under a detailed franchise contract. Co-operatives form a strategy for smaller organisations to gain some competitive stature by working together, to achieve critical mass in areas such as buying power. Large buyers such as Wal-Mart achieve coordination and control (an administered VMS) with their tight supply chain management system and sets of contractual relationships.

Employees

Internal stakeholders are vital and staff motivation and commitment are characteristics of successful organisations. Internal stakeholders can be segmented by features such as job level or job function. In internal marketing initiatives, such as during the management of change, attitude segmentation variables (e.g. positive, negative and apathetic) may be useful.

There is a spectrum of possible reactions to any proposed change:

◆ Enthusiastic co-operation and support, acceptance, or co-operation under pressure from management.

◆ Passive resignation – indifference, apathy, loss of interest, minimal contribution.

◆ Passive resistance – regressive behaviour, non-learning behaviour.

◆ Active resistance – protests, working to rule, minimal work, slowing down, personal withdrawal, committing errors intentionally, sabotage.

Monitoring the marketing environment

The problem with management is that there is too much data and not enough good relevant information.

> **Marketing information** – any information used or required to support marketing decisions – often drawn from a computerised 'Marketing Information System'. (CIM)

The Marketing Information System (MkIS) is not just a range of computer programs. People are needed to collect certain data. You can machine-read a bar code but not a customer complaint. Having collected the data, the system must evaluate the degree of confidence one might place in it (e.g. there may be some reservations about a sample scheme with market research). The data needs to be analysed and interpreted to generate relevant useful information.

There are a number of issues to be considered when formulating an appropriate MkIS for a given situation:

◆ What data needs to be collected?

◆   How can it be collected efficiently?

◆   What use is to be made of the information?

The macro environment and microenvironment need to be monitored, as does the efficiency of our own value chain and those of our competitors, including the relevant marketing mix issues. Market research may be conducted on an ongoing basis to track market trends (e.g. TV viewing habits) or for specific issues (to evaluate if falling sales are due to changes in customer perception of the brand). The research may be quantitative (how many people take part in an activity) or qualitative (how do consumers feel about the product). If appropriate secondary desk sources do not exist, more expensive primary research will have to be commissioned.

Market scanning

Marketing intelligence is a critical source of data for the organisation. Competitors' websites and annual reports are useful sources. Mystery shopping in the competitors' and one's own outlets can provide useful data for a retail organisation. The trade press provides a continual flow of industry 'gossip': who is moving to a new company, new investment plans and product launches, and the like. On a practical note, nobody except the commissioning company takes as much interest in marketing trials as the competition!

Specific research is needed to support a unique project such as a product launch. However, knowing how the market is moving (e.g. whether a new product launch is required) needs a continuous flow of data and information. A key activity is not only monitoring changes with customers, but also competitors' activities. New launches and new advertising campaigns will impact on the business, and if the organisation were to wait six months to see what happens, it will be too late to act.

Specialist trade magazines may be expensive but they do contain the industry 'hot' gossip. Who has moved from one company to another (watching competitor recruitment gives you an idea of what skills they are strengthening for future projects) and other key news such as product launches and capital plans. For new products in technology-rich areas, patent abstracts are useful. Company websites, annual reports, advertisements and other publications are all useful sources of information. One of the key reasons for attending a trade conference is to gain competitor and market intelligence.

Every visit to a customer is a chance to gain intelligence. For example, an organisation uses a given company to provide photocopiers; the organisation becomes dissatisfied with the existing supplier and decides to trial a competitor company. The technician from the original supplier arrives to repair the existing photocopiers and notices the competitor's machine. He then informs his boss, and a representative arrives the next day to see if there are any problems.

A major technical activity for many organisations is the reverse-engineering of products. A company produces a new DVD drive or a new washing powder. The first thing for the competitor is to obtain samples, get them into the laboratory and strip them down to see how they have been built. This is, in part, to check the strength of the competition (market leaders) and to (where legal) copy with a counter-type (a typical activity for a supermarket's own brand). This can also be applied to services, with researchers acting as 'mystery travellers' on an airline, for example.

Collection of secondary data

> **Secondary data** – marketing research data that already exists, and was collected for a purpose other than the current research process.

Vast amounts of internal data are collected by EPOS systems and loyalty cards. This can give accurate profiles of consumers (the purchase of cat food and pet litter may indicate that you are a ripe candidate for a pet insurance mailshot). Apart from computer data systems (accounts, etc.), care must be taken to capture 'soft' data such as customer complaints and sales visit reports which are not so easily converted into simple numbers but provide vital evidence of not only 'how much?' but 'why?'.

All data needs to be evaluated for accuracy and relevance so should in some way formally pass through the analytical system:

◆ If the pound is rising, the cost of imported materials from last year is fine when calculating last year's profits but not when pricing next year's production.

◆ Often some adjustment needs to be made to make certain that appropriate comparisons are being made. If we are analysing sales trends, it is important to know if the changes are due to price or volume changes as different corrective action may be needed.

◆ In comparing the results for a given week this year with that of the same one last year, care needs to be taken to ensure that there are not odd effects that may distort the figures (e.g. it may be relevant to note that Easter is early in some years and late in others).

It is often useful to note not only the physical value but also some appropriate ratio. When comparing the sales from two different sized shops in the same organisation, it may be appropriate to calculate the sales per square metre.

Activity 2.5

Look again at the case study in Chapter 1 relating to Tesco's Clubcard, to see how secondary data can be used.

Practice objective test questions

A   The value chain model can be used to analyse:

1   The external environment

2   The internal environment

3   The internal and external environments

B   In the value chain model, 'operations' is a:

1   Primary activity

2   Secondary activity

3   Support activity

C In the value chain model, 'marketing and sales' is a:

1 Primary activity

2 Secondary activity

3 Support activity

D In the value chain model, which activity covers 'the purchase of the inputs to the value chain'?

1 Inbound logistics

2 Operations

3 Procurement

E Which of the following tools can be used to analyse the external marketing environment?

1 The value chain

2 PESTEL

3 C2C

F In the PESTEL model, the two 'Es' are:

1 Effort and expenditure

2 Economy and efficiency

3 Economic and environmental

G In the PESTEL model, under which heading is taxation normally considered?

1 Political

2 Economic

3 Legal

H Marketing research data that already exists, and was collected for a purpose other than the current research process is known as:

1 Primary research data

2 Secondary research data

3 Company research data

Further work

1 Produce a value chain model for your organisation, or one with which you are familiar.

2 Produce a PESTEL analysis of the environment of your organisation, or one with which you are familiar.

3 Identify the stakeholders of your organisation, or one with which you are familiar.

4 Search the Internet for online specialist and trade magazines that are relevant to the industry of your organisation or one with which you are familiar.

The marketing mix

The importance of the marketing mix

Overview

It is obvious from the preceding sections that successful marketing strategies and plans can only be crafted with a clear focus on satisfying (meeting) customer needs and wants. Customers must be central to everything an organisation does. Approximately 30 years ago it became accepted that in this quest for a customer-driven approach, organisations had four basic marketing dimensions. These became known more commonly as known as 'the Four Ps';

◆ Product (or service)

◆ Price

◆ Promotion

◆ Place (distribution).

Marketing guru Philip Kotler would add at least one, P, that of People, and more recently two other factors (Process and Physical evidence) have been added to this basic listing to give a total of seven.

The term 'marketing mix' was first applied at the Harvard Business School to explain the range of marketing decisions and elements that must be balanced to achieve maximum impact. The Marketing mix represents the 'tool kit' for marketing practitioners who attempt to 'blend' the Ps. The apportionment of effort, the precise combination, and the integration of all four elements to achieve organisational objectives represent an organisation's own marketing programme or 'mix'. The marketer therefore is a mixer of these ingredients – procedures and policies to produce a profitable enterprise.

Kotler and Lane Keller (2006) define the marketing mix as:

> **Marketing mix** – the set of controllable variables and their levels that the firm uses to influence the target market.

The manager must address these fundamentals areas, so that all 'the Ps' combine to emphasise marketing as a total system of coordinating organisational activity focused on satisfying customer needs. For the majority of private sector organisations the aim of marketing is, generally speaking, synonymous with the overall purpose of maximising financial returns. There are clearly a wide variety of possible combinations of marketing variables which management can select. Inevitably some combinations will earn greater financial returns than others. The crucial combination of factors comprising the marketing mix is therefore of high significance.

Re-mixing the mix

The 'design' of the marketing mix will normally be decided on the basis of management intuition and judgement, together with information provided by marketing research.

Altering one component of the mix impacts upon most, if not all, of the others. For instance, the quality of advertising may need to be raised if the selling price of products is increased.

A manufacturer may also need a marketing mix for the end consumer, and an additional mix for the customer to whom they actually sell the product. Each mix will change as the marketing environment changes.

Product

> **Product** – the quality and attributes of a purchase (product or service) as perceived by the customer. (Kotler)

Product embraces:
◆ Product quality and durability
◆ Product design
◆ Brand name
◆ Logo
◆ Packaging
◆ The product range
◆ After-sales service
◆ Optional extras
◆ Guarantees and warranties.

For service rather than product-based organisations, this category includes the nature of the service including its key features.

Product in this context also includes associated services. Marketing a product involves product design, concept testing and product launch.

The starting point should of course not be with the product, but instead with the customer. By understanding their needs and wants an appropriate product or service can be developed to fulfil these desires. Potential customers need to be satisfied with an organisation's product or service or they are unlikely to buy it. This means that the product or service must fulfil their need and should clearly be of a quality that suits its purpose. This final sentence has two implications for the organisation:

◆ It needs systems to monitor customer perceptions of the product or service

◆ Product quality must meet the 'fitness for purpose' test.

Features and benefits

It is worth noting a key marketing concept: that the customer does not buy a product, but seeks to satisfy a need or a want. This is important for the organisation to understand so that it can concentrate on marketing the *benefits* of its product rather than its *features*.

Useful questions from a marketing point of view include:

◆ Are customers satisfied with existing products and services?

◆ Do these products or services fulfil their future needs?

◆ How are competitors addressing themselves to the same questions?

◆ Can competitors' products satisfy customers' future needs?

Activity 3.1

As customers buy the benefits of a product not its features, identify a recent purchase you have made and consider both its features and benefits.

Core, augmented and potential product

In marketing a product, more often than not, we do not market the core benefits. These are 'hygiene' properties. If we go to a hotel and find the toilets clean and well kept, we do not rush to reception to heap praise upon the management. If we find the reverse and the facilities are dirty and neglected, we will inform the management and possibly check out and tell all our friends. In a hotel advertisement, you will not see the message 'all of our rooms contain beds'. These core benefits are taken as read, but it is with the higher levels of service/product that we gain the business. This facet of product can be linked in the broadest sense to the general concepts, researched in other contexts, advanced by Maslow and Hertzberg in their motivation theories.

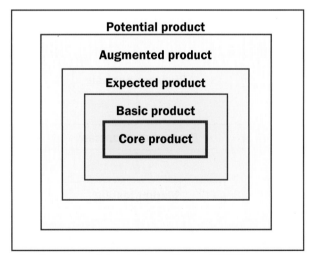

Figure 3.1: Levels of product. Adapted from Kotler (2000)

Figure 3.1 shows the customer value hierarchy framework. At the lower levels, customers are provided with what they expect; all providers must supply this or they gain no business at all. To gain a competitive edge, one must provide something of benefit value to the customer above and beyond the expected benefit set. This target is not static since customers' expectations grow; what delighted them five years ago is now taken for granted (e.g. in business hotels five years ago Internet access in all rooms would have been an 'extra', now it is expected).

The ultimate product is that which satisfies the dream needs of the customer. People do not want detergents; the ultimate product would be self-cleaning clothes that never needed ironing. The core benefit of a car is travel but people expect comfort not just a seat on a chassis. Today, cars are providing an ever-increasing number of electronic features (cruise control, global positioning systems and in-car entertainment systems). The ultimate potential product will be the car that provides total comfort and drives itself.

New product development

In business and engineering, new product development (NPD) is the term used to describe the complete process of bringing a new product or service to market. There are two parallel paths involved in the NPD process (Figure 3.2): one involves the idea generation, product design, and detail engineering; the other involves market research and marketing analysis. Companies typically see new product development as the first stage in generating and commercialising new products within the overall strategic process of product life cycle management used to maintain or grow their market share.

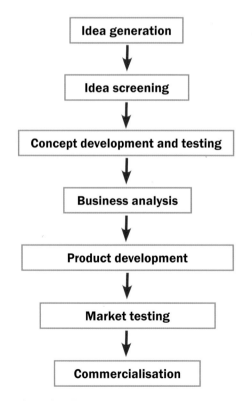

Figure 3.2: The new product development process

The process of NPD is outlined as follows:

1   Idea generation (The 'fuzzy front end' of the NPD process)

♦ Ideas for new products can be obtained from customers (through user innovation), designers, the R&D department, competitors, focus groups, employees, salespeople, corporate spies, trade shows, or through a policy of Open Innovation.

♦ Formal idea generation techniques can be used, such as attribute listing, forced relationships, brainstorming, morphological analysis and problem analysis.

2   Idea screening

♦ The object is to eliminate unsound concepts prior to devoting resources to them.

♦ The screeners must ask at least three questions:

• Will the customer in the target market benefit from the product?

• Is it technically feasible to manufacture the product?

• Will the product be profitable when manufactured and delivered to the customer at the target price?

3   Concept development and testing

♦ Develop the marketing and engineering details

• Who is the target market and who is the decision-maker in the buying process?

• What product features must the product incorporate?

• What benefits will the product provide?

• How will consumers react to the product?

• How will the product be produced most cost-effectively?

• Prove feasibility through virtual computer aided rendering, and rapid prototyping

• What will it cost to produce it?

♦ Test the concept by asking a sample of prospective customers what they think of the idea

4   Business analysis

♦ Estimate likely selling price based upon competition and customer feedback

♦ Estimate sales volume based upon size of market

♦ Estimate profitability and breakeven point

5   Product development

♦ Depending upon costs, produce a physical prototype or mock-up based on the previous concept development

♦ Test the product (and its packaging) in typical usage situations

♦ Make adjustments where necessary

6   Market testing

♦ Produce an initial run of the product and sell it in a test market area to determine customer acceptance

♦ Test the channels, media and price

♦ Fine tuning of all elements of the offering

7 **Commercialisation** (often considered post-NPD)

♦ Launch the product

♦ Produce and place advertisements and other promotions

♦ Fill the distribution pipeline with product

♦ Critical path analysis is most useful at this stage

These steps may be iterated as needed. Some may be eliminated. To reduce the time that the NPD process takes, many companies tackle several steps at once (referred to as concurrent engineering or time to market). Most industry leaders see new product development as a proactive process where resources are allocated to identify market changes and seize upon product opportunities before they occur (in contrast to a reactive strategy in which nothing is done until problems arise or a competitor introduces an innovation). Many industry leaders see new product development as an ongoing process (referred to as continuous development) in which the entire organisation is always looking for opportunities.

Source: Adapted from Wikipedia

Product extension

This is a strategy commonly used towards the end of a product's life cycle, with the aim of extending the product's life so further (high margin) sales can be made, and any remaining stocks cleared. Product extension may also fill any 'gap' between the tail end of one product's life and the successful launch and growth of its successor.

Product extension is common in the car industry, where a 'special edition' is often launched shortly before a car model is discontinued. This allows the manufacturer to use up any remaining components, and to earn a high margin on what is becoming an obsolete product. One such example was Ford's 'Crusader' variant at the end of the life-cycle of the Cortina.

Insight

Compact fluorescents are hot sellers, and Congress has passed a bill banning incandescent bulbs by 2014. So why is GE planning to sell a new high-efficiency incandescent? It's a case of 'last gasp' inspiration, says Harvard Business School professor Daniel Snow in January's *Harvard Business Review*. Snow says last gasps are common when new technologies are poised to replace older ones, partly because some of the new technology can benefit existing products. Carburettors, he says, lasted an extra decade or so by adapting electronics designed for the fuel injectors that replaced them. 'New-tech companies can't count out old players,' he says. Both must expect surprises in transition periods.

Source: Newsweek (2008)

Product modification

There are several general categories of new products. Some are new to the market (e.g. DVD players into the home movie market), some are new to the company (e.g. Game consoles for Sony), some are completely novel and create totally new markets (e.g. the airline industry). When viewed against a different criterion, some new product concepts are merely minor modifications of existing products while some are completely innovative to the company:

◆　　Changes to augmented product

◆　　Repositioning a current product into a new market or segment

◆　　Core product revision

◆　　Line extensions

◆　　New product lines

◆　　Completely new products.

Activity 3.2

Identify examples of real product developments that fit each of the above categories.

Price

Of the seven Ps comprising the marketing mix, price is the one most directly linked to generating income. Price setting is all-important especially for a financially orientated firm. Pricing includes;

◆　　Basic price levels

◆　　Discounts and allowances

◆　　Payment terms and credit policy.

It is easy to view price from a mathematical viewpoint and to fix a price based on 'cost plus'. The need to recover costs, and to earn a profit is, a powerful consideration. However, customers need to see price as 'fair' (not necessarily cheap). Pricing therefore needs to meet both the organisation's financial and marketing aspirations.

It is perhaps illuminating to consider the issue from three perspectives (Lancaster and Withey, 2005):

◆　　**The economic view** – Suppliers are in the business of profit maximisation. A market is a place where supply and demand comes into contact. Price is the mechanism whereby demand and supply are brought into equilibrium.

◆　　**The accountancy view** – Price is set to recover costs and make profit. Pricing should be guided by the use of ratios and techniques such as breakeven analysis.

◆　　**The marketing view** – Price is only one factor influencing demand, it does however have an impact on an organisation's competitive market position, including sales, and market share. A good price measure might be what 'the market will bear'.

Pricing strategies

In practice all these viewpoints should be considered to some degree. In addition an appropriate blending of the other factors of the marketing mix will also help establish the price. There are a number of methodologies that can help determine selling price.

◆　　**Competitive** – Setting a price by reference to the prices of competitive products

◆ **Cost plus** – Adding a mark-up to costs of production which may incorporate desired return on investment

◆ **Market based** – (or perceived value). Setting a price based on the value of the product in the perception of the customer

◆ **Penetration** – Setting a low selling price in order to gain market share

◆ **Predatory** – Setting a low selling price in order to damage competition

◆ **Premium** – Achieving a 'high' price due to differentiation of the product

◆ **Price skimming** – Setting a high price in order to maximise short-term profitability (e.g. the introduction of a novel product)

◆ **Selective** – Setting different prices for the same product in different markets

◆ **Selective: category** – Cosmetic modifications to allow variations to take place

◆ **Selective: consumer** – Modifying the price to take account of certain groups (e.g. junior or OAP)

◆ **Selective: peak** – Setting a price which varies according to level of demand (e.g. happy hours, premium rate calls, etc.)

Competitor pricing – monitoring

It is important that, as part of the pricing decision, the organisation continually monitors the prices charged by competitors. These prices should be compared to the benefits perceived by the customers for each product offering.

Competitor pricing – responding

Reference was made earlier to generic competitive strategy and the possibility of an organisation competing on the basis of price. If this is the chosen strategy it is important that excess production costs are squeezed with the overall aim that the organisation will be cost leader within their market. These savings could be passed on to the customer and might be reflected in low prices. Larger, well-established businesses are better able to compete on price. This is generally as a result of two basic concepts:

◆ **The experience curve** – Reductions in the average unit cost price as a result of learning from past experiences how to perform processes more cheaply.

◆ **Economies of scale** – Reductions in the average unit cost price as a result of size of operation.

There can after all only be one price leader in a market. It may be more advisable therefore to add value to the product so differentiating it from the competitors offering in some way. Alternatively, part of the market (a segment) might be identified where the competition will find it hard to access. Here the organisation is in a position to price on the basis of 'what the market will bear'.

There may be several other considerations when fixing price and some of which include:

◆ **The nature of competition** – If the competitor is the price leader pricing levels may be determined by 'follow the leader' pricing. So, for instance, if the largest oil company cuts the price of fuel, others are likely to follow suit.

◆ **The nature of the market** – By way of example, a company may find itself in the fortunate position of being the sole producer of a product due to a monopoly of 'know-how', resources or raw materials, etc.

◆ **Pricing as a result of a short-term promotion** – This may lead to 'loss leader' pricing on certain items to generate either customer loyalty or more sales of other products. This is particularly popular in pricing consumables in supermarkets.

◆ **Pricing as a competitive weapon** – The pricing of product may be set in order to crush competitors rather than achieve returns in revenue.

Price competition is a key issue in customers' perception of value. Motorists will travel miles to save a few pence a litre. Where accurate price comparisons can be made, consumers become very price sensitive and shop around. For a major purchase, once a consumer has decided on manufacturer and models, increasingly the next step is not to go to a shop and purchase but complete an Internet search for the best possible price. The 'dot-com' companies were not wrong in understanding that the Internet is changing purchasing habits, however what they did often get wrong was the timescales and the way the market actually developed. People are also now able to make price comparisons across international borders and can see where companies are operating different pricing policies. Companies have a dilemma in that different markets have differing perceptions of value and affordability so differential pricing may be necessary.

Customer expectations

Customers' feelings about a product or service are reflected in what they are prepared to pay, so getting pricing 'right' is crucial. Ultimately the manager must address the issue of whether customers believe the price is fair, commensurate with the quality of the product or service.

CIM makes the point that existing customers are generally less price sensitive than new ones. (This is one reason why it is vital to retain existing customers. A truism is that it is preferable to retain existing customers rather than having to find new ones.)

For the customer, price can imply quality. Pricing that is too low can have a detrimental effect on purchasing decisions and overall sales levels. Conversely, the higher the price, the more customers will expect in terms of product and service (whether packaging, the shopping environment, or promotional material, etc.).

Place

Getting 'place' right in marketing terms means effective distribution: getting the right products into the right places at the right time. The movement of goods from production to consumption points is key. Place therefore refers to:

◆ Distribution channels

◆ Distribution coverage

◆ The types of transportation vehicle

◆ Locations of sales outlets, the arrangements of sales areas

◆　　Stock levels

◆　　Warehouse locations.

Research indicates that delivery performance is one of the main criteria for businesses choosing a particular supplier.

Questions from a marketing point of view include:

◆　　Is the place of purchase convenient to customers and does it fulfil their needs?

◆　　Is the means of distribution appropriate?

◆　　Is the product available in the right quantities?

Contemporary developments have dictated that there is a changing emphasis on 'place' within the marketing mix, with advances in direct marketing and interactive marketing. These issues are dealt with later in this coursebook.

Role of distribution

Three aspects need to be considered:

◆　　Transport (physical delivery of the service or product)

◆　　The standard of service/inventory required

◆　　Geographical cover.

Nature of distribution

Delivery of physical products was transformed in the second half of the twentieth century. It is now possible and economic to source raw materials and manufactured products on a global basis:

◆　　It is more economic to make consumer electronics in China than to manufacture in Europe.

◆　　In the United Kingdom, deep mining of coal declined and imports of low-cost coal soared.

◆　　Transport by sea was revolutionised by containerisation, providing door-to-door delivery of manufactured goods to B2B customers on a global basis at economic cost.

◆　　Specialised transport provides solutions for the mass transportation of particular products (e.g. cars).

For some products, hybridised solutions evolved. For over 100 years, the railways provided overnight distribution of newspapers in the United Kingdom. Now papers can be transmitted digitally to regional printing centres providing a more efficient, timely service with reduced environmental impact.

People in different locations may want the same benefits but physical delivery may be different. An isolated hotel in the mountains may want gas (the fuel of choice for chefs in the kitchen) and broadband access. Gas pipes may not be feasible and, being remote from a town, fibre-optic links may not be available. The solution may be bulk delivery of liquid gas and satellite uplink or other radio technology for Internet access.

Distribution channels

Some products such as fresh foodstuff clearly benefit from short distribution channels. In the countryside it is often possible to buy produce directly from the farm. Alternatively, the farm may deliver daily to the supermarket. A specialist foreign car might, however, need to be imported, here the distribution is relatively lengthy and may take time.

The precise method of distribution chosen will vary depending upon the nature of the product and the degree of market exposure required. The greater the market an organisation wishes to access the longer and more complicated the distribution channel.

Campbell (1997) identified the most commonly observed channels as follows:

◆   Producer to customer

◆   Producer to retailer to customer

◆   Producer to wholesaler to retailer to customer

◆   Producer to agent to wholesaler to retailer to customer.

Maximising accessibility (differing customer needs)

Figure 3.3 shows some patterns of distribution for consumer goods. The blocks represent stages where stock is held. This may be short term in a distribution centre or longer term for a distributor of imported goods. The arrows represent the physical transport process: in general, taking goods from the stock area, loading the goods, transportation, unloading the goods and storage.

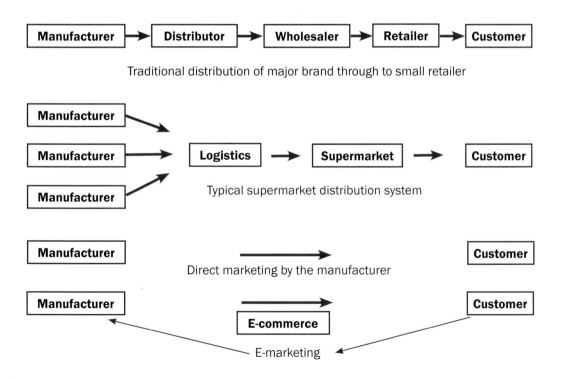

Figure 3.3: Some channel models

The message is simple: each arrow, each block, represents costs and unless these costs also add customer value the strategic pricing gap we discussed earlier is being eroded. The top distribution layer represents the distribution of an imported product sold through small retail outlets. The next shows the situation typical for a supermarket: manufacturers deliver products to a logistics centre; the assorted products for a given store are loaded into a vehicle (a supermarket may have over 10,000 lines but 10,000 vehicles do not arrive each day at every branch) and are delivered to the store. The supermarket system provides a vast array of products at reduced distribution cost. The small independent retailer has a huge mountain to climb to provide sufficient increased customer value to offset their increased costs (hence the death of the village shop/post office).

For appropriate goods (e.g. Dell with computers), the manufacturer can supply the goods direct. Here e-commerce can be seen as nothing totally new, it augments postal and telephone ordering. However, it is much more convenient and 'alive' for the customer, and the transaction costs are much lower. The manufacturer does not need a distribution system; this can be contracted out to one of the specialist operators (e.g. DHL, UPS, etc.). However, this does not provide the customer with a wide range of products, just those made by one manufacturer.

The changing role of logistics

In an earlier section, it was noted that newspapers are now distributed via a mixture of traditional and digital distribution (digital transmission to the regions, then local printing and physical distribution). The general distribution problem is to find cost-effective solutions that provide the customer with maximum convenience.

The 'hot potato' of the early twenty-first century is digital entertainment. More money is spent on computer games than is taken in box-office receipts at the cinema. Films, music and computer games are, in terms of distribution, one and the same thing: large computer files. With broadband access, we need never go to the record shop or hire a video or DVD. The technology is here and now (and very alive with pirate editions). The issue for the copyright owners is how to preserve their property rights, yet provide convenience to the customers.

Online and offline purchasing

Enter the 'dot-com' company: A central 'dot-com' e-commerce company takes the order and, in an ideal world, does not play any part in the manufacture, storage or transport of the goods (e.g. an e-travel company does not own hotels or airlines). Here there is maximum customer satisfaction (armchair shopping with a wide assortment of goods) and efficient delivery with minimum transaction costs. Of course, the 'trick' is in that single arrow in the e-marketing model.

Part of the problem of the 'dot-com' bubble was people were blinded by the glitz of the capabilities of the new communications channel and forgot the basics: that bargain PlayStation is no use if it arrives three days after the birthday and is damaged. Even if part-time marketers conduct much of the distribution, it is essential to customer satisfaction and it must form an integrated element of the marketing mix.

Activity 3.3

In the first wave of the dot-com age, only a minority of households had Internet connections, and domestic broadband access was not generally available. Now the majority of UK households have access to the Internet and much of that access is now over high-speed broadband access. Evaluate how this capability might change methods and channels of distribution for various goods and services to the digital home.

Promotion

Promotion – includes the tools available to communicate with customers and potential customers about a product or service.

A clear focus on customers and communication is central to modern marketing. Increasingly organisations attempt to understand customers and design communications to effectively and efficiently meet their needs. Once the organisation has determined what they believe the customers see as the main benefits of their product or service (see earlier) these aspects are focused upon when promotion takes place.

Promotion can take many forms and generally operates at one of three levels:

◆ Non-personal and mass, typically aimed at a market segment at large

◆ Personal and direct, typically one-way communication with a potential customer (e.g. by sending a letter)

◆ Personal and interactive, involving some one-to-one dialogue between the salesperson and the potential customer.

Promotion (irrespective of form) involves persuasion: ways of communicating convincingly the benefits of an organisation's products or services to customers and potential customers.

There are many individual promotional tools available and possibly these constitute the most visible dimension of marketing. These communication mechanisms need 'blending' by an organisation to develop its own promotional mix. The main promotional tools are briefly considered here.

◆ **Advertising** is the non-personal presentation and promotion of ideas, goods, or services but targeted at a specific market through some media channel. The mass media such as TV, press, radio or newspapers might be used as well as more traditional forms such as posters, hoardings and fliers.

◆ **Sales promotion** is impersonal and short-term by nature, involving the offering of incentives to encourage sales. Sales promotion is therefore a marketing activity aimed at stimulating consumer purchasing. It can involve the use of coupons, offers, giveaways, discounts, competitions, or BOGOFs (buy one get one free) products. Other non-routine promotional events include displays, exhibitions, demonstrations, and product sponsorship.

◆ **Publicity and public relations** is 'non-personal stimulation of demand for a product, service, or business unit by planting commercially significant news about it in a published medium, or obtaining favourable presentation of it upon radio, TV or stage. Whilst it is not paid for by the sponsor in the way that media time or space is paid for advertising, there may be costs in informing journalists and other types of opinion leader.' (The Chartered Institute of Marketing, 2004). This is an often-underestimated tool that can also include company open days, press releases and conferences.

◆ **Personal selling** often involves one-to-one contact with potential customers most commonly by telephone. The salesperson verbally presents the benefits of the product or service in the hope of making a sale.

◆ **Direct mailing** of promotional literature. Databases allow messages to be personalised to include the prospective customer's name. Normally, messages are personally targeted using either the traditional mail systems (often referred to as junk mail) or the e-mail media (often referred to as spam).

There is also a case to include direct marketing and packaging into this listing as both tools can contribute to the communication of the products benefits. (Packaging includes package, label, and description design). Other promotional activities include branding and producing literature and brochures.

Just as promotional tools need to be blended to form a promotional or communication mix, so promotion itself needs to be blended with the other Ps comprising the marketing mix. For instance, a reduction in promotional activity may be possible if a wider range or larger number of sales outlets is developed. (This implies a heavier mix of place at the expense of promotion.)

The traditional 'push' marketing policy is concerned with transferring goods out to wholesalers and retailers who then have the task of selling them to ultimate final customers. The emphasis of a 'push' policy is therefore on getting dealers to accept goods. A 'pull' policy by comparison is one of influencing final consumer attitudes so that a consumer demand is created which dealers are obliged to satisfy. A 'pull' policy usually involves heavy expenditure on advertising, but holds the potential of stimulating a much higher demand. For example, producers of convenience food and alcohol advertise their products nationally rather than relying on supermarkets to promote these products.

This represents consumer advertising as part of consumer marketing, and should be distinguished from trade and corporate advertising. Lancaster and Withey (2005) differentiate advertising according to uses and types as follows:

◆ Advertising products and services (e.g. Ford cars)

◆ Advertising ideas and issues (e.g. Greenpeace)

◆ Advertising people (e.g. Jennifer Lopez)

◆ Trade type (e.g. B&Q: 'warehouses for professional decorators')

◆ Consumer type (e.g. Robinson Barley Water: 'refresh your ideas')

◆ Corporate type (e.g. Shell: 'the caring company').

Communicating the marketing proposition

We noted earlier that it is not just customers we have to communicate with, but all relevant stakeholders. Therefore for a consumer product, the best advertising campaign (pull element of the strategy) is a waste of time if the B2B marketing to the channels has not succeeded in getting the product onto the shelf (the push element of the strategy). Sometimes in the literature on communications, stakeholders may be referred to as publics or audiences. We need to define what the corporate and brand values are before we get to the details. These set the tone and atmosphere of all policies and activities. It will then be possible to set the messages and propositions.

The first stage of communications activities is to verify the stakeholder analysis to ensure that it is complete and does not need revising or updating. The profiling process should not be reserved for the customers alone, but for all the stakeholders, so that we can understand their agendas (in American terms 'where they are coming from'). Later, we will see how important it is that communications intended for one audience (stakeholder group) may be received by another with a different agenda, who will put a completely different 'spin' on the message.

Sales

The selling mix concentrates on point-of-sale activity and involves several dimensions of promotion including:

◆ Logos, special storage and branding

◆ Locally devised packaging

◆ A personal selling approach

◆ Merchandising and display

◆ Point-of-sale advertising

◆ Distribution policy, especially dealer areas and competition limitations.

Advertising

It is estimated that within Western Europe every adult has up to 3000 'advertising encounters' every day. With so much expenditure on advertising it is perhaps surprising that there is any controversy over whether a company advertises or not. Lancaster and Withey (2005) articulate the diverse opinions surrounding the value of advertising as part of an organisation's promotional mix. Although most marketers agree that advertising has a role to play, some believe that it is an ineffective way of getting customers to purchase products. Two polar opposite positions can be identified as follows:

◆ Advertising is ineffective and a waste of money, only adding to company (and hence eventually customer) costs. Brands such as Body Shop, Pizza Express and Red Bull do not see a need to use advertising in their promotional campaigns relying instead on other sources of information in order to form positive attitudes towards their products. In any case, some might think that advertising demeans a particular product or company. In some cases advertising may seem unethical.

◆ Advertising is so powerful and effective as to be essential. Consumers, it could be argued, will rarely purchase unadvertised brands so by not advertising a company will be at a serious disadvantage compared to competitors. The results of advertising campaigns have been undeniably successful including for brands such as Orange, Walkers Crisps, Tango and French Connection.

Lancaster and Withey (2005) conclude that some brands may be strong enough to sell on their own merits only if they are long-established and have strong brand-loyal users. For advertising to be successful it needs to be:

◆ Well planned and executed

◆ Part of an effective promotional mix

◆ Effective as a communication tool

◆ Consistent with the values and mission of the organisation.

Activity 3.4

Reflect on why two of the companies cited, Body Shop and Pizza Express can afford not to advertise. Hint: (Think of the other compensating aspects associated with their operation such as PR within the promotional mix and place visibility.)

Sales promotion

Sales promotion – a range of techniques used to engage the purchaser. These may include discounting, coupons, guarantees, free gifts, competitions, vouchers, demonstrations, bonus commission and sponsorship. (CIM)

The key issue with promotion is that it is an invitation and incentive to act now; *everyday low prices* is not a promotion. This is a pricing strategy and should be considered as an element of the pricing aspect of the marketing mix. However, a *two for one* (BOGOF) promotion for a post-holiday, slow sales period is a promotional activity. There are a whole range of options including competitions and gifts. Sales promotion efforts are key in inducing trial of a new product, for example, using various forms of sampling to consumers.

In the B2B sector, promotion still has its part to play. Competitions can be used to motivate sales staff as distributors. When introducing a new computer product, free training could be offered.

Public relations

Public relations – the function or activity that aims to establish and protect the reputation of a company or brand, and to create mutual understanding between the organisation and the segments of the public with whom it needs to communicate. (CIM)

Some of the communications needed by an organisation are not best conducted by mass media. Therefore, for the management of political publics (e.g. planning application for a supermarket) it may be appropriate to have briefing sessions for local key decision-makers (e.g. local politicians).

Many organisations may not have a formal marketing department but will have a communications and public relations function (e.g. the police). In this context, a key responsibility will be agreeing, maintaining (here internal marketing may be key) and enforcing the corporate-communications manual. Often event management will be the responsibility of

PR specialists. The opening of new facilities or a product launch are activities that most marketers will get involved with sometime in their careers.

A key aspect is developing and maintaining good relations with the media publics/stakeholders. This is not achieved by sending out a press release commenting on the annual report, but is a continual process of developing and maintaining contacts. Here personal professional integrity is vital. One definition of PR is, 'the truth told well'. This is the very opposite of 'spin'. Your job is to get over the organisation's message; the media's responsibility is to get news. Taking airlines as an example, their press communications may one day be good news about the launch of a new route, the next, the worst of news, an accident or safety scare. PR contingency plans are, therefore, vital. The long-term relationship built up with the media is key to this. If the experience is that the organisation has been 'economical with the truth' then it should be no surprise that trust will be lacking.

Direct marketing

> **Direct marketing** – all activities which make it possible to offer goods or services or to transmit other messages to a segment of the population by post, telephone, e-mail or other direct means. (CIM)

The links in a distribution channel involve the manufacturer selling to a retailer who then acts as an intermediary to the final customer. Under this model the customer would have no direct dealings with the manufacturer. Where there is only one intermediary link in the chain the activity is referred to as a 'one level channel'. This generally applies to most consumer goods such as branded foodstuff and clothing.

Often there are several intermediaries in the chain ('two level channel') making manufacturer and ultimate customer contact even more unlikely. The further the manufacturer is from the final customer the less control the manufacturer has over marketing effort.

Direct marketing refers to a 'zero level channel' where the manufacturer interacts directly with the customer. Under these conditions 'place' becomes cyberspace. Examples include the web-based company Amazon.com and the direct booking of air travel on line. The Chartered Institute of Marketing (2004) comments that direct marketing:

> is becoming increasingly important, particularly as technology advances. It involves such techniques as direct mail shots, telesales, etc.

Even in the e-commerce age, direct mail is still a major tool. The first and most important issue is to obtain 'clean' contact address lists. These can come from an organisation's data retrieval form, an effective in-house MkIS (e.g. profiles constructed from purchases using a loyalty card) or from purchased lists (e.g. lists bought from learned societies for professionals interested in specific areas such as analytical instruments). In this area, there are significant conformance issues, and the legal issues regarding data protection are quite restrictive (the interpretation of data protection legislation is an evolving area and the law is different in different countries). If in doubt, the legal authorities should be consulted.

Care must be taken to get copyright and determine what will be an attractive proposition to the target. Given the limitations, the work and the costs, one might ask, 'Is it all worth it?' A key issue is that a good list can be highly targeted with minimum waste. Thus, though the costs per thousand are very high, when compared to many other options, the targeting and the quality of the presentation may make all the effort rewarding.

E-communications

E-communications have not changed the laws of marketing. It does not matter whether the order comes by e-mail or snail mail if you get the product to the customer late and damaged.

E-commerce is a very powerful addition to the integrated communications mix and just as jet travel made long-haul holidays affordable in price and feasible in travel time, it has created entirely new business opportunities. The key is to understand what is different about e-communications and how the differences can be exploited by an organisation and, more importantly, by other stakeholders (pressure groups have been quick on the uptake).

Some key differences are noted in Table 3.1.

Table 3.1: E-communications – selected differences

Issue	E-commerce	Traditional
Cost per hit	Near zero. Site costs fixed rather than variable	Cost of postage and brochure printing for traditional direct mail very high
Time	Quick and 24/7/365	Slow and needs people so not 24/7/365
Ability to update	With good organisation can be near real-time	Brochures once printed are pretty much fixed for the season without vast additional cost
Amount of content	With care, almost unlimited	Limited by the size of the document. Selectivity is not possible. Supplier has to cover the cost of providing 99% of content that is not relevant to the customer
Selectivity	With good navigation and key words, excellent	Hard work as often only indexed one way
Feedback and control	Sophisticated tracking tools can be built into the system using cookies and so on.	Mail shots can be tracked but the process is slower and more labour-intensive and expensive
Security	Probably high but customers are still concerned, a major issue for financial transactions	With registered post can be high but so are the costs of insurance
Two-way communications	Good but need care to manage responses	'Clunky' with snail mail but can be minimised with fax-back forms

There are clearly many major advantages to e-commerce but a number of issues that need to be kept in mind. The best website is of no value if people do not find their way there. Building 'hooks' into the site so that it appears early in searches is vital for sites where 'cold' discovery is important (e.g. a customer requiring a maintenance service for emergencies is not going to look through 20 screens).

In an integrated mix, traditional communications methods can be used to point people to the website. In addition, many sites have paid search engines like Google, Yahoo or Alta Vista to pull their address up in the first 10 or 20 responses to a general search. Product information on a pack should point to the appropriate part of the website as well as the helpline. Calls are expensive; the more the customers can do for themselves, the better it keeps transaction costs down.

Technological advances and the introduction of large organisational databases have enabled companies to identify customers, their behaviours and characteristics and build profiles of individual households including how they are made up and their collective interests. This has led to more accurate targeting of marketing communications and direct marketing to take place. (Thus direct marketing impinges on two aspects of the marketing mix: place and promotion.)

With the adoption of personal computers in the home, firms are increasingly dealing directly with customers who can buy virtually anything online without leaving their home. Supermarket shopping, for instance, need not be a physical event instead it can involve a 'mouse to house' transaction (borrowing the strap line from a supermarket chain). This has been facilitated by adoption of the technology in the home, acceptance of credit cards, and organisations developing efficient supply and distribution systems.

Activity 3.5

Identify what you believe to be some of the advantages of the Internet as a marketing channel.

Developments in communication technology, specifically cable, satellite and digital technologies have provided a platform for another form of home shopping via the television. Advantages over web-based selling include complete user familiarity with the equipment (the TV) and the ability to extensively demonstrate/advertise the products visually on a dedicated channel.

Telephone technology is not new but ownership is more widespread than ever. Within the UK virtually all businesses, most homes and increasingly individual teenagers and adults have a telephone. This provides the potential for contact to be made by telemarketing either to stimulate product interest, sell directly or arrange for a visit to be made by a salesperson.

There has of late been great emphasis in providing specialist training for telesales personnel including coaching on accent and responses to questions raised by customers. A contemporary trend is also the development of large call centres sometimes based overseas. ('M-marketing' refers to the technique being adopted using mobile telephones.) This type of selling involves the initiative being taken by the vendor and is unsolicited. As such it may be unwelcome, intrusive even and naturally ethical concerns can surface. Impolite approaches or 'pushy' sales techniques being employed are particularly distasteful.

Personal selling

This is often not included in the marketing budget, but if all the costs of personal selling were added up, the spend would far exceed the spend on advertising. For major consumer purchases (cars, mortgages, etc.), this element of the mix is vital. In B2B, the sales role is usually one of the more important elements of the communications mix.

If personal selling tends to be more important for B2B situations, point of sale (POS) is often key for the FMCG sector. This is, in effect, the opportunity to close the sale. The product must be displayed in as attractive a way as possible with as much convenience for both the buyer and the retailer (e.g. the confectionery display next to the pay point in the convenience store). Care must be taken with not only the style but also the location of display in the store. Proper grouping of products will increase overall sales. Attractive POS material may be offered free of charge for a minimum order value.

People

Relationship marketing is founded on the bedrock that people buy the service that is provided by other people. The effectiveness and efficiency of this process depends on relationships. Companies do not have relationships, people in companies do business and have relationships with other people in other companies. For effective service delivery, relationships must be good not only between the front-line staff and the customer, but also with all the internal stakeholders in the organisation supporting the front-line contact for all the part-time marketers. Many companies often state, 'People are our most valuable asset'.

Service delivery

People include both staff and customers. An organisation's people come into contact with customers and can have a massive impact on customer satisfaction levels. In the customers' eyes, staff are generally inseparable from the total service. This implies the need for well trained, motivated staff mindful of the adage 'the customer is always right'. It is important therefore that every member of staff contribute to the marketing philosophy and support the firm's external marketing activities.

As organisations introduce streamlined hierarchies and more flexible working practices, marketing offers the opportunity for their employees to operate in interdisciplinary teams furthering an overall marketing philosophy. Corporate investment in their most valuable asset, employees, through training and development supports the processes of creating and defending competitive advantages gained from successful marketing.

In terms of customers, good research should reveal vital, personal, cultural, social and psychological profiles of potential customers. This data can be exploited when applying other aspects of the marketing mix.

Transactional marketing

Transactional marketing is marketing aimed at individual transactions (or one-off sales), rather than at creating a long-standing customer relationship. Transactional marketing is most appropriate when marketing relatively low value consumer products, when the product is a commodity, when switching costs are low, when customers prefer single transactions to relationships, and when customer involvement in production is low. When the reverse of all the above is true, as in typical industrial and service markets, then relationship marketing can be more appropriate. Most firms should be blending the two approaches to match their portfolio of products and services. Virtually all products have a service component to them and this service component has been getting larger in recent decades.

Customer relationships

Relationship marketing is a form of marketing developed from direct response marketing campaigns conducted in the 1960s and 1980s. It emphasises customer retention and continual satisfaction rather than individual transactions and per-case customer resolution.

Relationship marketing differs from other forms of marketing in that it targets an audience with more directly suited information on products or services which suit retained customer's interests, as opposed to direct or 'intrusion' marketing, which focuses upon acquisition of new clients by targeting majority demographics based upon prospective client lists.

Process

Process refers to systems involved in providing a service focused upon 'identifying, anticipating and satisfying customer requirements'. So for instance, useful considerations might include the processes implied by the following questions:

◆　Do customers have to queue or wait to be dealt with?

◆　How are customers kept informed?

◆　Is the service conducted efficiently?

Processes assume greater significance in certain sectors such as banking and financial institutions. Much of the content of the Process P was covered in the section on the value chain in Unit 2.

Delivering the customer proposition

The customer value proposition consists of the sum total of benefits which a vendor promises that a customer will receive in return for the customer's associated payment (or other value-transfer). In simple words:

value proposition = what the customer gets for what the customer pays

Accordingly, a customer can evaluate a company's value-proposition on two broad dimensions with multiple subsets:

◆　Relative performance: what the customer gets from the company relative to a competitor's offering;

◆　Price: which consists of the payment the customer makes to acquire the product or service, plus the access cost

The company's marketing and sales efforts offer customers a value proposition; its delivery and customer-service processes then (hopefully) fulfil that value proposition.

End-to-end service support

The delivery of a service typically involves six factors:

1　The accountable service provider and its service suppliers (e.g. the people)

2　Equipment used to provide the service (e.g. vehicles, cash registers)

3　The physical facilities (e.g. buildings, parking, waiting rooms)

4　The consumer requesting service

5　Other customers at the service delivery location

6　Customer contact.

The service encounter is defined as all activities involved in the service delivery process. Some service managers use the term 'moment of truth' to indicate that defining point in a specific service encounter where interactions are most intense. However, service is a process that extends from the initial contact with the customer through to the customer's 'death' (in marketing terms, when they cease to be a customer for whatever reason).

Physical evidence

As one of the features of a service is that it is intangible by nature it cannot (unlike a product) be experienced before it is delivered. This means that potential customers may perceive greater risk. To overcome these feelings, service organisations can give reassurance by way of testimonials and references from past satisfied customers as a substitute for physical evidence.

Many services have small 'products' associated with them. The classic example is a ticket (e.g. travel, theatre, car park, etc.). The design and quality all make a communications statement. An invoice is not only a request for money but, in relationship-marketing terms, also an opportunity to communicate. An area where there has been much consumer dissatisfaction has been insurance policies and guarantees (the 'small-print syndrome'). These were (and still are by some poor companies) simply seen as legal documents. Of course they are, but they are also customer communications; if they are written in a language the customer does not understand, they have failed (every time you insure your car you do not want to consult your solicitor for a translation of the policy document).

In many contexts, products may be a substantial element in service provision. The quality of training manuals in a distance learning course or the food in a restaurant are all key to actual and perceived quality.

Tangible clues are an essential part of the service: you do not get onto the aircraft without your boarding pass. Facilitating goods are products that are associated with the service, which may or may not be supplied by the service provider. A golfer may have their own clubs or hire a set for the day. An opera-goer may purchase a copy of the opera libretto to add to their enjoyment or they may bring their own copy. Again, this should be viewed like a spectrum. A Manchester United shirt may be worn to the game as part of the ceremony surrounding the event. The coffee mug is a brand extension. Fine distinctions as to where you classify the product in the model are not too important. What is important is that such products are often major sources of income. The National Trust and museums exploit their 'service' brand image with a wide variety of goods, a major additional income stream to grants and subsidies.

Physical checks can be made on the standard of facilities (e.g. in a hotel washroom you may see a sign along the lines 'These toilets were inspected by #### at ####, any problems contact #####'). Plans can be made to refurbish to an agreed timetable. New styles (e.g. concept stores) can be test-marketed at just a few locations to see if they achieve the desired objectives. Tangible clues and facilitating goods are products, so they can be checked by normal product means.

Environment and ambiance

Services are intangible; physical evidence provides something tangible enabling people to 'feel' the quality of the service. How many people come into a shop? How long do they spend in the shop? What they buy is affected by the ambience and physical layout of the store. Lighting, heating, sound, colour and even smell (remember your last trip to the bakery) all contribute. This can be large-scale, such as the construction of a shopping mall, to the physical display of goods (there is no sharp dividing line between environment and point of sale for a shop). Airlines, theatres and museums all take care with their physical environment. Appropriate environments and even music can speed up recovery rates in hospitals.

Corporate image

A corporate image refers to how a corporation is perceived. It is a generally accepted image of what a company 'stands for' The creation of a corporate image is an exercise in perception management. The image is created primarily by marketing experts, who use public relations and other forms of promotion to suggest a mental picture to the public. Typically, a corporate image is designed to be appealing to the public, so that the company can spark an interest among consumers, generate brand equity, and thus facilitate product sales.

A corporation's image is not solely created by the company: other contributors to a company's image could include news media, journalists, labour unions, environmental organisations, and other NGOs.

Practice objective test questions

A Which were the original '4 Ps' of the marketing mix?
1 Product, Place, Packaging and Price
2 Product, Place, Price and Promotion
3 Product, Price, People and Processes

B According to Kotler, the marketing mix is the set of controllable marketing variables and their levels that a firm uses to influence the:
1 target market
2 level of spending on marketing
3 price of goods

C Which part of the marketing mix normally covers brand names and logos?
1 Packaging
2 Promotion
3 Product

D An organisation should concentrate on marketing:
1 Features rather than benefits
2 Neither benefits nor features
3 Benefits rather than features

E In a typical new product development process, which of the following stages is normally carried out earliest?
1 Idea screening
2 Beta testing
3 Business analysis

F   In a typical new product development process, which of the following stages normally contains the production of a prototype?

1   Concept testing

2   Idea screening

3   Beta testing

G   Which of the following methods seeks to gain market share by setting a low price?

1   Penetration

2   Predatory

3   Premium

H   In which part of the marketing mix do we normally consider distribution?

1   Process

2   Place

3   People

I   Public Relations (PR) is part of the:

1   Product mix

2   Promotional mix

3   Process mix

J   Offering discounts to wholesalers is an example of:

1   Push promotion

2   Pull promotion

3   Direct marketing

K   Which part of the marketing mix normally covers communication of the marketing proposition?

1   Price

2   Promotion

3   Product

L   Transactional marketing is most appropriate when marketing:

1   High value products

2   B2B products

3   Commodity products

M   The value chain model can be used to analyse:

1   People

2   Process

3   Physical evidence

Further work

Search on the Internet for details of the marketing activities carried out by a range of different organisations in different industries. Categorise the activities of each under the marketing mix headings. Why do the marketing mixes of organisations vary so much?

Unit 4
Marketing in different organisational contexts

Customers and buying decisions

Customers do not buy products, they buy *benefits*. I do not want a packet of detergent, I want clean clothes. Accountants see price, customers want to experience *value and affordability*. If they do not, there is no sale. Place involves decisions such as the nature of the outlet from which the product will be sold and the physical distribution (delivery) of the product to the outlets and finally to the consumer. However, customers are not interested in the organisation's smart supply chain logistics. They wish to experience *convenience* with the right product, in the right place, at the right time and in the right condition for the customer's use.

The firm wants to promote products, and to persuade people to buy their products. Consumers need to experience *communications* to persuade them that they want these benefits, that they can afford the product which is good value and convenient to obtain.

The service extension of the marketing mix (people, physical evidence and process) provides reassurance and confirmation of the quality of the service which, of necessity, is intangible (you do not walk away with a physical object).

The buying decision-making process

The process of making a purchase decision consists of a number of stages (Figure 4.1), each of which is considered in detail in the following sections.

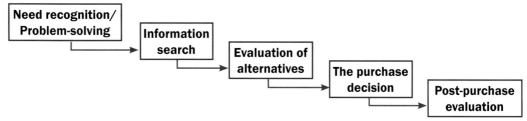

Figure 4.1: The buying decision

Need recognition/problem-solving

Recognising that, as a consumer, you need to purchase a product or service can happen for a number of reasons. It may be that you need to replace something you already own, which no longer fulfils your needs. A new father of twins may realise that his two-seater sports car is no longer the ideal car for him to own.

Other changes in your life may result in new purchases – a change of job requiring you to work from home will result in your needing office and IT facilities, or maybe you have just made a new set of friends who go skiing three times a year so you need the equipment to join them.

Outside influences also lead to us recognising a need. The knowledge that the population is ageing and today's 40-year-olds will probably not receive a sufficient state pension is prompting many to top up their personal pension plans. On a different scale, did we know that we needed a disposable toilet brush before we saw one advertised on TV? Communications can be the single most powerful influence if used well.

Needs arise for different reasons and different people will be aware of different needs, but once the need has been recognised then the consumer will be in a state of heightened attention, more likely to take notice of products/services that fulfil their needs or solve their problems.

Let us follow through an example of a couple booking their honeymoon, and see what messages and media they will be aware of as they progress through the buying process.

Information search

In this state of heightened awareness, in this case for an exotic and memorable holiday, the couple will start searching for information about their ideal honeymoon destination and itinerary.

They will search the Internet, look out for newspaper and magazine articles and advertising, walk the high street to interrogate the travel agents, listen to the radio, watch TV travel programmes and ask their friends and work colleagues about their experiences. At this stage, the message needs to be about the holiday resort. The strapline needs to conjure up the feeling of being on holiday and the visual needs to feature a long white beach, turquoise sea and palm trees.

The media will need to be carefully chosen to reach the target group – a bridal magazine will reach this couple but not other consumers for an exotic holiday.

Evaluation of alternatives

Having collated a plethora of information, the couple now need to sift through that information to make a considered decision. They will start considering their important criteria in order to sift the information – which country, which resort, hotel or self-catering, duration of flight, departing airport. At this stage, they will find information gaps and need to gain additional, more detailed information on certain options.

Websites and the travel agent can provide this information but it needs to be easily accessible for them to retain interest in a particular holiday package. They are also looking for a USP or differentiating factor that will make their choice easier. This could be a complimentary bottle of champagne on arrival or a limo to the airport.

Whichever is likely to appeal to this couple is what the holiday company needs to be finding out and communicating to them. This message is unlikely to be the banner headline for the company but in all the brochures, websites and travel agents it does need to be contained within the communication from the organisation. The key objective here is to *inform* detail.

The purchase decision

In most cases it is the salesperson either in a shop or on the phone that will move the consumer towards making a final purchase decision. In the case of online purchasing, the ease of access and navigability of the site will aid the purchase transaction, but a site that shows positive customer feedback and comprehensive resort guides will help the purchaser towards the final purchase.

It is important at this stage that there are no last minute hitches to put off the purchaser. A crowded travel agent, ever-ringing phone or an unavailable website will mean the couple do not see the final purchase decision through and could lead to them reconsidering their decision.

Added value gained at the point of purchase can also sway a decision. A third week free could encourage people to lengthen their stay; free travel insurance can encourage them to consider another company. It is important that the messages received by the consumer at this stage help to confirm in their minds that they have made the right decision and they feel secure in their choice. The key objective here is to *differentiate*.

Post-purchase evaluation

We cannot forget the consumer once they have made their purchase. What happens after purchase will affect their repurchasing decisions and the feedback that they give to family and friends. There need to be feedback devices incorporated within any communication so that problems can be detected early and acted upon. Front-line staff need to be competent in dealing with problems and complaints. The message here needs to be one of reassurance that problems will be sorted out and there are available resources to enable that to happen. Only if this occurs can customer satisfaction arise. The key objective here is to continue the *differentiation* to *remind* the couple why they made this choice.

The buying decision-making unit

In B2B marketing, it may be relevant for an organisation to communicate not only with the purchaser but also with others who could be involved in the decision to purchase. The people involved in the purchase decision tend to have quite formal and closely defined roles; these individuals who make and influence buying decisions in a B2B environment are known as the decision-making unit, the DMU (Figure 4.2).

For example, a firm that supplies photocopiers to small businesses needs to communicate with a variety of people, including the admin assistant who will use the machine, the office manager who has encountered other machines working in other organisations, and the finance director who will be interested in how much it will cost. These are not direct customers, but may influence the decision to buy and therefore need to be communicated with.

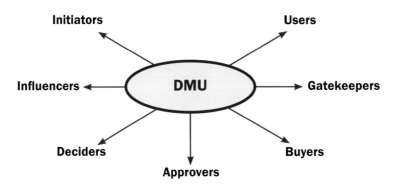

Figure 4.2: The DMU

Various roles have been identified:

◆ In the case of a substantial organisation, the **initiators** might be senior management needing technology to reduce costs.

◆ **Influencers** would include technical staff such as maintenance technicians.

◆ **Deciders** in this case might well be a small committee that advise the board on the purchase decision.

◆ **Approvers** would include senior financial staff (e.g. financial aspects of contracts including penalty clauses for late delivery).

◆ The **buyers** in this case will be strongly influenced by the control of the deciders, with little flexibility to switch vendors or change the contract.

◆ **Gatekeepers** would include such functions as safety (compliance of equipment with local and company safety policy, e.g. VDU use).

◆ The **users** are the operators and the like.

The reason for this DMU analysis is that not all the DMU participants will meet sales staff and so the literature and the rest of the integrated communications must carry the company message to them. The members of the DMU are key stakeholders with whom the selling organisation needs to build strong links/relationships.

Using the marketing mix

Concentrating on any single element of the mix is pointless. The advertising campaign is not going to be effective if the product does not work, is not in the shops or costs more than people are prepared to pay for it. Moreover, the elements of the mix must be in harmony and consistent as they interact. When considering the appropriate communications mix, the marketer needs to ensure that all the other elements of the marketing mix can communicate.

The brand imagery communicated in the advertisements needs to be carried over onto the packaging, an element of product. For luxury and exclusive products, a low price would not sustain the exclusivity proposition. In the same way, if the product were available in every cut-price outlet, it would be difficult to sustain the luxury image.

In developing the detailed plans for one element such as product, it is necessary to consider issues such as point-of-sale ideas. For example, some soft drinks are sold from racks that grip a collar around the neck of the bottle; integrated design was needed for both the product and the point-of-sale promotional stand.

The marketing mix in different types of organisation

Hopefully, the business contexts within which marketing principles can be usefully applied are apparent. A few of these contexts are discussed here to give a flavour of the particular considerations including buying decisions and consumer behaviour. These contexts are:

◆ Fast-moving consumer goods

◆ Business-to-business

◆ Services

◆ Voluntary and not-for-profit (NFP) organisations

◆ Online businesses.

Fast moving consumer goods organisations

Consumer goods can take two forms:

◆ Durable goods

◆ Fast-moving consumer goods (FMCGs).

The decision to purchase high-cost durable goods such as televisions, computers, cars and furniture and the frequency of repurchase will be influenced by changing technical features, fashions and wearing-out of the old product.

FMCGs are by comparison purchased for personal reasons and generally involve relatively low financial outlays. For FMCGs like canned foods, soft drinks and confectionery there may be habitual purchasing but products tend to have short life cycles. It follows therefore that the marketing mix will differ considerably between both types of consumer good. Understanding consumers involves appreciating the factors that affect buying decisions as well as types of buying behaviour.

Of particular relevance to FMCG is advertising, branding and packaging. Lancaster and Withey (2005) identify the following key factors influencing FMCG purchasing behaviour:

◆ personal factors (age, gender, income, etc.)

◆ psychological factors (perceptions, motives, attitudes)

◆ social/cultural factors (family influence, reference groups, etc.).

Business-to-business organisations

For organisations that market goods and services to other intermediary organisations (rather than direct to ultimate consumers), the implication of buyer behaviour, the assessment of marketing opportunities and industrial market segmentation take on heightened significance.

Business-to-business (B2B) marketing differs from business-to-consumer (B2C) marketing in a number of key respects, not least the purchaser makes purchasing decisions for organisational rather than personal reasons. In addition many people are involved in the B2B buying decision including:

◆ Initiators who start the buying process. (It might be for instance a department who identify a need to replace a piece of equipment.)

◆ Influencers who affect the buying decision often based on their particular technical expertise.

◆ Buyers who raise orders and sanction payment and although they may enter into negotiation they may be guided heavily by others in the organisation.

◆ Users who ultimately operate the equipment.

Activity 4.1

On what basis are B2B purchasing decisions made?

Service organisation

Recognition should be given to the fact that there are fundamental differences between products and services; hence the marketing of a service assumes a different emphasis.

Mullins (2005) identified the main differentiating features as:

◆ The consumer is a participant in the service process.

◆ Services are perishable. If there is no sale on Monday it cannot (unlike a tin of fruit) be sold on Tuesday: that sale is lost forever.

◆ Services are intangible, so communication is made more difficult when explaining the benefits.

◆ Services are people orientated and the characteristics of the workforce determine the effectiveness of the service.

◆ Output measurement is less easy to evidence.

Activity 4.2

Using the above features identify examples of services and the implications of these features on service marketing.

This thinking can be directly applied to the marketing mix, for instance:

◆ The 'product' will consider in particular issues of type and range of service offered.

◆ Pricing will be mindful of perishability of the service.

◆ Promotion might emphasise personal selling.

◆ Place will take account of the fact that the consumer is a participant in the service.

For service organisations it is worth noting the heightened emphasis on the augmentation of the four 'Ps' already identified namely:

- **People** – As employees interface with customers and can have a massive impact on customer satisfaction levels.

- **Processes** – Systems involved in providing a service.

- **Physical evidence** – Organisations can give reassurance by way of testimonials and references from past satisfied customers as a substitute for physical evidence.

Lancaster and Withey (2005) explain that the banking industry took a long time to wake up to the need to be customer oriented and the benefits of using the marketing tools and techniques in the same way that fast-moving consumer goods did. They identify a dramatic change over the past decade concluding that 'the global banking sector is one of the success stories in recent years of the application and implementation of the marketing concept'. Some of the changes include:

- Market research and analysis designed to keep in touch with customer needs and customer satisfaction levels

- Organisational and marketing structures based around customer requirements

- Marketing planning and control systems including market segmentation and targeting

- A need for increased quality, service and customer care, and

- An awareness of wider environmental factors, including its ethical and social responsibilities towards customers.

Voluntary and not-for-profit organisations

For other service organisations, such as not-for-profit (NFP) organisations including charities, hospitals, political parties and universities and local authorities, marketing has been embraced with varying degrees of enthusiasm and success. It is beyond the scope of this material to discuss the marketing implications of each in turn but it is worthwhile perhaps highlighting the particular features associated with NFP organisations, namely:

- NFPs are subject to tighter legislative requirements

- Heightened issues of achieving value for money often arise;

- Customers may be a different grouping from those paying for the service.

Online business organisations

According to Otlacan (www.teawithedge.com) e-marketing strategy is often based upon the principles that govern traditional, offline marketing – the well-known marketing mix. Otlacan proposes an extended 'E-marketing mix', based on a 2P + 2C+ 3S formula:

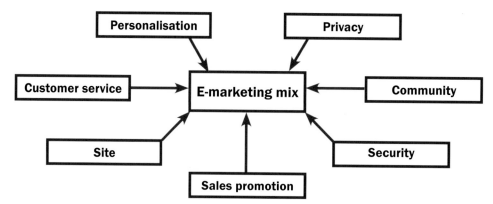

Figure 4.3: The E-marketing mix (Otlacan)

Personalisation

The fundamental concept of personalisation as a part of the e-marketing mix lies in the need of recognising and identifying each customer in order to establish relations. It is crucial to be able to identify customers onan individual level and to gather all possible information about them, with the purpose of knowing the market and to be able to develop customised, personalised products and services.

For example, a cookie strategically placed on the website visitor's computer can let the marketer know vital information concerning the access speed available: in consequence, if it is known that the visitor is using a slow connection (e.g. dial-up) a low-volume variation of the website will be offered, with reduced graphic content and no multimedia or flash applications. This will ease the customer's experience on the website and he or she will be less likely to leave the website for the reason that it takes too long to load its pages.

Privacy

Privacy is an element of the mix very much connected to the previous one – personalisation. When we gather and store information about our customers and potential customers (in other words, when we perform the personalisation part of the e-marketing mix) a crucial issue arises: that of the way this information will be used, and by whom. A major task when implementing an e-marketing strategy is that of creating and developing a policy on access procedures to the collected information.

It is a duty and a must for any conscientious marketer to consider all aspects of privacy, as long as data about individuals is collected and stored. Privacy is even more important when establishing the e-marketing mix since there are many regulations and legal aspects to be considered, e.g. the Data Protection Act, regarding collection and usage of such information.

Customer service

Customer service is one of the necessary and required support function activities in transactional situations. When switching from a situational perspective to a relational one (and e-marketing is mostly based on a relational perspective) marketers find themselves somehow forced into considering support and assistance on a non-temporal level, permanently, over time.

For these reasons, we should consider the customer service function (in its fullest and largest definition) as an essential one within the e-marketing mix.

Community

The value of a network is given by the number of its components. More exactly the value of a network equals the square of the number of components. We can apply this simple law to communities, since they are a network. Thus the value of a community rises with the number of its members.

The customers of a business can be seen as part of a community where they interact (either independent or influenced by the marketer), therefore developing a community is a task to be performed by any business, even though it is not always seen as essential.

Site

E-marketing interactions take place on a digital medium – the Internet. But such interactions and relations also need a proper location, to be available at any moment and from any place – a digital location for digital interactions.

Such a location is what we call a 'site', which is the most widespread name for it. It is now the time to mention that the 'website' is just one form of site. The 'site' can take other forms too, such as a Palm Pilot or any other handheld device, for example.

Security

The security function emerged as an essential function of e-marketing once transactions began to be performed through Internet channels.

What we need to keep in mind as marketers are the following two security issues:

◆ security during transactions performed on our website, where we have to take all possible precautions that third parties will not be able to access any part of a developing transaction;

◆ security of data collected and stored, about our customers and visitors.

A honest marketer will have to consider these possible causes of further trouble and has to co-operate with the company's IT department in order to be able to give convincing messages to the customers that their personal details are protected from unauthorised eyes.

Sales promotion

Last but not least, we have to consider sales promotions when we build an e-marketing strategy. Sales promotions are widely used in traditional marketing, and are an excellent, efficient, strategy to achieve immediate sales goals in terms of volume.

This function counts on the marketer's ability to think creatively: a lot of work and inspiration is required in order to find new possibilities and new approaches for developing an efficient promotion plan. On the other hand, the marketer needs to continuously keep up with the latest Internet technologies and applications so that he or she can fully exploit them.

E-marketing thus implies new dimensions to be considered alongside those inherited from traditional marketing.

Practice objective test questions

A Which is the most appropriate sequence of stages in the buying decision-making process?

1 Need recognition, information search, evaluation, decision
2 Need recognition, evaluation, information search, decision
3 Information search, need recognition, evaluation, decision

B A USP is a:

1 Target market
2 Differentiating factor
3 Type of retailer

C Which of the following is a role in the DMU?

1 Suppliers
2 Advertisers
3 Gatekeepers

D Consumer goods can take the form of:

1 Hard or soft goods
2 FMCGs or durables
3 Basic or augmented goods

E The main difference between B2C and B2B marketing is that, in B2B marketing:

1 The purchaser makes decisions for personal reasons
2 The purchaser makes decisions for organisational reasons
3 The purchaser does not make decisions

F In Otlacan's e-marketing mix, the 2Cs are?

1 Concept and consumer
2 Customer and consumer
3 Customer service and community

Further work

For an Internet-based organisation with which you are familiar, identify the organisation's marketing activities and classify them according to Otlacan's e-marketing mix.

Compare the marketing mix of a B2B organisation with that of a B2C organisation.

Compare the marketing mix of a FMCG organisation with that of a service organisation.

Using the Internet, analyse the marketing mix of a not-for-profit organisation such as a charity.

Unit 5
Review: What is marketing?

Using this unit

This unit is a summary of units 1 to 4, for revision purposes. It has two components:

◆ Revision notes, for you to revise before the assessment, and to give you clues and hints while practising objective-test questions. These notes will allow you to quickly review the key points of each section.

◆ Overview diagrams showing the key points. These can be used as the basis for your own final revision tools. You should supplement them, not with notes based on this text, but with additional material found by looking at other sources, or at relevant organisations.

Marketing as an exchange process

◆ **Definitions of marketing**

 ♦ The management process responsible for identifying, anticipating and satisfying customer requirements profitably. (CIM)

 ♦ It is all about getting the right product or service to the customer at the right price, in the right place, at the right time. (Kotler/CIM)

◆ **The exchange process**

 ♦ The process of marketing is concerned with the establishment and maintenance of mutually satisfying exchange relationships. (Baker)

 ♦ Communication is key

 ♦ Stakeholder relationships are key

Marketing and customer satisfaction

◆ **Marketing, analysis and planning**

   ◆ Current and changing customer requirements
   ◆ Effectiveness of marketing
   ◆ Customer satisfaction objective
   ◆ Marketing impact of strategic options

◆ **Making customer satisfaction a business objective**

   ◆ Satisfying customers is at the heart of marketing
   ◆ Marketing is a shared business ethos
   ◆ Orientations
       • Production
       • Product
       • Sales
       • Marketing
   ◆ What is marketing?
   ◆ Department/function
   ◆ Culture/ethos
   ◆ The evolution of marketing:
       • The production era
       • The sales era
       • The marketing era
       • The relationship era

◆ **Ensuring marketing practices secure customer retention**

- ◆ Customer retention is key
- ◆ Retaining customers is much cheaper than getting new ones
- ◆ Retention needs a strategy

Marketing as a cross-functional activity

◆ **Marketing and the organisation**

- ◆ Marketing does not just happen within the marketing department
- ◆ Dialogue is necessary between marketing and each of the other functions
- ◆ Marketing is both customer and supplier to other functions
- ◆ Information must be complete, accurate and on time

◆ **Research and development**

- ◆ Customer needs
- ◆ Timings

◆ **Human resource management**

- ◆ Planned marketing activity
- ◆ Organisational design

◆ **Finance**

- ◆ Budgeting
- ◆ Activity and performance
- ◆ New projects

◆ **Operations**

- ◆ Demand
- ◆ Quality
- ◆ Stock

◆ **Information technology**

- ◆ Content
- ◆ Customer service
- ◆ Design

◆ **Customer services**

- ◆ Feedback
- ◆ Product/service features and benefits

Internal marketing

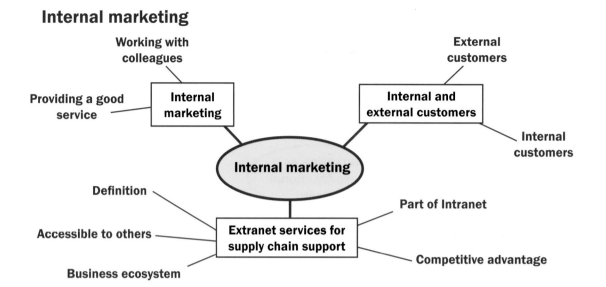

- ◆ **Internal and external customers**
  - ◆ **External customers**
    - ◦ B2C
    - ◦ B2B
    - ◦ C2C
  - ◆ **Internal customers**
    - ◦ Other functions
    - ◦ Line manager
    - ◦ Colleagues within marketing
- ◆ **Internal marketing**
  - ◆ Working together with colleagues
  - ◆ Providing them with a good service
- ◆ **Extranet services for supply chain support**
  - ◆ An extranet can be defined as a collaborative network that uses Intranet technology to link businesses with their suppliers, customers, and other businesses that share common goals. (CIMA)
  - ◆ Part of a company's intranet
  - ◆ Accessible to other companies
  - ◆ May lead to competitive advantage
  - ◆ Business ecosystem
    - ◦ Creative ideas
    - ◦ New products
    - ◦ Manufacturing agility
    - ◦ Customer focus

The importance of the marketing environment

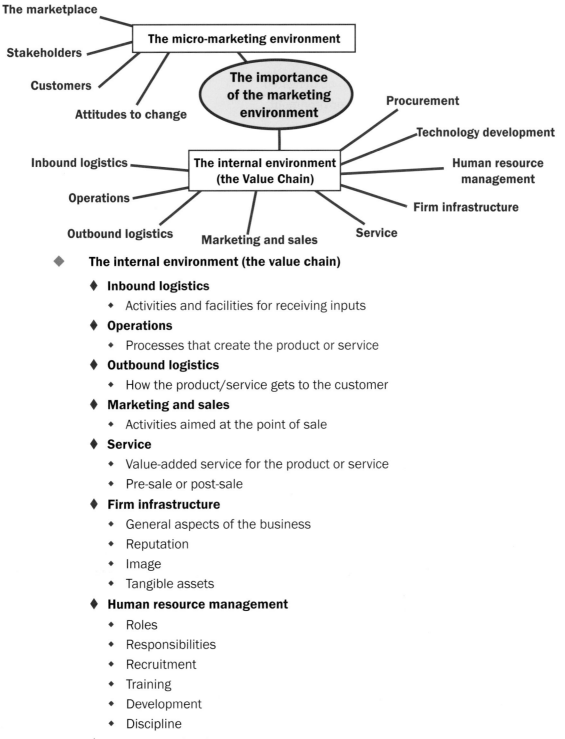

- ◆ **The internal environment (the value chain)**
  - ◆ **Inbound logistics**
    - Activities and facilities for receiving inputs
  - ◆ **Operations**
    - Processes that create the product or service
  - ◆ **Outbound logistics**
    - How the product/service gets to the customer
  - ◆ **Marketing and sales**
    - Activities aimed at the point of sale
  - ◆ **Service**
    - Value-added service for the product or service
    - Pre-sale or post-sale
  - ◆ **Firm infrastructure**
    - General aspects of the business
    - Reputation
    - Image
    - Tangible assets
  - ◆ **Human resource management**
    - Roles
    - Responsibilities
    - Recruitment
    - Training
    - Development
    - Discipline
  - ◆ **Technology development**
    - Information and communications systems
    - Internets, intranets and extranets

◆ **Procurement**
  • The purchase of the inputs to the value chain
◆ **Controllable and uncontrollable environmental factors**
  • All factors are uncontrollable
  • Can be influenced
  • Their impact can be mitigated
◈ **The micro-marketing environment**
◆ **The marketplace**
  • Buyers
  • Users
  • Buyers can exert power
  • Marketing strategies
  • Push strategy
  • Pull strategy
◆ **Stakeholders**
  • Customers
  • Consumers
  • Regulators
  • Suppliers
  • Trade associations
  • Media
  • Competitors
  • Employees
◆ **Attitudes to change**
  • Enthusiastic co-operation and support
  • Passive resignation
  • Passive resistance
  • Active resistance

The PESTEL model

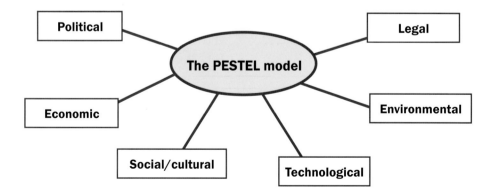

◆ **Political**

 ♦ Stability
 ♦ Attitudes to industry
 ♦ Attitudes to competition
 ♦ Climate for 'free trade'
 ♦ Attitudes to foreign investors

◆ **Economic**

 ♦ Business cycle
 ♦ Inflation rates
 ♦ Interest rates
 ♦ Disposable income
 ♦ Wealth distribution
 ♦ Consumer spending patterns
 ♦ Credit availability
 ♦ Employment levels
 ♦ Exchange rates
 ♦ Taxation

◆ **Social/cultural**

 ♦ Demographics
 ♦ Society
 ♦ Culture

◆ **Technological**

 ♦ Inventions
 ♦ Discoveries
 ♦ Information technologies

◆ **Environmental**

 ♦ Consumer pressure
 ♦ Volatile organic compounds (VOC)
 ♦ Persistent organic pollutants (POP)
 ♦ Ozone depletion/CFCs
 ♦ Global warming
 ♦ Genetic engineering issues
 ♦ Environmental fate
 ♦ Sustainable development
 ♦ Life cycle analysis

◆ **Legal**

 ♦ Monopolies and mergers
 ♦ Competition
 ♦ Consumer legislation

- Health and safety
- Consumer safety (e.g. strict liability)
- Employment law
- Environmental law
- Regulations (e.g. labelling)
- Codes of conduct
- Self-regulation

Monitoring the marketing environment

- **Marketing information system (MkIS)**
  - Macro-environment
  - What data needs to be collected?
  - How can it be collected efficiently?
  - What use is to be made of the information?
  - Micro-environment
- **Market scanning**
  - Marketing intelligence
  - Competitors' websites
  - Annual reports
  - Mystery shopping
  - Trade press
  - Specific research
  - Specialist trade magazines
  - Customer visits
  - Reverse engineering
- **Collection of secondary data**
  - EPOS systems and loyalty cards
  - Evaluate for accuracy and relevance

The importance of the marketing mix

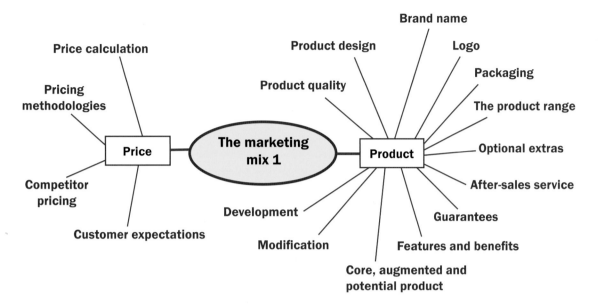

◆ **The marketing mix** –The set of controllable variables and their levels that the firm uses to influence the target market. (Kotler)

◆ **Product**

   ◆ Product quality and durability
   ◆ Product design
   ◆ Brand name
   ◆ Logo
   ◆ Packaging
   ◆ The product range
   ◆ After-sales service
   ◆ Optional extras
   ◆ Guarantees and warranties
   ◆ Features and benefits
      ◆ Are customers satisfied with existing products and services?
      ◆ Do these products or services fulfil their future needs?
      ◆ How are competitors addressing themselves to the same questions?
      ◆ Can competitors' products satisfy customers' future needs?
   ◆ Core, augmented and potential product
      ◆ Core benefits are 'hygiene' properties
      ◆ Levels of product
   ◆ New product development
      ◆ Idea generation (The 'fuzzy front end' of the NPD process)
      ◆ Idea screening

- Concept development and testing
- Business analysis
- Product development
- Market testing
- Commercialisation (often considered post-NPD)
- ◆ Product modification
  - Changes to augmented product
  - Repositioning a current product into a new market or segment
  - Core product revision
  - Line extensions
  - New product lines
  - Completely new products
- ◆ **Price**
  - Basic price levels
  - Discounts and allowances
  - Payment terms and credit policy
- ◆ Price calculation
  - The economic view
  - The accountancy view
  - The marketing view
- ◆ Pricing methodologies
  - Competitive
  - Cost plus
  - Market based
  - Penetration
  - Predatory
  - Premium
  - Price skimming
  - Selective: category; consumer; peak
- ◆ Competitor pricing
  - Aim for cost leadership
  - The experience curve
  - Economies of scale
  - Add value to the product
  - Differentiate it from the competitor's offering
  - Focus on a segment
- ◆ Customer expectations
  - What will they pay?
  - Existing customers are less price sensitive
  - Price can imply quality

◆ **Place**

- ◆ Role of distribution
  - ◆ Transport (physical delivery of the service or product)
  - ◆ The standard of service/inventory required
  - ◆ Geographical cover
- ◆ Nature of distribution
  - ◆ Delivery options
  - ◆ Hybrid solutions
  - ◆ Multiple methods
- ◆ Distribution channels
  - ◆ Producer to customer
  - ◆ Producer to retailer to customer
  - ◆ Producer to wholesaler to retailer to customer
  - ◆ Producer to agent to wholesaler to retailer to customer
- ◆ The changing role of logistics
  - ◆ Digital transmission
  - ◆ Direct sales
- ◆ Online and offline purchasing
  - ◆ The 'dot-com' company

◆ **Promotion**

- ◆ The selling mix
  - ◆ Logos, special storage and branding
  - ◆ Locally devised packaging
  - ◆ A personal selling approach
  - ◆ Merchandising and display
  - ◆ Point-of-sale advertising
  - ◆ Distribution policy

- Advertising
  - Critical success factors
  - Well planned and executed
  - Part of an effective promotional mix
  - Effective as a communication tool
  - Consistent with the values and mission of the organisation
- Sales promotion
  - Competitions and gifts
  - Special offers
  - Short-term low price
- Public relations
  - Communications with: customers, media
  - Good publicity
  - Bad publicity
- Direct marketing
  - A 'zero level channel'
  - Get clean customer data
  - Get copyright
  - Find an attractive selling proposition
- E-communications
  - Benefits
  - Cost per hit
  - Time
  - Ability to update
  - Amount of content
  - Selectivity
  - Feedback and control
  - Security
  - Two-way communications
  - Methods
  - Web
  - Telephone
  - TV
  - Mobile telephones
- Personal selling
  - B2B
  - Durables
  - FMCG

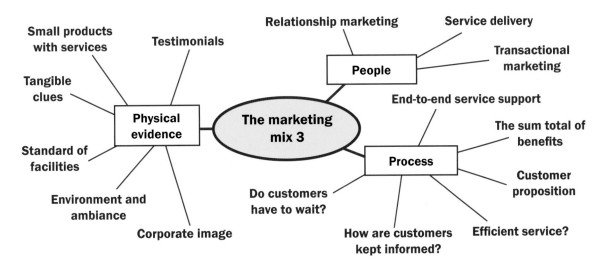

- ◆ **People**
  - ◆ Relationship marketing
    - • People in companies do business
    - • Front-line staff
    - • Part-time marketers
  - ◆ Service delivery
    - • Staff
    - • Customers
  - ◆ Transactional marketing
    - • Aimed at individual transactions (or one-off sales)
    - • Opposite of relationship marketing
    - • Used when
      - • Relatively low-value consumer products
      - • The product is a commodity
      - • Switching costs are low
      - • Customers prefer single transactions
      - • Customer involvement in production is low
- ◆ **Process**
  - ◆ Do customers have to queue or wait to be dealt with?
  - ◆ How are customers kept informed?
  - ◆ Is the service conducted efficiently?
  - ◆ Delivering the customer proposition
  - ◆ The sum total of benefits
    - • Evaluated by: relative performance and
    - • Relative price
  - ◆ End-to-end service support
    - • The delivery of a service
    - • The people

- Equipment
- The physical facilities
- The consumer
- Other customers
- Customer contact

◆ **Physical evidence**

- Testimonials
- Small products with services
- Tangible clues
- Standard of facilities
- Environment and ambiance
  - Ambience
  - Physical layout
  - Lighting
  - Heating
  - Sound
  - Colour
  - Smell
- Corporate image
  - What a company 'stands for'
  - An exercise in perception management
  - Public relations and promotion
  - Other contributors
  - News media
  - Journalists
  - Labour unions
  - Environmental organisations
  - NGOs

Customers and buying decisions

- ◆ **Customers buy benefits**
  - ♦ They wish to experience convenience
  - ♦ Consumers need communications to persuade them
- ◆ **The buying decision-making process**
  - ♦ Need recognition/problem-solving
  - ♦ Information search
  - ♦ Evaluation of alternatives
  - ♦ The purchase decision
  - ♦ Post-purchase evaluation
- ◆ **B2B marketing**
  - ♦ The buying decision-making unit
    - ◆ DMU roles
      - ◆ Initiators
      - ◆ Influencers
      - ◆ Deciders
      - ◆ Approvers
      - ◆ Buyers
      - ◆ Gatekeepers
      - ◆ Users
    - ◆ Members of the DMU are key stakeholders

Using the marketing mix

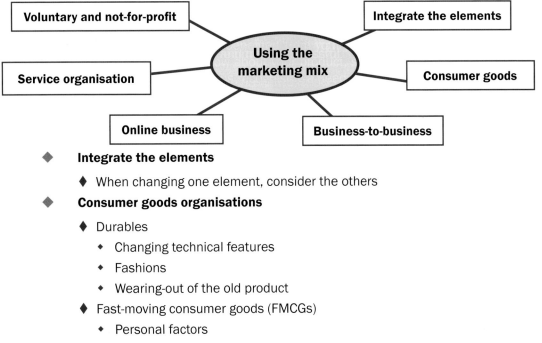

- ◆ **Integrate the elements**
  - ♦ When changing one element, consider the others
- ◆ **Consumer goods organisations**
  - ♦ Durables
    - ◆ Changing technical features
    - ◆ Fashions
    - ◆ Wearing-out of the old product
  - ♦ Fast-moving consumer goods (FMCGs)
    - ◆ Personal factors
    - ◆ Psychological factors
    - ◆ Social/cultural factors

- **Business-to-business organisations**
  - Industrial segmentation
  - DMU
- **Service organisation**
  - The consumer is a participant
  - Services are perishable
  - Services are intangible
  - Services are people orientated
  - Output measurement is less easy
- **Voluntary and not-for-profit organisations**
  - Subject to tighter legislative requirements
  - Heightened issues of achieving value for money
  - Customers not consumers
- **Online business organisations**
  - 2P + 2C+ 3S
    - Personalisation
    - Privacy
    - Customer service
    - Community
    - Site
    - Security
    - Sales Promotion

Assessment information

Both units will have their own assessment and be as follows:

Unit 1 – What is Marketing?: A 1 hour online test, consisting of objective format questions

Unit 2 – Understanding Customer Relationships: A written project made up of a number of short work-based tasks

Success in an assessment associated with each unit will lead to the award of that unit. Students who wish to be awarded the CIM Introductory Certificate will have to successfully complete the assessments associated with both units.

Practice objective test questions

A Marketing is defined as the identification, anticipation and satisfaction of customer:

1 Service

2 Needs

3 Demand

B   A business offers a product or service and the customer offers a sum of money in return for it. In marketing terms this is know as:

1   The cost and benefit process

2   The purchase process

3   The exchange process

C   In order to be marketing focused an organisation must:

1   Promote its goods and services aggressively

2   Satisfy customer needs and wants

3   Sell low-cost highly demanded goods

D   Which of the following statements is true of the new product development (NPD) process?

1   Concept testing comes after idea generation, but before the screening of new ideas.

2   Business analysis comes after the screening of new ideas, but before test marketing.

3   Idea generation comes after concept testing, but before test marketing.

E   Which of the following types of media is likely to be most appropriate for advertising in a small geographical area?

1   Web advertising

2   Hoardings

3   Television

F   Which of the following factors is an example of the MICRO marketing environment?

1   Economic factors

2   Competitor factors

3   Political factors

G   Which of the following statements is true in relation to the sale of goods?

1   A wholesaler sells to retailers.

2   A firm which sells its products to the final consumers on the Internet is classified as a wholesaler.

3   A firm which sells its products via telephone selling is classified as an agent.

H   Which one of the following is an example of an *economic* factor?

1   Exchange rates

2   Population age distribution

3   Product innovations and developments

I   Which of the statements below underlies the Sale of Goods Act?

1   Selling goods that are subject to unreasonable price increases.

2   Selling goods to underage consumers.

3   Selling goods that are not as described.

Part 2
Understanding customer relations

Overview

The second half of this book covers Unit 2 of the Introductory Certificate in Marketing syllabus.

This part of the sylllabus focuses on developing an understanding of internal and external customers, and considers how a knowledge and understanding of customers can assist in designing appropriate marketing activities to engage and support customers to achieve long-term customer loyalty.

It also provides some insight into the practicalities of developing internal and external relationships, including consideration of networking, collaboration and co-operation in order to reduce the potential for conflict.

Developing effective tactical communications and effective customer service support is essential to harmonious relationships in both B2B and B2C organisations, and as a result the syllabus here considers the contributions that these activities can make to developing relationships for marketing and business success.

It explains why organisations need to know and understand their customers and how successful relationships can be developed through effective communications and strong customer service and support.

Overarching learning outcomes

By the end of this unit, students should be able to:

◆ Explain the importance of understanding customers, and how marketing information aids the better development of marketing activities to achieve customer satisfaction

◆ Explain the value and importance of internal and external relationships of the organisation and the importance of networking, collaboration and co-operation in order to develop and maintain relationships

◆ Recognise the importance of internal relationships as an aid to the marketing function establishing its cross-functional presence

◆ Explain the different ways in which to communicate with both internal and external customers in order to develop, maintain and strengthen customer relationships

◆ Explain the requirements for developing effective and efficient customer service and customer care in order to maintain successful relationships

Learning outcomes and syllabus content

Chapter 6

Understanding customers (weighting 20%)

1.1 Discuss the need for organisations to understand about the needs of the customer and the benefits of a marketing orientated approach

1.2 Recognise the importance of collecting information to gain a better understanding of customer needs.

1.3 Explain how information collected from a range of sources can be stored in order to create and maintain a customer database.

1.4 Explain how customer information can help with identifying customer needs and developing appropriate marketing mix activities.

Chapter 7

Building and maintaining effective internal and external customer relationships (weighting 30%)

2.1 Explain the different types and characteristics of people with which an organisation develops relationships.

2.2 Describe the links between the marketing concept, a customer focus and the relationship marketing.

2.3 Explain how marketing activities help to support relationships with customers.

2.4   Explain the importance of developing and sustaining customer, supplier and distributor relationships.

2.5   Describe approaches used to build and develop relationships both within the marketing function and across the organisation.

2.6   Identify key colleagues within the organisation with whom it is important to develop relationships.

2.7   Identify potential areas of conflict that can occur between the functions of an organisation.

2.8   Describe the methods that can be used to overcome conflict between organisational functions:

2.9   Discuss the need to take into account the views of others within the organisation when undertaking marketing activities:

Chapter 8

Communicating with internal and external customers (weighting 30%)

3.1   Explain the importance of communication as a tool to aid the development and maintenance of long-term relationships.

3.2   Explain the nature and scope of the communications cycle.

3.3   Explain the various business formats required for communicating both internally and externally with customers.

3.4   Explain the importance of good verbal and non-verbal communications.

3.5   Identify the strengths and weakness of promotional activities in a range of different marketing scenarios designed to aid relationship **management**.

3.6   Describe the processes involved in undertaking a range of tactical direct marketing campaigns.

3.7   Discuss how customer databases can be used to support tactical marketing communications activities.

3.8   Explain the process used for effectively managing a communications budget for specific communications tasks, including apportioning costs effectively.

3.9   Identify and explain the different methods available for monitoring and measuring the success of internal and external tactical communications campaigns.

Chapter 9

Providing customer service for internal and external customers (weighting 20%)

4.1   Describe the concept of customer care and customer service and its importance in different sectors.

4.2   Explain the relationship between customer care, customer focus, relationship marketing.

4.3   Describe the different stages of a customer care programme and discuss why these programmes are important to delivering a consistent level of customer service and customer support.

4.4   Explain the importance of obtaining formal and informal customer feedback and identify a range of methods for collecting information.

4.5   Describe the measures that can be used to monitor the success of customer service support activities.

4.6   Explain how an understanding of information technology and databases is essential to managing customer care and customer service activities.

4.7   Explain the process for managing own self in a disciplined, time orderly and customer conscious way.

Unit 6 Understanding customers

Customers and needs

The difference between customer and user

In the traditional sense of the word, *customers* are the people who buy an organisation's products and services. To communicate with them effectively, an organisation needs to know who they are, what needs the products or services are required to meet, where they are located and the most cost-effective methods of communicating with them. By doing this, it will be easier to develop effective communications, such as advertising, sales literature, packaging and product instructions, that appeal to, and are understood by, the customer. However, there are some discreet differences between customers that will have an effect on how we can communicate with them effectively.

Customer

> **Customer** – a person or company who purchases goods or services. (CIM)

These are individuals who have no connection with an organisation, other than that they may have purchased goods or services in the past, or are purchasing at present. They can be either the traditional customer/consumer who buys a multitude of goods and services for their own use or that of their family, this category is referred to as business-to-consumer market (or B2C) or the business consumer who is buying on behalf of their organisation, known as business-to-business (B2B).

The consumer/user

> **Consumer/user** – an individual who (buys and) uses a product or service. (CIM)

While the most obvious customer is the person who purchases the product or service, the consumer is the end-user – the person who actually uses the product or service and is sometimes different from the purchaser. Therefore, although the person who pays for the product may also be the user or the consumer of the product this is not always the case.

For example, a manufacturer of toys needs to communicate with both the children who will use the product, so they will exert pressure on parents, and the parents themselves, as they will be the purchaser/decision-maker. The required message therefore has a dual purpose – first to *persuade* the children how exciting the toy is and second to *inform* the parents of its educational value.

When the purchase becomes more important and/or more expensive, such as a car, holiday or furniture, then again more people become involved in the purchase and certain members of the family become members of the DMU. Each member of the DMU will have a different perspective and often take on similar, but less formal, roles to those identified for B2B purchases.

Differing needs and wants

In any purchase where the customer and consumer/user are different, there are likely to be conflicting needs. Often, the customer is most interested in a value-for-money proposition, whereas the consumer/user may be more concerned with product features and/or benefits.

Activity 6.1

How might the needs of the customer and consumer differ in the following purchases?

Pet food, bought by the pet's owner

A child's bicycle, bought by a parent

A laptop PC, bought for a manager by the IT department

The benefits of a marketing oriented approach

In Unit 1 we defined marketing as: 'the management process responsible for identifying, anticipating and satisfying customer requirements profitably.' (CIM)

We also said that a marketing orientation 'starts with the philosophy that only if the organisation understands the benefit needs and wants of the consumer can it devise products and services that satisfy the marketplace.'

You will notice that, in these two definitions, there appears to be a conflict between customer and consumer. In reality, this is not the case. A marketing-oriented organisation, that serves a market where customer and consumer differ, would aim to identify, anticipate and satisfy customer *and* consumer needs. Indeed, an organisation with a different orientation might not even recognise the significance of the difference.

Of course, before we can begin to satisfy customer (or consumer) needs, we must understand what they are.

Collecting information about customer needs

Internal and external sources

For the company value chain to operate normally, lots of information needs to be collected (e.g. production figures for accounts and raw materials ordering). These are a vital input into the system. The warning has already been given that it is necessary to check (on the basis of collection and calculation) to ensure that the figures are appropriate for the marketing decision in hand. For example, historical costs will not necessarily be appropriate for that export order to be delivered in three months' time. Apart from the obvious sources such as data from EPOS and so on, care should be taken to collect more informal data which may be of considerable value; for example, customer complaints can be a stimulus for new product developments.

Marketing research activity can be divided into two types: primary research and secondary research.

◆ Primary research is where you go out into the field to collect new data using appropriate research methods (e.g. a questionnaire).

◆ Secondary research is where you actively research existing data, which is available from a rich variety of sources (e.g. government statistics).

Primary research that is generated by the organisation itself (because such data does not currently exist) can emanate from a number of sources. Leading research companies can be employed for the purpose and methods of data collection and analysis are again helped by technology (for example the use of scanners, observational equipment and sophisticated databases may all have a role to play).

Confusingly, secondary research should be completed before primary research, since primary marketing research is expensive in both time and physical resources. Having defined the issue(s) and information needed in the outline, the first stage is to see what information may already exist. This may, in part, answer the problem (if you are lucky, possibly completely). If not, it will give you a better understanding of the issues and enable you to be more focused and pursue the primary research more effectively and efficiently. There is no substitute for market sense. Secondary research and informal investigations provide the foundation for primary research. The most difficult issue in marketing research is developing sufficient understanding of the relevant issues so as to be able to ask the *right* questions.

Secondary data sources

Secondary research is usually much less expensive and enables primary research to be more successfully completed. Thus, it is the appropriate place to start. Increasingly much of this is now available online. Below are some selected issues to consider when using secondary sources:

◆ **Date of the research** – When was the data collected? In fast-moving market situations, research can quickly become outdated. If you pull a piece of fresh chicken out of the fridge, the first thing you do is check the use-by date. The danger is that secondary data does not come with warning signs and use-by dates. Government statistics are often interesting as they are collected regularly on a more or less consistent basis and so give information about trends.

◆ **How was the data collected?** If possible, check on where the sample was taken and how the research was conducted. It may have been sufficient for the original researcher's needs, but is it right for your new context? International market research can be difficult as criteria can be defined differently in various countries (e.g. the age at which you may drive a car differs in some countries).

◆ **'Political' research**: this is where the researchers have deliberately, or simply through ignorance, framed the research in such a way that they get the 'right' result. The newspaper survey is a typical situation: *Look at the pretty pictures of Arctic seals, send in this coupon if you think these nasty big people should not kill them.* Not surprising the next day you get the headlines '99 per cent of our readers support the ban' – who was that one person who does not like cute seal pictures?

Technological advances and the potential offered by IT have assisted data gathering techniques considerably. The Internet can provide access secondary research data sources, and universities typically have effective databases allowing for research and analysis of customer behaviour.

The limitations of data

The key limitation of data is that it is unstructured. Whereas 'information' has been put into a form that is suitable for use, 'data' is in the form in which it is collected.

Elsewhere in your studies you may have been introduced to the 'qualities of information' – those characteristics that information should possess, in order to be of value for decision making. In general terms, information should be;

◆ Timely

◆ Accurate

◆ Complete

◆ Concise

◆ Understandable

◆ Relevant

◆ Economical.

If these qualities are applied to research data, a number of issues can be identified:

◆ Research data, particularly that from secondary sources, can be out of date. The marketing environment is changing at such a rate that data might be obsolete by the time it is published, or may have been in existence for some time before it is found.

◆ Secondary data may come from sources that are not professional or thorough. It may therefore contain errors or omissions that make it of little value.

◆ Secondary data often has its origins in primary research, but the purpose of that research may differ greatly from the purpose of the current research. For example, data originally collected to evaluate the success of a product launch might not be valid if we are now looking at buyer behaviour.

Clean up the data

Data can be affected by the way in which it was collected and it may be necessary to adjust (and there must be a valid reason for the adjustment), or transform it in some way.

Issues of date – One problem is looking at trends in sales such as travel, hotel bookings or visitor attractions, where the marketer is concerned with how things are on a year-on-year basis. It may be OK to compare the second week of February with the second week of February last year. But take care in springtime, as the date of Easter moves and this year's week may not include a bank holiday where last year's did. Clearly, what needs to be compared is the Easter performance not the calendar weeks in this situation.

Issues of number – Consider the situation where a company runs an annual staff attitude survey. The analyst reports to the board that there is a big problem, since twice as many people are dissatisfied with their job as there were last year. Well is there? If there had been a fourfold increase of staff over the last year, this actually might be good news. What is required is a percentage figure. 'Good news – work dissatisfaction down by 50 per cent!'

Creating a customer database

Creating a database

What is of concern to a manager is the management of information. If the systems engineers ensure security, it is up to managers to make certain that the staff enter accurate data or that appropriate equipment (e.g. scanners) is available. This is particularly important in e-commerce, where marketing, Logistics and IT must ensure a fusion of product that looks good on the screen, works fast on customers' systems, is secure and has a back-up system that ensures customers get their products.

In devising systems, potential future use of the information needs to be considered (for data protection reasons as well). A special database of particular importance is the mailing list. This has a high data protection profile and is difficult to keep clean and updated.

The 'bits and bytes' of database management should be left to the computer experts. Key issues to be assured of are data security (both unauthorised access and loss/corruption) and ease of access. With ever-increasing data protection regulation, managers must ensure that both the database and the specific application are legal (e.g. it may not be possible, in certain circumstances, to use a database constructed for one purpose for another).

A typical database on customers might contain the following:

- **Name** – note issues such as formal names and 'known' name: a person christened Robert may be known in the working context as Bob. On an airline ticket the passport name will be required; in other cases it may be more appropriate to use Bob.

- **Contact information** – addresses, these may be segmented so they can be searched (e.g. keeping city as a specific field, telephone(s), fax, e-mail).

- **Role/occupation**

- **Profile information** – as appropriate (e.g. age, etc., for a consumer database, role for a B2B database).

- **Purchase records** – (e.g. value of purchases, type of purchases – from sales records).

- **Media profile** – plus past responses to promotions.

There are two key aspects of database management (from the marketer's point of view) and they are related to the issue of whether we get the message to all the right people (high percentage of cover) with minimum wastage. First, this implies that the database is clean (e.g. dead addresses eliminated) and has the selection criteria we may need to build into the structure (e.g. make the address searchable not just a character 'string'). The second is that when we present the information to the person, the communication is relevant and persuasive. This profile of interests and past purchases allows us to tailor the message.

As with most systems, when you use consultants and everyone is enthusiastic about a new project, constructing a new database can seem hard work but, with care, is usually done well. The problem is one of continual maintenance and tracking of address changes and the like. People change address and jobs every few years and it is typical to find that 20–50 per cent of entries will need amending each year. A 'dirty' database is a waste of money and damages the reputation of the organisation.

Controlling access

Information is a vital asset for a company. To manage the future you need to be able to effectively and efficiently manage information. The company's core information will most often be under the control of IT specialists who will take care of security (both against loss and 'hacking') and legal aspects (data protection legislation) on core databases such as payroll and so on. However, with each person controlling a PC on their desk and having wide Internet access, all staff need to be alert and professional. That handy personal database you have set up without any password may fall within the jurisdiction of data protection legislation and may be vulnerable to unauthorised access. For smaller organisations with no formal IT function, there is still the need for virus protection and the like. Take specialist advice when appropriate; a marketer may not always be a computer consultant.

The value of customer information

Identifying the factors that influence decision-making

Customers do not operate within a vacuum merely deciding what they are going to go out and buy that day. They have a range of influences and constraints imposed upon them that will affect their buying decisions.

Some are external influences, economic conditions will determine how much disposable income they have. There have been various articles expressing concern on the level of consumer spending on credit but people generally consider what they can afford rather than just go out and buy. The increasing effect of technology on the home may mean a consumer is encouraged to upgrade the family PC to enable them to access better services.

The consumer also has internal influences that will affect their buying decision. Peer group pressure is a strong influence and organizations should recognize that word-of-mouth recommendations are a powerful communications tool. We need to gain an understanding of these to fully appreciate what our communications message has to achieve.

Activity 6.2

Have a look at the goods and services you purchase. For how many of those purchases were you influenced by family and friends?

Insight: The Teen market

Teenagers have always been a regularly targeted group who place great importance on the products purchased by their friends and other social groups. Every generation has a teenage 'look' that is copied to the finest detail within that age group.

Nike and Adidas have recognized the existence of global youth culture, where the 15-year-old in the United Kingdom, United States, Asia and Africa will aspire to buy the same product and achieve the same look.

A recently emerged group is Pre-Teens – especially amongst the female population where 9- to 12-year-olds are now making the same level of product choice previously associated with the older age group.

A growth in media opportunities has enabled the advertisers to effectively target this impressionable group, although research by the advertising agency Ogilvy and Mather suggests that mothers need to be targeted too, as often the relationship between mother and daughter is open, sharing interests and sometimes purchases, especially in the cosmetics market.

And, of course, mother has the disposable income that the teenager does not.

Identifying differing needs and wants

Recognition that as a consumer you need to purchase a product or service can arise for a number of reasons. It may be that you need to replace something you already own, which no longer fulfils your needs. A new father of twins may realise that his two-seater sports car is no longer the ideal car for him to own.

Other changes in your life may result in new purchases – a change of job requiring you to work from home so that you need office and IT facilities, or maybe you have made a new set of friends who go skiing three times a year so you need the equipment to join them.

Outside influences also lead to us recognising a need. The knowledge that the population is ageing and today's 40-year-olds will probably not receive a sufficient state pension is prompting many to top up their personal pension plans. On a different scale, did we know that we needed a disposable toilet brush before we saw one advertised on TV? Communications can be the single most powerful influence if used well.

Needs arise for different reasons and different people will be aware of different needs, but once the need has been recognised then the consumer will be in a state of heightened attention, more likely to take notice of products/services that fulfil their needs or solve their problems.

Having a comprehensive customer database can help us to identify the wide range of needs that customers are trying to satisfy when they make a purchase. If we can identify a number of different reasons why customers purchase a product, integrated marketing campaigns can be designed for each.

Developing marketing mix activities to meet customer needs

In Chapters 3 and 4 we saw how the marketing mix can be used to create a series of unique 'blends' of marketing variables. Although we tend to look at how the marketing mix is used to position different products, it can also be used to position the same product for different target markets.

If we recognise that different market segments have different needs that can be satisfied by the same product, we can effectively market that product differently to each type of customer, thus persuading them that the product perfectly satisfies their needs. This is done with many products, for example, soap powders are all fairly similar, but are positioned to appeal to customers looking for whiter whites, colour-fast colours, or stain removal.

Practice work-based tasks

Role

Your manager is interested in developing a better understanding of the organisation's internal and external customers and wishes to know how this can assist in designing appropriate marketing activities that will engage and support customers, and in this way achieve long-term customer loyalty.

During a meeting with the marketing team, it was felt that it would be useful to review different approaches that a range of other organisations use to develop their internal and external customer relationships.

In your role as a marketing assistant, you have been asked to review the article reprinted on pages 101 to 104, which profiles different organisations and their individual approaches to managing customer relationships. Using this supporting material, and your knowledge of your own (or another) organisation, address the following tasks:

Task 1: Identifying customer needs (25% weighting)

Using the resources provided on pages 101 to 104, produce a presentation consisting of TEN slides with supporting notes, suitable for presentation to the marketing team.

The presentation should:

◆ Briefly describe the specific initiatives adopted, by the various organisations described in the article, to identify and gather information about customer needs.

◆ Compare these initiatives with those adopted by your organisation, or one with which you are familiar.

◆ Identify the strengths and weaknesses of your organisation's approach to information gathering about customer needs.

◆ Explain what your organisation can learn from the approaches taken by the organisations described.

Word count 750 words, excluding relevant appendices

Task 2: Information for marketing decisions (35% weighting)

You are required by your manager to produce an informal report for circulation to relevant departments to demonstrate how a better understanding of customer needs can benefit the organisation.

For your organisation, or one with which you are familiar, prepare a report that covers the following tasks, using examples to illustrate your points:

◆ Provide a brief background to your chosen organisation, its customer base and product/service range (two sides of A4 maximum, as an appendix to the report).

◆ Identify the needs of *two* different customer groups.

◆ Describe how internal and external information sources can help the organisation to understand the buying behaviour of these *two* customer groups.

◆ Identify the internal departments to which your report should be circulated, giving reasons for your choice.

Word count 750 words, excluding relevant appendices

Comments on practice work-based tasks

A case study approach has been adopted for this assignment. Material provided refers to particular industries/sectors and a range of organisations. The intention is to offer candidates a wealth of examples, so that they can contextualise their answers, even if they are not working within a marketing department.

It is envisaged that the material provided will form the basis of group discussion and candidates should be encouraged to use other material and information sources in addition to what is provided. The case study material can be used to reinforce the theoretical concepts and encourage the candidates to be more analytical in their approach.

Group analysis and discussion of the case material is acceptable, although it is very important that the assignment tasks are undertaken individually, and not as part of a group. The examiners will be expecting to see originality of thought in the interpretation and application of the assessment tasks.

Task 1

This task is designed to allow the candidate to identify different methods of gathering information relating to customer needs. It would also be interesting to put this in context by looking at initiatives adopted by other organisations.

Determining which initiatives could be used successfully in another organisation could either be related to the candidate's own organisation, or another organisation that they are familiar with if they are not currently in a suitable role. A level of justification with regard to why certain initiatives would or would not be possible, alongside a brief consideration of the benefits delivered, would be expected for the higher grades.

The wording used within this task is designed to allow the candidates a degree of flexibility in their approach and to allow them to demonstrate their ability to understand what motivates customers to purchase. Any answer is in theory as valid as another, as long as the thinking is supported by valid argument.

Candidates should be encouraged to think about the presentation format and how this could be presented. In their job role they may be expected to have PowerPoint skills and to be able to produce speaker's notes to accompany the slides.

Task 2

This task is designed to cover the information-gathering aspects of the syllabus, in terms of secondary and primary data.

It is preferable, where possible, that candidates choose two very different customer groups (B2B & B2C, or two very different market segments, would be a good combination) as this allows the clear demonstration of the differences in buying behaviour between them.

The candidates need to be able to follow the process of assessing what is known through existing information, what can be sourced, and therefore what information gaps exist.

Finally, the candidates need to consider the value of the report to other departments within the organisation, with a justification of their choice possibly including the benefits that other departments could gain, and actions that could be taken as a result of this report.

Further work

Look at how customer needs can differ for any product with which you are familiar. Investigate how organisations position their products to apparently satisfy those needs by creating a range of different marketing mixes.

For any product or service with which you are familiar, identify some primary data sources that might help you to identify customer and consumer needs. What might the problems be with using such data?

Support material: Are your customers being served?

When Colin Marshall strode into the boardroom of British Airways (BA) in 1983, the airline was a publicly owned, strike-riven and loss-making disaster. Within the space of a few years he had helped transform the newly privatised carrier from what was popularly dubbed 'Bloody Awful' into the 'The world's favourite airline'. He did this through the now legendary Putting People First employee training programme. And he led from the front: not only did he travel much of the time in the economy section of BA planes, but he also talked regularly to passengers and staff about their experiences. But BA's crown has slipped: it is not coincidental that its reputation for losing bags and declining customer service has developed during a period characterised by strikes and industrial unrest. Does new chief executive Willie Walsh talk to his customers and staff? Judging by the rumour that his e-mail address is a closely-guarded secret to prevent people writing to him directly to complain, the answer is 'probably not'.

Back in the mid-1990s, Unilever suffered considerable embarrassment when mounting complaints about the damage its much-hyped new laundry detergent Persil Power was causing to clothes, led to the product being withdrawn. The then-chief executive Niall FitzGerald was reported to have finally cut the post-mortem discussion dead by asking the assembled senior managers whether they ever washed their own clothes.

Needless to say, not one of them did. There's no mystery. When those who sit around the boardroom table of any company have a deep understanding of their customers, the company thrives. But those companies where directors sit in ivory towers removed from the real world of customers and staff, face a very uncertain future. How can you possibly develop products and services that customers want and will keep buying unless you understand them and the way they make decisions, asks Jean Carr, a management consultant specialising in qualitative research. 'The customer should be part of the regular board agenda,' she says. 'Measuring your success with customers should be as standard a metric as sales. Discussion about who your customers are, why you have attracted those customers, where you can get more from, and whether you actually want these customers or different ones, should be routine.'

While marketers should act as the customer's representative in the boardroom, they need to convince the rest of their board colleagues of the need for greater customer centricity, she argues.

'When I work with clients I try to get the board as a whole to take responsibility for customers and actually get them in front of customers as soon as possible,' says Carr. 'The first step is to let them see focus groups so they can witness at fi rst hand just what their products and services stand for in consumers' lives. Most companies seem to assume that customers are as preoccupied with their products and services as they are themselves.'

The next step is to get them out experiencing their brand with customers in the real world: 'When board members go "back to the floor" or work in a branch for a day, heads usually roll afterwards.'

It was Carr's involvement that led to B&Q putting 'wise old men' in charge of the stores' different departments. 'People used to go to B&Q and end up buying just a packet of wallpaper paste because they couldn't find the right advice or the right wallpaper. Now customers stay longer and buy more.'

Carr also got the board at B&Q to imagine they were going to decorate their own, their mothers' or their daughters' houses using supplies from B&Q. 'It really made them sit back on their heels and think "if it's not good enough for me, who is it good enough for?" But that is exactly what boards need to do – put themselves in customers' shoes.'

If more boards did see their business through their customers' eyes, you've got to think that customer service would improve. It's probably been some considerable time since GNER chief executive Christopher Garnett tried to buy a standard-class ticket on one of his trains via the company's website or over the phone, or since BT boss Ben Verwaayen used the normal customer channels to query some aspect of his account. Loyalty expert Frederick Riechheld has shown that it costs ten times more to win a new customer than it does to keep an existing one, yet most marketers continue to focus their efforts on acquisition rather than ensuring that their current customers are happy. And while complaints are one of the best sources of intelligence on how well products and services are being received, few companies appear to have mechanisms for feeding these complaints back to the marketing department. It's a disconnect that smacks of an outmoded silo mentality – HR, operations and marketing operating in splendid isolation from each other.

As Carr concludes: 'Unless you know what your brand stands for compared to the competition, you are going to be in the dark.'

And that's a dangerous place to be. Fed up with poor customer service and having their complaints fall on deaf ears, consumers are increasingly airing their grievances to a receptive audience of millions via the Internet.

Companies providing poor service have nowhere to hide. A recent survey by the Institute of Customer Service (ICS) and HR consultancy TMA found that four out of five customers would spread the word if a complaint had been handled badly, and poor complaints handling is the chief reason customers switch suppliers. But despite steadily rising numbers of complaints, only one in four employees feels qualified to deal with them, the report found.

Laurie Young, a marketing consultant specialising in service businesses, believes that companies are starting to take customer service more seriously again, rather than just paying lip service to it. 'Most senior business people understand that the quality of the service they provide affects their future profitability. And there are phases of history where they get reminded of that', he says.

One such phase was the late 1980s, when Tom Peters was preaching his message of customer focus in *In Search of Excellence*. But though many companies made serious efforts to get closer to customers, the recession of the early 1990s saw them retrench and cut costs wherever they could. It was a myopic approach: iconic brands such as IBM, Marks & Spencer, Levi's and Sainsbury's all suffered financially by closing their ears to customer concerns.

The problem this time round is that many companies are trying to become 'customer-centric' on the cheap, since creating a well-paid, well-trained 'human' service organisation requires considerable commitment and investment.

A recent survey by US-based management consulting firm Katzenbach Partners found that much of the accepted wisdom about customer service is incomplete and can actually undermine service rather than enhance it. Three of the most common mistakes include:

◆ Adopting a customer-comes-first ethos at the expense of employees

◆ Providing scripted responses for customer interactions

◆ Relegating customer service to a cost-centre status.

Getting employees on side is the often-forgotten but arguably most critical element in delivering great service, whether in consumer-facing or business-to-business companies.

It's not forgotten at construction and services company Alfred McAlpine, though. Group director of human resources Tor Farquhar says: 'The person who knows the customer best is the employee, so we work hard to make sure that the people who deliver our services are committed to the company.'

Farquhar explains: 'What we sell is our people. Our product is the person within the company delivering our services every day, so our brand is represented through the attitude and motivation of that person. We are an upside-down organisation. The customers are at the top, feeding all their wishes into the front-line staff, and then those staff feed back into the management of the company.'

Service is a powerful differentiator. Paul Dickinson, sales and marketing director of Virgin Atlantic, points out that because Virgin is small, with only 40 planes, providing excellent service is the only chance it has to stand out.

Unlike some of its competitors, the airline doesn't charge customers for booking over the phone rather than the Internet. 'We don't penalise them for calling us,' says Dickinson. Interestingly, the average transaction value in the call centre is higher than the self-service web option.

Dickinson agrees that having engaged staff is key, claiming that over 85 per cent of employees are 'very proud' to work for Virgin, and the rest 'quite proud'.

Given their pivotal position as interface between the market and the company, marketers are the obvious people to spearhead the drive for better customer service.

And there are signs that a new breed of marketer is emerging in response to service challenges, particularly in the USA, where the title 'chief marketing officer' (CMO) is gaining more credence. The 2007 Marketing Outlook Survey from the CMO Council found that marketing is changing significantly in response to demands from chief executives for marketers to improve the relevance, accountability and performance of their activities.

In addition to managing traditional functions such as branding, websites, advertising and public relations, large minorities are now reporting jurisdiction over business development (44%), distribution and channels (37%), pricing (37%) and product management (30%). They are also busy adding new competencies and capabilities in areas such as financial accountability, analytics and customer-centricity.

However, the gap between what marketers believe to be their top three accomplishments in 2006 – which are predominantly brandfocused – and the challenges they face in 2007 shows there is still some way to go.

A further sign that companies are waking up to the need to instil customer-centricity throughout the organisation is the rise in the number of companies that are appointing 'customer champions'. This new breed comes in a range of different guises, from 'vice-president of customer experience' to 'chief customer officer' (CCO).

The cynical might see this as another desperate attempt by firms suffering from a consumer backlash to stick plasters over the wound. And the demands of the position are not for the faint-hearted.

As customer expert Patricia Seybold, founder and chief executive of the Patricia Seybold Group, puts it: 'No matter how high you try to put these customer experience people in the organisation, the fact of the matter is that most of the stuff that affects the customer that they need to infl uence or ideally control is outside their purview.'

If more proof of the benefits of being customer-centric were needed, you only have to look at Tesco's recent results. In April 2007, the retailer reported record profits of £2.6bn, up 13% on the previous year. It is no accident that Tesco's core purpose is 'to create value for customers to earn their lifetime loyalty'. It expresses the way it does that through two values – 'No one tries harder for customers' and 'Treat people as we like to be treated'. It regularly asks customers and staff what it can do to make shopping with it and working with it that little bit better, something encapsulated in its 'Every little helps' strategy. Satisfied staff make for satisfied customers.

Everyone at Tesco is customer focused, but the marketing team 'owns' the relationships with customers and works closely with other departments to provide a seamless customer experience.

Unless marketers in other companies raise their game, suggests Paul Cooper, director of the ICS, 'in ten years' time they will be reporting to customer service. Customer centricity will be everything.'

Source: Are your customers being served?, Laura Mazur and Jennifer Small, *The Marketer*, May 2007

Building and maintaining customer relationships

Internal and external customers

In the traditional sense of the word, *customers* are the people who buy an organisation's products and services. To communicate with them effectively, an organisation needs to know who they are, what needs the products or services are required to meet, where they are located and the most cost-effective methods of communicating with them. By doing this, it will be easier to develop effective communications, such as advertising, sales literature, packaging and product instructions, that appeal to, and are understood by, the customer. However, there are some discreet differences between customers that will have an effect on how we can communicate with them effectively.

Customers fall into two main categories, external and internal – each having very different needs and expectations of the organisation. We will deal first with these two distinct categories and then discuss how some of the boundaries are becoming less distinct in today's competitive environment.

External customers

These are individuals who have no connection with an organisation, other than that they may have purchased goods or services in the past, or are purchasing at present. They can be either the traditional customer/consumer who buys a multitude of goods and services for their own use or that of their family – the business-to-consumer market (B2C); the business consumer who is buying on behalf of their organisation – the business-to-business (B2B), or individuals selling to one another (C2C).

Internal customers

Consider your internal customers and how important it is that there is good internal communication in an organisation. Think about how sometimes you are the customer and someone else is the service provider.

For example, as an employee, when you receive your pay slip from the finance department, you are the customer and expect it to be correct, to be delivered on time and the salary payment actually credited into your bank account. If there is a problem, you expect to be dealt with courteously and promptly. You do not expect to have to engage in lengthy correspondence to rectify a mistake. If you do receive information from the finance department – say, for example, about a new profit-related pay scheme – you expect it to be clearly written and well presented.

At other times, you could be the service provider to your colleagues or line manager; for instance, when you are asked to cost the production of a sales promotion item as part of a future promotional campaign. Your internal customers will expect you to have completed the task on time, accurately, and to present it clearly at the next planning meeting.

So internal marketing is about working together with colleagues and providing them with a good service so that, as a team, your organisation achieves its goals.

Users

The most obvious customer is the person who purchases the product or service; the end-user (or consumer) is the person who actually uses the product or service and is sometimes different from the purchaser. Therefore, although the person who pays for the product may also be the user or the consumer of the product this is not always the case.

For example, a manufacturer of toys needs to communicate with both the children who will use the product, so they will exert pressure on parents, and the parents themselves, as they will be the purchaser/decision-maker. The required message therefore has a dual purpose – first to *persuade* the children how exciting the toy is and second to *inform* the parents of its educational value.

When the purchase becomes more important and/or more expensive, such as a car, holiday or furniture, then again more people become involved in the purchase and certain members of the family become members of the decision-making unit (DMU). Each member of the DMU will have a different perspective and often take on similar, but less formal, roles to those identified below for B2B purchases.

Stakeholders

Stakeholders – those persons and organisations that have an interest in the strategy of the organisation. Stakeholders normally include shareholders, customers, staff and the local community. (CIMA)

As such we can consider them to be people and organisations who have a say in:

◆ What you are to do

◆ What resources you have

◆ What you should achieve.

Most organisations also have a mix of stakeholders or publics, that is; internal and external individuals or groups, who come into contact with an organisation or who affect or are affected by its activities. From a communication point of view, they can be considered as important customers or target audiences with whom the organisation must communicate.

It is important to appreciate the importance of knowing about an organisation's stakeholders and why they might want to communicate with them. An organisation may choose to communicate with these publics, such as the media or the local community, because it is good for its public relations image and ultimately good for its business. Or it could be a legal requirement for an organisation to produce an annual report for shareholders. It is often essential for an organisation to form a close relationship with suppliers or distributors, in order to become more competitive. Thus an organisation may establish an extranet to provide suppliers with up-to-date stock requirements or provide distributors with automatic access to orders to help them plan their distribution schedules.

In addition, most organisations wish to communicate effectively with current and potential employees to attract and retain the best staff in the marketplace.

Let's consider the example of a car manufacturer such as Land Rover, which, although it is (for now) part of the American company Ford, has a UK manufacturing plant in Solihull.

◆ Its **customers** will receive many forms of communication ranging from national advertising to attract new customers to direct mail shots targeting existing users to upgrade. Traditionally, communications within marketing was concerned only about communicating with this group. However, the potential customers' interaction with the other stakeholders may influence their purchasing decision. An employee of a supplier will be more likely to consider buying a Land Rover if the relationship between the two organisations is a good one.

◆ The **financial supporters**, such as the banks and city analysts, will be concerned not only about the financial health and viability of the owner company, this can be communicated via the annual report, but also by the level and type of media coverage the organisation receives. These stakeholders are usually communicated via PR techniques.

◆ The **suppliers and distributors** are heavily dependent upon Land Rover's survival for their own financial stability, they will need to ensure that their own systems are as efficient and effective as possible in order to lower costs and be closely attuned to current and future customer needs. Regular communication is required often using an intranet facility to replace many paper-driven processes such as ordering from suppliers and analysing stock availability.

◆ The **local community** will be interested in the stability due to the need for jobs and the financial well-being of the community, both now and in the future, for their children. Land Rover, who employ 3000 people in Solihull, can build links with the community by sponsoring local events or teams to engender a more pastoral edge to their corporate image.

◆ **Employees** will need to be reassured of the company's ability to provide work. They need to be told what the company's plans for the future are and how that will affect them personally. Employees who feel positive about who they work for are more likely to be motivated and happy in their work.

Marketing and customer relationships

Increasingly, marketers are deepening their conviction that closing the sale is only one of the important milestones in an ongoing relationship. Thus, a car dealership is not only interested in selling you a car but servicing it and, in a few years' time, supplying you with a replacement. This is building a relationship between the client, the staff at the local distributorship and the manufacturer's brand. Viewed in this context, the 18,000-mile service is not only seen to be a chance to make a sale (the income from the service), but a marketing opportunity to maintain and develop the relationship.

Thus, the reception team and the motor technicians are involved in building the relationship through their contact with the customer. Another key concept of relationship marketing is that of the 'part-time marketer' (e.g. any customer-facing staff). Much of the relationship building does not take part with the full-time marketers. In supermarkets, the full-time marketers may be comparatively remote. How the shopping experience feels will be greatly affected for better or worse by the interaction between customers and front-line staff at the checkout and others in customer contact roles – the 'part-time marketers'.

Although relationship marketing is important in consumer marketing, it is critical in B2B marketing. Organisations do not do business with organisations. People in one organisation do business with other people in another organisation. Thus, a key strength of an advertising agency, for example, is the quality of the relationships between the creative staff and the key personalities in the commissioning organisation. It is a very old saying that 'first you make them your friend, and then you make them your customer'.

This often involves many people interacting with many other people in the linking organisations. A network of interacting relationships is formed between the organisations, which then have to be maintained and sustained both internally (internal marketing) and externally. Thus, in considering the marketing action plan, the impact on all the relevant stakeholders is important.

Relationship management focuses on how these relationships may be positively sustained and developed. Marketing is not seen as a mechanistic set of actions, intellectual cogs in an industry machine but as an activity that depends on a network of human relationships to support the organisation's mission and objectives.

The move to relationship marketing can be seen as the leading edge in developing from a production orientation (any colour you like as long as it is black) to sales (all we need to do is push harder) to developing long-term relationships of positive benefit to both parties. In traditional sales negotiations, you could end up with winner–loser outcomes. In a relationship-marketing context, only creating and sustaining win–win outcomes will nurture and develop the relationship and future profit opportunities.

Customer acquisition and customer retention

As far as marketers are concerned, there are two different groups of customers to whom marketing messages are targeted; existing customers (for whom repeat purchase and increased purchase frequency are the objectives) and new customers (for whom a first purchase is the objective). These two groups of customers necessarily require different information, and might even be reached by different media. The organisation therefore needs two very different communications strategies to reach them.

The benefits of retaining customers

Everyone wants to retain their existing customers. Few companies, however, are implementing positive strategies aimed at retention. Most companies are organised for customer acquisition. Their advertising and sales programmes are designed to find and promote their products and services to new customers. The companies are organised on a product or brand basis, not on a customer segment basis. While they all have customer service departments, and most have a customer service free-phome number, they lack an integrated marketing strategy that is directed at retention, and that defines retention as the measurement of success.

You have probably heard it said that 'It's ten times cheaper to keep a customer than it is to get a new one.' Most people would agree with this statement, even though they have no way of proving it. Indeed, the majority of large organisations today are experimenting with database marketing programmes aimed, in large part, at retention. Most of these companies are not yet sure whether their experiments will be successful.

Pareto theory

The Pareto principle (also known as 'the 80/20 rule', the 'law of the vital few', or the 'principle of factor sparsity') states that, for many events, 80 per cent of the effects come from 20 per cent of the causes. Business management thinker Joseph Juran suggested the principle, and named it after Italian economist Vilfredo Pareto, who observed that 80 per cent of income in Italy went to 20 per cent of the population.

What it is

The '80/20 Rule' is a simple way of looking at your sales and profit figures and identifying the largest sources of contribution. This technique can be used for finding which of your customers are profitable, which channels to market you use are most profitable, and which products and services are profitable.

Why it is important

Just as people aren't all the same, neither are your customers. Some are more important than others and some cost you more than others. Knowing which customers are the most profitable helps in a number of ways:

◆ You can make sure you are really looking after those customers

◆ You can understand what it is about them that is making them profitable

◆ You can then use that information to find other customers who are like them

◆ You can gradually build up the number of profitable customers and reduce the number of less profitable ones

What you need to know

The Pareto principle can be applied to many aspects of your business such as profits and sales. For example:

◆ 80 per cent of your profits may come from just 20 per cent of your customers

◆ 80 per cent of your sales may come from just 20 per cent of your products and services

This simple rule has little scientific basis but it invites you to analyse how productive your marketing effort is. It often leads to some interesting and useful insights into how you operate now and where you should be focusing your efforts in the future.

The 80 per cent and 20 per cent are not magical figures that work out exactly in all situations, nor do they need to add up to 100 per cent. Ratios such as 80/35, 80/25 or even 80/10 may equally apply, although you will be surprised to find just how close to 80/20 the relationship often is. The principle is that, in each case, we are seeking to find the source of the majority of whatever activity is being measured.

Obviously, if the 'most valuable' 20 per cent of the customer base can be identified, marketing activity can be targeted at those customers. In this way, a limited marketing budget can be spent more efficiently.

The ladder of loyalty

The model shown in Figure 7.1 is used to describe the development of a business relationship between its customers. Relationship marketing is used to move customers up the ladder. The essence of relationship marketing is communicating directly with the customers and asking them to respond in a tangible way. It provides the means for the customer to respond, and is set up to fulfil the response.

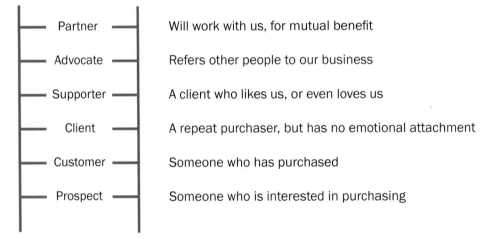

Partner	Will work with us, for mutual benefit
Advocate	Refers other people to our business
Supporter	A client who likes us, or even loves us
Client	A repeat purchaser, but has no emotional attachment
Customer	Someone who has purchased
Prospect	Someone who is interested in purchasing

Figure 7.1: The Ladder of Loyalty

Marketing and customer loyalty

How marketing activities aid customer retention and loyalty

There are a number of techniques that can be used to move customers from 'prospect' to 'partner'. The main techniques can be summarised as follows:

◆ **Customer satisfaction** - In a competitive marketplace, customer satisfaction is the best way to ensure that buyers return repeatedly. To achieve high levels of satisfaction requires the effort of all functions within an organisation. However, there are many cases of companies that have not developed any explicit relationship marketing programme, but nevertheless achieve very high levels of customer advocacy.

Of course, many companies enjoy a high level of repeat business without providing high levels of customer satisfaction. Many customers of train companies may complain about the price and reliability of their train service, but return to it because they have no realistic alternative. Even companies which have an apparently poor standard of service can achieve high levels of repeat business by charging low prices.

Insight: Developing loyalty

The chocolate retailer Thorntons has developed strong loyalty from customers who return to its shops for indulgence and gift purchases of chocolate, despite having no formally stated relationship marketing programme.

Retail chains such as Aldi and Lidl have developed strong loyalty from price-sensitive customers who consider that the total service offer (access to the store, range of products, cleanliness, and friendliness, etc.) are acceptable in return for the price that they have paid.

◆ **Adding value to a relationship** – A relationship, to be sustainable, must add value in the eyes of customers. This value can come about in a number of ways, including:

  ◆ Making reordering of goods and services easier (for example many hotels record guests' details and preferences so that they do not have to be re-entered each time that a guest checks in).

  ◆ Offering privileges to customers who wish to enter into some type of formal relationship (for example, many retailers hold special preview events for card holders, and send a free copy of the store's magazine).

  ◆ Developing an ability to solve problems jointly. For example, a car repair garage may take on board identifying exactly what the problem is that a customer seeks fixing, rather than leaving it to the customer to have to specify the work that they require to be carried out. Such joint problem solving requires a considerable level of trust to have been developed between the parties.

◆ **Loyalty programmes** - Loyalty programmes work on the basis of providing rewards to customers in return for their continuing patronage. For the customer, a loyalty programme can add to the value of a relationships in the ways described above. For the seller, the main attractions are based on the ability to gather large amounts of information about identifiable individuals, rather than aggregate level data about the 'average' customer. A loyalty programme can also have the effect of 'tying-in' a customer, at least in the short term while the customer collects sufficient points in order to obtain a reward. For example some coffee shops offer 'buy 10 get the 11th free' – and stamp the first two places on the card for free, to build return visits.

◆ **Creating barriers to exit** – Companies can try to keep their customers by making it difficult for them to defect to a competitor. Suppliers of industrial machinery create ongoing relationships where they are the sole supplier of spare parts or consumable items which the purchaser must buy if they are to continue using their equipment. Many companies negotiate exclusive supply agreements with a supplier in return for a promise of preferential treatment. In both cases, the customer is dependent in the short term. However, such ties can usually be broken eventually (for example when the machinery is replaced or when an exclusive supply contract comes up for renewal), and it is at that point that the true loyalty of a customer is put to the test.

Supply chain marketing

What is supply chain marketing?

The supply chain – The network of suppliers, manufacturers and distributors involved in the production and delivery of a product. (CIM)

Developing networking skills

Earlier in this unit, it was stated that the distinction between the internal and the external customer is becoming more blurred in many organisations. This has largely occurred due to the increased use of ICT replacing less efficient written and verbal communication processes. Good customer communication goes beyond your own immediate organisation. The relationship your staff have with your organisation's suppliers, distributors and the like can have a critical impact on the service your customers enjoy. More efficient communication via ICT using intranets and extranets results in quicker, cheaper and more effective use of resources for all members of the distribution channel, especially when linked into quality systems such as just-in-time (JIT).

For example, the Body Shop, the retail chain that sells health and beauty products, ensures that its staff work closely with the firm it retains to distribute its merchandise to its retail network, and the distributor actually has office space within the Body Shop factory. This arrangement ensures that close relationships and good communication are achieved.

This improved communication can result in staff enjoying as close a relationship with someone working for a supplier or distributor as the person at the next desk. This is where the difficulty of deciding where the boundaries between internal and external customers arises, with some groups previously considered external now becoming part of the extended organisation.

Even end-users, although still very much categorised as external customers, are now able to order goods and services through digital, web-based or voice-activated systems requiring little, if any, human intervention.

Activity 7.1

Review the internal communication that you as an employee receive from your own organisation. Consider if you fully understand all the messages sent and how relevant they are to you personally.

How could both the message and the method of communication be improved?

If you work for an organisation that does not communicate, consider the minimum amount of information that you would like to receive and the method of communication that should be used.

Collaboration and co-ordination between intermediaries

A good working relationship with suppliers and other 'partners' can produce dramatic effects, such as:

◆ Innovation

◆ Improved performance

◆ Lower costs

◆ More holistic solutions to problems

◆ Better understanding of the needs of all parties

◆ New ways of working together

◆ More co-operation.

Case study: Argos

Argos is one of the United Kingdom's largest non-food retail chains with annual sales exceeding £3 billion. In 1998, a successful, but hostile, takeover by GUS plc led to a change in management. It was the role of the new Managing Director, Terry Duddy, to reverse a previously disappointing performance.

One of his key areas of focus was concerned with the level of customer service. However he realised that to enable change he had to create an environment within Argos that motivated staff to work with him.

His new approach to make Argos more customer-focused was concerned with creating a new set of attitudes and beliefs for the employees to buy into. Those values are encapsulated in the newly created 'employer brand' which seeks to confirm:

◆ Change makes us better and more successful

◆ We are impatient to win

◆ As much opportunity as you can handle

◆ Teams work.

This approach was successful in gaining the commitment of Argos employees. Individual training programmes were set up to achieve the cultural change needed. All employees' progress was tracked through training modules and individual performance objectives set. Performance against objectives was regularly discussed in appraisal sessions with their line managers.

Performance was rewarded with numerous bonus and incentive schemes that are used to encourage employees to deliver good customer service and high levels of sales.

In its 2003 Speak Out survey, Argos found that amongst its employees:

◆ 82 per cent believe the company wants to beat its competitors.

◆ 74 per cent believe strong teamwork is a major contributor to Argos's improved performance.

◆ 77 per cent believe the business is customer-focused.

◆ 80 per cent of employees say they clearly understand the company's goals and objectives.

◆ 89 per cent of employees say they know what is expected of them in their job.

Reward for Argos came in the shape of the *Retail Week* magazine award as 'Retailer of the Year – 2003'. Another reward is that Argos are able to fill 80 per cent of their management vacancies through internal appointments.

Negotiation within the supply chain

Organisational power can be defined most simply as 'potential force' i.e. it is the ability to get things done, to achieve goals and outcomes to one's own standards. We can apply this idea to the supply chain.

A supply chain member can be said to be powerful if:

◆ Other members are dependent upon them for essential components

◆ They have control over significant financial resource

◆ They play a central part in the network

◆ What they supply is not substitutable, or

◆ hey have the ability to reduce uncertainty for the other players.

It is worth remembering that business is about appropriating value for one's own company and stakeholders and, hopefully, building a strategic position where competitors, buyers and suppliers do not pose a threat to that value position. With that in mind, we might want to consider that companies need to find a position where they are able to exercise power over other members of the supply chain. This contradicts much of what is said in the literature about 'lean' supply chain management, which should be based on equity, trust and openness. We can summarise the position in which a buyer may find themselves under four categories: buyer dominance, interdependence, independence and supplier dominance. This position will depend upon the relative utility and the relative scarcity of the goods or services that are being traded.

◆ Buyer dominance is likely to occur where there are few buyers and many suppliers and the supplier is highly dependent upon the buyer for revenue. The buyer will almost certainly have low switching costs relative to the supplier.

◆ Interdependence will occur when there are relatively few buyers and sellers and both have high switching costs.

◆ Independence will occur when there are many buyers and sellers and both buyer and seller have low switching costs.

◆ Supplier dominance occurs where there are relatively few suppliers and the buyer has high switching costs relative to the supplier.

Insight: Supermarkets and suppliers

Take as an example a typical supermarket such as Tesco, Sainsbury or Morrisons, each of whom have a considerable market share in the UK. There are many customers going into each of the stores and they are independent of those supermarket chains. However, when we look at the relationships that the supermarkets have with suppliers of prepared packaged foods we have an example of buyer dominance. The relative size of the supermarket and the likelihood that the supermarket business is a significant percentage of the food supplier's revenue makes the supermarket dominant. When we consider the relationship between the food supplier and the supplier of customised plastic packaging for the product it is likely to be one of interdependence. Most probably the food supplier and the packaging firm have collaborated on the design of the packaging and may even have shared the cost of the moulds for manufacture.

Building and developing relationships

Internal co-operation

Just as individuals have internal customers, such as colleagues and line managers, that they have to deal with, organisations have internal customers in the form of their staff.

From an organisation's perspective, internal communication is vital to internal marketing, and the maintenance of employee motivation and company competitiveness. Simple methods of communication can be used to keep staff informed about new products/ services, internal restructuring or how well (or not) the organisation is doing. In dynamic environments, where firms need to manage change effectively, communication needs to be harnessed to help staff adapt and become familiar with changes in their working environment.

According to Berry and Parasuraman (1992), who are widely credited with recognising the importance of internal marketing,

> A service company can be only as good as its people: if they aren't sold, customers won't be either.

The point here being that most organisations provide at least some level of customer service as part of their product offering and increasingly it is seen as a way of differentiating products in an overcrowded market. Without a culture of internal marketing and effective internal customer communications, the employees within an organisation face the following problems:

◆ Communication problems

◆ Frustration and non-cooperation

◆ Time-wasting and inefficiency

◆ Stress and lack of job satisfaction

◆ Poor quality of work.

All of these problems eventually lead to poor service to the external customer, which eventually leads to reduced profit in the long term.

115

Internal support for marketing initiatives

It is important for many marketers to market their department or services internally to colleagues and other departments. Problems can be raised by other people unaware of the department's full range of services and the contribution it can make to the business.

The changing environment in which organisations operate means that it may be difficult for some to communicate with staff in the traditional way, and pressures upon staff may mean that they are less inclined to be committed to the organisation's values and culture.

The combination of downsized organisations and flatter management structures has removed layers of management and this means that employees are nearer to the decision-makers and that the communication process is speeded up. However, staff that are less secure in their jobs and more pressured to work faster and harder are less likely to communicate openly with their colleagues and managers.

The trend of teleworking and home-based workers results in more people working away from the office, and this means it is more difficult to create a corporate culture and a sense of belonging where people feel happy to communicate on an informal basis.

The trend for some organisations to provide a 24/7 service often means that employees do not all meet each other and probably end up sharing personal space, such as a desk, with two others whom they have never met. This can be quite isolating.

The merging of companies across the United Kingdom and elsewhere in the world is creating global organisations that do not have local identities and which cross over into different cultures, languages and operating systems. This can make it difficult for senior managers to communicate effectively with employees.

Internal relationships

Within marketing

Before building relationships with others inside or outside the organisation, it is important for marketers to interact with their colleagues within the marketing function. In smaller organisations, where marketing staff might share an office or even a desk, this is unlikely to be a major problem. However, in larger ones, or those where the marketing function is decentralised, this might be a major issue.

Most marketing functions are organised along one of two lines:

◆ By product, service, customer or geographic location. In this case the organisation has a number of small, multi-disciplinary, marketing functions.

◆ By functional specialism, such as marketing research, communications, sales, etc.

In the first, where the marketing function consists of a number of small multidisciplinary departments, marketing staff must ensure that they avoid competition between departments, either for resources or for status. In the second, marketers must ensure that they understand each others' priorities and activities, and that they communicate across the functional boundaries.

Communication and relationships between marketing and other functions was covered in Unit 1. You may want to re-read that now.

Activity 7.2

Reflect on the relationships between the various departments within your organisation (or one with which you are familiar) and how each of them might adversely affect customers' perception of the organisation.

Sources of conflict

Conflict can be viewed as an inevitable feature of organisational life, and can result in both positive and negative outcomes. This section will consider the nature of conflict and the reasons as to why they occur. It will go on to explore the different ways that conflict can be managed within organisations.

Sometimes conflict is overt, as when it emerges in the form of a strike, or individuals refusing to communicate with each other at all. However, conflict can also be covert, with indifference and lack of cooperation occurring with no particular enthusiasm on the part of those involved. Either way, the management of conflict is likely to be easier and more effective if the symptoms of conflict can be recognised and dealt with at an earlier stage.

Case study: Conflict in Apple

A conflict at Apple Computer between the Apple II and Macintosh groups took place in 2002. Organisational factors that led to the conflict were physical separation of the two groups and different goals. The trigger for conflict was an annual meeting in which senior executives devoted most of the programme to Macintosh products and ignored Apple IIs innovations, which were the backbone of the company at that time. The consequence for Apple was poor morale and decreased performance in the Apple II division. Management responded by paying more attention to Apple II and by changing conditions so that the Apple II group would not be physically removed from the rest of the organisation.

Causes of conflict

There are a number of factors that may play a part in creating conflict (Figure 7.2):

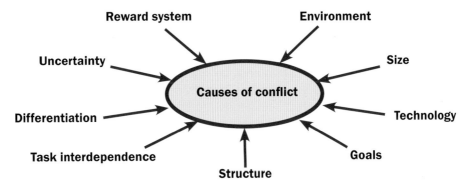

Figure 7.2: The causes of conflict

Environment

Departments are established to interact with major domains in the external environment. As the uncertainty and complexity of the environment increase, greater differences in skills, attitudes, power, and operative goals develop among departments. Each department is tailored to 'fit' its environmental domain and, thus, is differentiated from other organisational groups. Moreover, increased competition, both domestically and internationally, have led to demands for lower prices, improved quality, and better service. These demands exert more intense goal pressures within an organisation and, hence, greater conflict among departments.

Size

As organisations increase in size, subdivision into a larger number of departments takes place. Members of departments begin to think of themselves as separate, and they erect walls between themselves and other departments. Employees feel isolated from other people in the organisation. The lengthening hierarchy also heightens power and resource differences among departments.

Technology

Technology determines task allocation and interdependence among departments. Groups that have interdependent tasks interact more often and must share resources. Interdependence creates frequent situations that lead to conflict.

Goals

The overall goals of an organisation are broken down into operative goals that guide each department. Operative goals pursued by the marketing, accounting, legal and personnel departments often seem mutually exclusive. The accomplishment of operative goals by one may block goal accomplishment by other departments and hence cause conflict. Goals of innovation also often lead to conflict because change requires coordination across departments. Innovation goals cause more conflict than do goals of internal efficiency.

Goal incompatibility is probably the greatest cause of intergroup conflict in organisations. The operative goals of each department reflect the specific objectives members are trying to achieve. The achievement of one department's goal often interferes with another department's goals. University security personnel, for example, have a goal of providing a safe and secure campus. They can achieve their goal by locking all buildings on evenings and weekends and not distributing keys. Without easy access to buildings, however, progress toward the science department's research goals will proceed slowly. On the other hand, if scientists come and go at all hours and security is ignored, police goals for security will not be met. Goal incompatibility throws the departments into conflict with each other.

A typical example of goal conflict may arise between marketing and manufacturing departments. Marketing strives to increase the breadth of the product line to meet customer tastes for variety. A broad product line means short production runs, so manufacturing has to bear higher costs. Other areas of goal conflict are quality, cost control, and new products. Goal incompatibility exists among departments in most organisations.

Structure

Organisation structure reflects the division of labour as well as the systems to facilitate coordination and control. It defines departmental groupings and, hence, employee loyalty to the defined groups. The choice of a divisional structure, for example, means that divisions may be placed in competition for resources from headquarters, and headquarters may devise pay incentives based on competition among divisions.

Differentiation

This deals with the differences in cognitive and emotional orientations among managers in different functional departments. Functional specialisation requires people with specific education, skills, attitudes, and time horizons. For example, people may join a sales department because they have ability and aptitude consistent with sales work. After becoming members of the sales department, they are influenced by departmental norms and values. The underlying values and traits of personnel differ across departments, and these differences lead to horizontal conflicts.

Insight

Consider an encounter between a sales manager and an R&D scientist about a new product.

The sales manager may be outgoing and concerned with maintaining a warm, friendly relationship with the scientist. He may be put off because the scientist seems withdrawn and disinclined to talk about anything other than the problems in which she is interested. He may also be annoyed that the scientist seems to have such freedom in choosing what she will work on. Furthermore, the scientist is probably often late for appointments, which, from the salesman's point of view, is no way to run a business. Our scientist, for her part, may feel uncomfortable because the salesman seems to be pressing for immediate answers to technical questions that will take a long time to investigate. All the discomforts are concrete manifestations of the relatively wide differences between these two people in respect to their working and thinking.

Task interdependence

This refers to the dependence of one unit on another for materials, resources, or information.

◆ **Pooled** interdependence means little interaction;

◆ **Sequential** interdependence means that the output of one department goes to the next;

◆ **Reciprocal** interdependence means that departments mutually exchange materials and information.

Generally, as interdependence increases, the potential for conflict increases. In the case of pooled interdependence, units have little need to interact. Conflict is at a minimum. Sequential and reciprocal interdependence require employees to spend time coordinating and sharing information. Employees must communicate frequently, and differences in goals or attitudes will surface. Conflict is especially likely to occur when agreement is not reached about the coordination of services to each other. Greater interdependence means departments often exert pressure for a fast response because departmental work has to wait on other departments.

Uncertainty

When activities are predictable, departments know where they stand. They can rely on rules or previous decisions to resolve disputes that arise. When factors in the environment are rapidly changing, or when problems arise that are poorly understood, departments may have to renegotiate their respective tasks. Managers have to sort out how new problems should be handled. The boundaries of a department's territory or jurisdiction become indistinct. Members may reach out to take on more responsibility, only to find that other groups feel invaded. In a study of hospital purchasing decisions, managers reported significantly higher levels of conflict when purchases were non-routine than when they were routine. Generally, as uncertainty about departmental relationships increases, conflict can be expected to increase.

Reward system

The reward system governs the degree to which subgroups cooperate or conflict with one another.

Insight

An experiment with student groups illustrated how incentives influence conflict. In one half of the groups, called cooperative groups, each student's grade was the grade given for the group's project. All students in those groups, regardless of individual contribution, received the same grade. In the remaining groups, called competitive groups, students were rewarded on the basis of their personal contribution to the group project. Each student was graded individually and could receive a high or low grade regardless of the overall group score.

The outcome of these incentives on conflict was significant. When the incentive system rewarded members for accomplishing the group goal (cooperative groups), coordination among members was better, communication among members was better, productivity was greater, and the quality of the group product was better. When individuals were graded according to their personal contributions to the group (competitive groups), they communicated less with each other and were more frequently in conflict. Members tried to protect themselves and to succeed at the expense of others in the group. Quality of the group project and productivity were lower.

Incentives and rewards have a similar impact on conflict between organisational departments. When departmental managers are rewarded for achieving overall organisation goals rather than departmental goals, cooperation among departments is greater.

Bechtel, for example, provides a bonus system to division managers based upon the achievement of Bechtel's profit goals. Regardless of how well a manager's division does, the manager is not rewarded unless the corporation performs well. This incentive system motivates division managers to cooperate with each other. If departments are rewarded only for departmental performance, managers are motivated to excel at the expense of the rest of the organisation.

The effect of conflict

Whilst conflict can have negative consequences leading to dysfunctional behaviours, it can also have positive outcomes. The terms destructive and constructive conflict are used to differentiate between negative or positive outcomes. Daft (1989) noted that several negative consequences for organisations that may arise from conflict are as follows:

◆ **Diversion of energy** –Time and effort wasted in addressing a conflict rather than achieving organisation goals.

◆ **Altered judgement** – Judgement and perceptions become less accurate when conflict becomes more intense.

◆ **Loser effects** – The losers may deny or distort the reality of losing, withdraw, or seek scapegoats.

◆ **Poor coordination** – Under intense conflict, coordination does not happen. Collaboration across groups decreases – less contact, not sympathetic to other points of view – achieving departmental goals and defeating the enemy take priority. There is no room for compromise.

However, the positive outcomes of conflict can stimulate creative problem solving and generation of ideas, brings emotions out into the open, release hostile feelings and avoids complacency by challenging accepted/old fashioned ideas.

Overcoming conflict

A useful framework for classifying different ways of handling conflict has been produced by Thomas (1976). It is based on two conflict-management dimensions. These consist of

◆ The degree of assertiveness in pursuit of one's interests, and

◆ The level of cooperation in attempting to satisfy others' interests.

The strength of each of these in a particular situation can be regarded as lying along two continuums, respectively, as illustrated in Figure 7.3, and so producing five conflict-handling strategies.

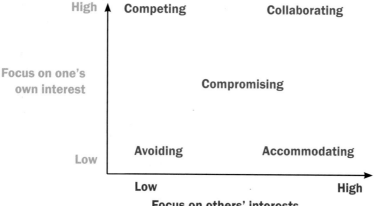

Figure 7.3: Conflict management strategies. Adapted from Thomas (1976) 'Conflict and Conflict Management', in M.D. Dunnette (ed.) *Handbook of Industrial and Organisational Psychology*, 1976, Wiley.

◆ **Avoidance** – One or more parties in conflict may seek to avoid, to suppress or to ignore the conflict. This is not recommended as it does not resolve the conflict which may break out again when the parties meet in the future.

◆ **Accommodation** – This involves one party putting the other's interests first and suppressing their own interest in order to preserve some form of stability and to suppress the conflict. Again, if the causes of conflict are endemic or lasting, the accommodation strategy may not resolve the differences. Also, the accommodating party may well lose out as a result.

◆ **Compromise** – Often seen as the optimum solution. Each party gives something up and a deal somewhere between the two is accepted after negotiation and debate. However, in compromise, both parties lose something and there may be a better alternative.

◆ **Competition** – This is a state where both or all parties do not cooperate, but instead seek to maximise their own interests and goals. It creates winners and losers. The resultant conflict can prove damaging to the organisation as well as to at least one of the parties. So, it is not recommended.

◆ **Collaboration** – From the perspective of all parties, this is likely to be the optimum solution. Differences are confronted and jointly resolved, novel solutions are sought and a win–win outcome is achieved.

Co-operation and collaboration

It is important for marketing staff to take into account the view of others within the organisation, and to work with them, when undertaking marketing activities.

Contributing constructive ideas

A dialogue between marketing and non-marketing staff will allow the development of marketing plans and activities that are more likely to be successful. The use of brainstorming techniques might be of benefit here.

> **Brainstorming** – a group creativity technique designed to generate a large number of ideas for the solution to a problem. The method was first popularised in the late 1930s by Alex Faickney Osborn, an advertising executive and one of the founders of BBDO, in a book called *Applied Imagination*. Osborn proposed that groups could double their creative output by using the method of brainstorming. (*Source:* Wikipedia)

Co-operating with others to follow plans

Once plans have been developed, they must be implemented. As we have already seen, marketing is a cross-functional activity, and the help and commitment of staff outside the marketing department will be needed if plans are to succeed.

The successful implementation of marketing plans might require the organisation to form one or more multidisciplinary project teams, tasked with the implementation of the plan, or parts of it. Such teams will necessarily include, and may indeed be led by, members of the marketing department.

Keeping commitments

It is very important that, whatever promises are made regarding services to be performed or information to be supplied, these promises are met. Most organisations now take a 'total quality' approach to activity:

> **Total Quality Management (TQM)** – a management approach for an organization, centered on quality, based on the participation of all its members and aiming at long-term success through customer satisfaction, and benefits to all members of the organization and to society. (ISO)

One of the main principles of TQM is that any product or service, whether delivered within or outside the organisation, should be 'right first time'. This principle applies to marketing information and activity as it does to any other aspect of business.

Practice work-based tasks

Role

Your manager is interested in developing a better understanding of the organisation's internal and external customers and wishes to know how this can assist in designing appropriate marketing activities that will engage and support customers, and in this way achieve long-term customer loyalty.

During a meeting with the marketing team, it was felt that it would be useful to review different approaches that a range of other organisations use to develop their internal and external customer relationships.

In your role as a marketing assistant, you have been asked to use your knowledge of your own (or another) organisation to address the following tasks:

Task 1: Customer loyalty (25% weighting)

You are required by your manager to produce a report to demonstrate how a better understanding of customers, and how to encourage their loyalty, can benefit the organisation.

For your organisation, or one with which you are familiar, prepare a report that covers the following tasks, using examples to illustrate your points:

◆ Provide a brief background to your chosen organisation, its customer base and product/service range (two sides of A4 maximum, as an appendix to the report)

◆ Identify TWO internal and FOUR external customer groups

◆ Distinguish between the customers and consumers of your organisation's products or services

◆ Explain how your organisation might persuade its external customers to 'climb the ladder of loyalty' by means of marketing activities designed to achieve this objective.

Word count 750 words, excluding relevant appendices

Task 2: Supply chain marketing (25% weighting)

Your Manager has asked you to produce an email for circulation internally to all supplier and customer-facing personnel that:

◆ Explains the concept of supply chain marketing

◆ Identifies those stakeholders in the organisation's supply chain with whom the organisation should develop relationships

◆ Recommends specific marketing activity to improve the relationships between the organisation and other members of its supply chain.

Word count 750 words, excluding relevant appendices

Comments on practice work-based tasks

Group discussion of tasks is acceptable, although it is very important that the assignment tasks are undertaken individually, and not as part of a group. The examiners will be expecting to see originality of thought in the interpretation and application of the assessment tasks.

Task 1

This task is designed to allow the candidate to identify the organisation's customers, and discuss ways of encouraging customer loyalty. It would also be interesting to put this in context by looking at initiatives adopted by other organisations. This task also allows the candidate to apply the 'ladder of loyalty' concept.

Determining which initiatives could be used successfully in an organisation could either be related to the candidate's own organisation, or another organisation that they are familiar with if they are not currently in a suitable role. A level of justification with regard to why certain initiatives would or would not be possible, alongside a brief consideration of the benefits delivered, would be expected for the higher grades.

The wording used within this task is designed to allow the candidates a degree of flexibility in their approach and to allow them to demonstrate their ability to understand how loyalty can be encouraged. Any answer is in theory as valid as another, as long as the thinking is supported by valid argument.

Task 2

This task is designed to allow the candidate to identify the organisation's supply chain, and discuss ways of marketing to the various participants. It would also be interesting to put this in context by looking at initiatives adopted by other organisations.

Determining which initiatives could be used successfully in an organisation could either be related to the candidate's own organisation, or another organisation that they are familiar with if they are not currently in a suitable role. A level of justification with regard to why certain initiatives would or would not be possible, alongside a brief consideration of the benefits delivered, would be expected for the higher grades.

A suitable format should be used, and the language and style of the e-mail should be appropriate for circulation within the organisation.

Further work

Investigate how a range of organisations use marketing tools to encourage customer loyalty.

Discuss situations where you have encountered, and successfully dealt with, conflict at work.

Unit 8
Communicating with customers

The importance of communication

The day-to-day communications of the marketer should not be viewed as something entirely separated to the formal marketing communications of the organisation. In an integrated view of communications, advertisements and others have their place. We must also consider the formal and informal communications that take place, and even our body language and posture. We send a message with everything we do!

However, in the buying process, some stages may need other communications, for example responding by e-mail to a query on goods damaged in transit at a 'dot-com company'. Even the communications within the organisation can be viewed not as something separate, but as internal marketing. Your internal markets (stakeholders) are key.

Exchanging information with customers and suppliers

A company letter or report is not normally written in isolation. A customer complaint may have arisen from extravagant expectations given in advertising and poor instructions on the packaging. A letter (or e-mail) attempting to resolve the issue may also draw on additional information on the company website. Additionally, the letter (or e-mail) will conform to organisational house rules (e.g. font used as well as headed paper or e-mail footer). The communication needs to be seen as part of two sets of integrated communications:

◆ The full range of communications sent out by the organisation

◆ The full range of communications received by the stakeholder.

If you consider with whom you communicate, why, how and how often, you may be surprised at just how many people there really are, and the balance between those inside your organisation and outside it. You should also consider the people and organisations from whom you receive information. How much of that do you actually use and take in? How effective is your communication in relaying the intended message accurately?

The main reasons for people to communicate in business organisations, internally and externally, are as follows:

◆ **To build relationships** – internally and externally, with individuals and groups.

◆ **To give specific instructions** to others on a range of business matters, both procedural and strategic.

◆ **To disseminate information** on a range of corporate matters such as the mission statement, policy issues or, in the case of the external market, on price changes or new promotional initiatives.

◆ **To share ideas and values** on general organisational issues, possibly to maintain or subtly change the corporate culture.

◆ **To negotiate** matters of policy such as a joint venture or merger.

◆ **To discuss** or negotiate personal or professional matters such as remuneration and other factors affecting their performance within the workplace.

◆ **To motivate, interest and stimulate** employees for commitment and loyalty to the firm.

◆ **To create an awareness** of the organisation, its products or services and *persuade* the external market, for example, to make a purchase decision or to request further information.

◆ **To establish a two-way communication process** to ensure messages sent are received and understood, and outstanding issues resolved through receiving *feedback*.

If, for instance, you are working in the marketing department of a firm that makes and sells garden furniture, and you have responsibility for the organisation's marketing communications, then in an average working day you may communicate with a large number of people in a variety of ways (Table 8.1),

Table 8.1: Communication methods

Method	With whom	Possible purpose of communication
Post	Customers	Complaining about an element of product or service
	Suppliers	Informing you of their services
Telephone	Suppliers	Chasing or placing or negotiating terms on an order
	Colleagues	Arranging meetings
		Clarifying information
	Media	Talking to the press about a forthcoming launch
E-mail	Suppliers	Confirming details of an order
	Colleagues	Confirming details of a meeting
		Clarifying information
		Providing information
	Distributors	Confirming details of their order
Fax or e-mail	Advertising agency	Confirming copy changes to a new press ad
Letters/direct mail	Customers	Informing the customer of a forthcoming price promotion
Formal meetings/ presentations	Colleagues	Presenting the last quarter's sales figures to the rest of the team
Informal ('water cooler') meetings	Colleagues	Office gossip, or valuable insight
Report	Colleagues	Presenting items for discussion before decisions made

Keeping customers up to date

As consumers we receive over 30 times the amount of messages we are physically able to process in any one day. Many of these are concerned with our everyday life and therefore will be accepted into our memory without problem. As marketing-focused organisations, we must ensure the messages sent to our customers are worthy of being remembered and are delivered to the recipient in the most effective and efficient manner, in order that the one chance we get maximises our opportunity.

Communication is, therefore, a core skill that marketing professionals need to use daily.

The purpose for any communication can be broken down into four main areas. Most communication will have at least one of these four factors as their main objective and it can be useful to analyse which of these are required when putting a message together. These factors can be remembered by the mnemonic *DRIP*.

◆ **Differentiate** – Identifies for the message receiver the key difference between the products/services you provide and those provided by competitor, for example Daz washes whiter.

◆ **Remind** – Includes within the message product/service attributes they may have forgotten, for example now it's winter, it's nice to drink hot chocolate.

◆ **Inform** – Includes within the message details of what the product/service can provide and any action required by them, for example now that the DVLA have an improved database of car owners, you will be fined if you do not renew your car tax on time.

◆ **Persuade** – Usually applied to products/services we want rather than need, giving us a reason to buy, for example Crunchie – get that Friday feeling.

Dyson manufactures a revolutionary (and premium-priced) type of vacuum cleaner and has 52 per cent of the UK market. Its communications have needed to:

◆ **Differentiate** it from conventional products – use of innovative technology.

◆ **Remind/reassure** customers that the cyclone system works better than any other and to resist the competition's attempts to gain top of mind awareness.

◆ **Inform** and educate the market about what is wrong with conventional appliances.

◆ **Persuade** potential customers to consider Dyson as the only option when next purchasing floor-cleaning appliances.

Activity 8.1

Look closely at a daily newspaper or weekly magazine and cut out at least ten different advertisements for a wide cross-section of products/services. Analyse how many of the DRIP factors you can apply to each advertisement and construct a table showing which advertisement incorporates which DRIP factors. Has your analysis allowed you to come to any conclusions about the types of messages that different categories of products/services tend to use when communicating with the consumer?

Communication and the AIDA model

All good marketers follow the AIDA model. The AIDA model stands for Attention, Interest, Desire, and Action (figure 8.1).

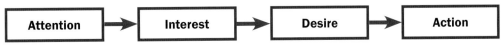

Figure 8.1: The AIDA model

Attention

If you want your sales letter or advertisement to have an impact on your audience, it must first get their attention. You can do this with a hard-hitting headline or lead paragraph that hits the nail directly on the head or you can even begin your mailing with a captivating question. For instance, 'Do you want to cut your electricity cost by 45%?'

An appropriate headline for a sales letter promoting a weight loss program might be: 'Now, you can lose 15 pounds in 2 weeks without having to starve; and it's easy and affordable!' This headline not only solves a problem, but also offers a quick and easy solution that keeps in mind the price-sensitive consumer.

Your audience will be interested only in knowing 'What's in it for me?', 'Why should I invest my time in reading on, or finding out more?'

Interest

You must get the readers/viewers' interest by showing them why they need your product or service. You have to create a want for it. Let them know how their lives will become easier with your product or service. Show them what they are missing by not even trying it.

Here, you need to sell the key specific benefits, or differentiating features, of your product or service. You can rest your case by using testimonials or case histories. You can provide feedback from users who have benefited from your product. Always remember that you know everything there is to know about your product, so 'stale news' to you can be fresh news to the other person.

Desire

Now you've got the readers/viewers' attention and hooked their interest. Next, you've got to create desire. Tell the readers how exactly they'll benefit from your product. Link the benefits to their daily life. Get them to realise how your product can benefit them, how convenient it is for them to get it, and how comfortable life will be for them afterwards.

Generalities are less convincing. Specific details are far more believable. For example, when you want to sell books on lowering employee theft . . . 'By the end of this quarter, you could see your percentage of employee theft drop by more than 37%. Imagine the spectacular effect it will have on your bottom line!'

Action

What do you want the reader/viewer to do next? Send in a reply card? Order the product or service? Call in asking for more information? Schedule an appointment? Notify them accordingly. It is amazing how many sales letters do not inform the reader about the subsequent step, and how many advertisements do not say where the product is available or how to contact the company.

You've worked hard so far. You have their attention, hooked interest, created desire. Isn't it appropriate to ask for action? Don't presume that your reader/viewer knows what to do next. As a support to getting the preferred action, you should always incorporate a reply card with your mailing.

Communications and stages

If you look at the overview of the AIDA model above, you will see that it is very difficult to create one communication that covers all the stages. It is very common to target an advertisement or direct mailing at just one or two stages of the model. For example, a TV advertisement for a new product might just seek to create attention and interest, while a direct mailing for a recognisable service might concentrate on desire and action.

Activity 8.2

Make notes on three communications that are targeted at you as a customer/consumer. Annotate those notes with comments about the stages of the AIDA model that the communications seem to be addressing.

The communications cycle

The Schramm model

Wilbur Schramm (1955) developed the most commonly known model of communication (Figure 8.2), which broke the process down into five clearly defined consecutive stages or dimensions.

These are as follows:

◆   The sender has the need to communicate.

◆   The need is translated into a message (encoding).

◆   The message is transmitted.

◆   The receiver gets the message (decoding).

◆   The receiver interprets the message and provides feedback to the sender.

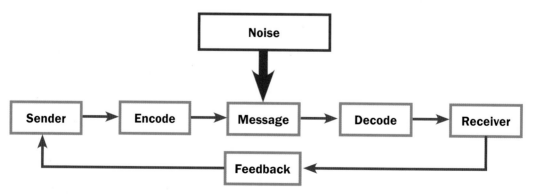

Figure 8.2: Schramm's communications cycle.

These stages can be considered in more detail, as follows:

1   The need to communicate business messages to your internal and external markets is an essential part of the marketing process. The DRIP factors help us to identify what kind of message is required at which stage of the product life cycle. In deciding to send out a message we must be clear what customer needs we are meeting and the objective behind the planned communication. Once this is clear, you can then move on to plan the message content.

2   Messages may be **expressed** in a number of different ways. It is usual that in any business communication the message content and method of communication is a result of careful planning rather than an off-the-cuff remark. Most promotional messages are more sophisticated than 'this product's good, so go and buy it'. In planning the message content, the sender will consider:

   ◆ The purpose of the communication
   ◆ The subject to be communicated
   ◆ The likely needs of the recipient
   ◆ The communication methods available for use.

   It is imperative that we communicate to the recipient in a way they will easily understand and will arouse interest. This process is known as *encoding* and involves a combination of words, pictures and symbols to represent the message to be transmitted. The first step to encoding is to decide what and how much to say; if a message contains too much information it is difficult to absorb, but if you do not include enough, it will not meet with the expectation of the recipient and may leave room for misinterpretation.

3   The **medium** you choose for transmission will depend on the message to be conveyed, location of the recipient, speed, convenience and degree of formality required. The usual internal methods are memo, report, e-mail, telephone and face-to-face interaction. External methods available will be determined by the media consumption habits of the recipient. For example, one of the best ways to communicate to 16–19-year-olds is by advertising in cinemas or SMS messaging.

4   **Decoding** is the interpretation of the message that has been received by the recipient. If the decoding message is the same as the encoded message then the communication will have achieved its objective. However, if the recipient decodes the message in another way, it may mean that the communication is entirely wasted. The degree of misinterpretation will need to be established before the message content is adapted.

5   **Feedback** (or lack of) is the response that the recipient sends back to the sender and is a key element in the communication process because it enables the sender to *evaluate* the effectiveness of the message. Feedback may take the form of verbal (telephone call, face-to-face interaction, etc.), non-verbal communication or action (body language, etc.) or written messages. The inclusion within the message of a response mechanism to establish two-way communication will aid this feedback. Marketing research is a more formal (and expensive) way of eliciting feedback.

Feedback is the key element that creates a cycle in the communication chain, enabling the information that is sent to be reviewed when it is received back. If the feedback shows that the communications objectives have not been met then corrective action, usually changing either the message content or communication method, can be taken.

Encoding the message

Messages to achieve objective

Again, there is a wide range of possibilities. Not much explicit planning is needed for: 'We have received your order.' However, a report to a client on a mix of advertising media to be used will need planning, as there may well be a basket of issues needing to be addressed to get the overall desired effect: 'Place your account with us.' It is important to understand both ends of the equation. The message must not only be appropriate to our needs but also meet the stakeholder needs and expectations. The message 'Buy our product as it is cheap' may not be right for a wealthy client more interested in green issues. In constructing the message, some anticipation of stakeholder reaction is needed.

Format and media

Increasingly, communications at the one-to-one level are moving into electronic media. E-mails provide audit trails (you can tell if an e-mail has been received but not an ordinary letter); they are quick, cheap and, with attachments, can carry vast amounts of data (reports, images, etc., can be attached as files). It is important to provide the communication in a medium that is convenient for the receiver. Poor quality format and construction detracts from the quality of the message.

Text should be written in clear language that is appropriate for the target audience.

- Keep your sentences short.
- Use active verbs.
- Use 'you' and 'we'.
- Choose words appropriate for the reader.
- Don't be afraid to give instructions.
- Avoid nominalisations.
- Use positive language.
- Use lists where appropriate.

The effects of noise

Noise, such as distractions or the interference that occurs as the communication is being encoded, transmitted and decoded, can obstruct the transmission of the message. There are many different types of noise that can render the message inaccurate, unclear or even mean that it is not received at all.

Technical noise

Technical noise can occur while the message is being transmitted; for example, when a poor telephone connection means the caller's voice cannot be heard, or when the fax machine breaks down. Now, slow broadband or not being able to pick up a mobile signal is just as problematic and frustrating and is also viewed as being a form of technical noise.

Physical noise

Physical noise can occur while the message is being transmitted; for example, people talking, traffic or noisy machinery could render a speaker's voice inaudible during a presentation.

Social noise

Social noise creates interference in the transmission and decoding of messages. It is caused when people are prejudiced against others because they are of a different age, gender or social class. For example, a young woman delivering a presentation on corporate funding to older businessmen may be perceived to lack credibility by some of the audience who are prejudiced because of her age and gender. Social noise can also be used to retain interest or differentiate the whole message.

Psychological noise

A person's emotional state or attitude could interfere with message transmission. A person's anger or hostile attitude can create psychological noise. For example, a customer whose goods have not been delivered may be unable to hear the reason why the goods have been delayed because he is so angry about the situation.

Insight: Communications barriers

A UK manufacturing company hosted a delegation from an associate company in Japan. The marketing manager was given the task of arranging the first day's activities, which were to include a two-hour long presentation about the history, structure and objectives of the firm, a tour of the main manufacturing site and lunch followed by a brainstorming session on how the two companies could forge closer links and benefit from future joint projects. However, little consideration was given to the communication barriers that arose during the visit:

◆ Cultural differences in the way Japanese people greet others, their degree of formality and taste in food.

◆ The language barrier in that many of the delegation did not speak English and none of the host company spoke Japanese.

◆ The unfamiliar technical environment and organisation of the company, which meant that the jargon and abbreviations specific to the host company that were used in the presentation, made the presentation incomprehensible to most of the delegation.

◆ The noisy manufacturing site meant that during the tour most of the visitors could not hear what was being said to them.

◆ The lengthy presentation meant that the visitors who understood English had 'information overload'. Most lost concentration and could not take in the overall message that was being conveyed.

◆ The delegation did not feel confident or comfortable with contributing to the brainstorming session.

For future visits, the marketing manager thought of a number of ways to eliminate the communication barriers:

- Employing an interpreter.

- Researching cultural differences and using this information to provide appropriate refreshments and use appropriate greetings, seating arrangements and so on.

- Ensuring that no jargon or colloquialisms are used by speakers.

- Using small groups to tour the factory at a quiet time so that visitors could hear what the guide is saying.

- Using a shorter presentation to prevent boredom and information overload.

- Using a different presentation approach, with visual media, such as slides or video and Powerpoint software.

- Increasing interaction with the audience with question and answer techniques to check understanding.

- Providing a pack of information in English and Japanese, containing key points about the company, such as its structure, objectives and current operations.

- Avoiding the brainstorming session as it is probably too ambitious an exercise. Replacing it with a more social event where individual host managers can be 'partnered' with visiting managers, and interpreters used to help exchange views in a less threatening context.

Business communication formats

Letters

Despite the growth of e-mail communication, letters still play an important role in the business world. Think about the covering letter that you send with your CV – if the letter isn't great, the CV won't even be read. The major sections of a typical letter are as follows:

- **The sender's address block** will contain the full contact information for the organisation (address with postcode, telephone and fax). This block may include website information or this may be printed as a 'footer' on the bottom of the headed paper. The printed heading may be customised a little with the personal contact information of the sender (e.g. direct telephone line and e-mail address).

- **The reference section** gives reference information to identify the document. In past days this might have been the typist and author. This is often now the location address for the letter's word-processing file.

- **The date** should be in the specific organisation's house style (e.g. US companies use a different format). Standard options are given in Word and other packages.

- **The recipient's address block** should contain the recipient's correct title (Dr., Rev., etc.), name and address (including postcode or zip). Word allows this block to be highlighted and then used to address an envelope or a label so full postal information is required.

- **The salutation** is the formal address line (e.g. Dear Dr Smith). The salutation and recipient's address block are almost invariably left justified.

◆   **The heading block** can be centred, left or right justified according to the organisation's house style. The reference and date blocks will usually be left or right justified, according to house style. The heading (if used) will often be in bold and may be left aligned or centred according to the house style.

◆   **The body of the letter** will generally contain a line or two of introduction and conclusion. The main body of the letter contains the substance. In the exam setting, this is where you will demonstrate your understanding and context-specific application of marketing knowledge.

◆   **The signature block** will contain an ending salutation (e.g. Yours sincerely,) followed by a space for the sender's signature. Often handwritten signatures are illegible, so the name and qualifications (where relevant, e.g. FCIM, Chartered Marketer) need to be added below the signature, with the position (normally one line below), and if only general Internet information is given in the heading the personal direct e-mail contact information should be given below that.

◆   If the letter has **supporting documentation** (e.g. reports, specifications, etc.) this may be listed at the foot of the page. If other people have been sent copies of the letter, the circulation list may also be given.

Reports

The single most important format in business, and for a CIM candidate, is report format. Different contexts demand different house styles and the general framework given below should be adapted as required.

◆   **Title page** – including title of project and date. For CIM integrative assignments, the question number should be included. Lavish colour graphics are not required; presentation is no substitute for content. A good, clear, professional presentation is required.

◆   **Executive summary** – focused and brief (150–300 words), should include key words for computer indexing of the project for more formal academic reports, and is important for longer formal reports in the business context. Provides senior management with an overview and directs further selective reading.

◆   **Acknowledgments** – assistance may have been given with resources (e.g. with running focus groups) or other support. It is good manners to acknowledge support.

◆   **Contents** – helps people find their way around a longer project. Longer academic projects might include page numbers of main topic headings, appendices and lists of diagrams, figures, tables and illustrations. Reports should be page-numbered.

◆   **Brief introduction** – a clear definition of the hypothesis, issue(s) or problems covered in the report.

◆   **Body of the report** – with full use of headings and subheadings. In academic reports, the more formal style should be used (e.g. 'the view is advanced' rather than 'I suggest'). For business reports, the organisation's house style should be followed (e.g. in less formal companies the view might be that you take ownership of your recommendations and write, 'I recommend'. For a typical academic project, the major section headings might be 'Literature review', 'Primary research' and 'Conclusions & recommendations'.

◆ **Conclusions and recommendations** – this section should summarise the findings and, if appropriate, give recommended courses of action (e.g. in a CIM assignment how the selected organisation might improve its operations in the area covered in the report).

◆ **References** – these are particularly important in academic work. Failure to properly reference work quoted can leave a suspicion of plagiarism. The CIM framework expects candidates to read around the subject and keep up with developments. References provide evidence that you have done this. Tables 8.1 (books), 8.2 (journals) and 8.3 (websites) give the accepted referencing system used professionally and in academic institutions. The 'Harvard' system for referencing in the body of the report is the most widely used in business and academic work. In academic works the references tend to be at the end (in a separate section) whereas in business reports it is more common to use footnotes on each page.

In business, full referencing is generally not required, but indication where information has been obtained from is usually good practice (e.g. source of statistical data in a table). In the exam setting, full referencing can be too time-consuming, but where you use a theory, you may wish to briefly acknowledge the source, for example 'Value Chain (Porter)'. References are the sources that you used directly in writing your report.

◆ **Bibliography** – the same conventions in referencing the source apply, but this is the more general material that you consulted in your overall research but have not used directly and quoted in the body of your report.

◆ **Appendices** – should be restricted to essential support material. For CIM company-based assignments, a brief overview of the company context is helpful. Complete copies of annual reports and others are generally not required. If some primary research was conducted with a questionnaire, then an example copy of a completed questionnaire might be appropriate. If in doubt, consult your tutor.

◆ **Exam reports** – In general, only the briefest of headings should be given, with introductions and conclusion short and focused. It is the quality of the content of the body of your report that will score high marks. As noted above, there may not be time for full references. The CIM website provides good examples of specimen reports in a range of exam contexts.

◆ **Company reports** – Most organisations have their own house styles and conventions. This may be contained in a company style manual. If not, when you come to write your first report, talk to your manager and ask for the report that is considered to have been the best in recent past. This will give you an indication of the company style. The submission cover page will normally be replaced with a front page giving the title, author(s), date of submission, edition (if taken though various drafts), executive summary and the distribution list. The summary and title pages are not necessary in this context, as all the information will be contained on one page.

◆ **Font style** – You should follow house style for company reports. For CIM reports, 12-point proportional type is recommended. Times New Roman and Arial are good, popular type styles, whereas Tahoma is often used when there is a risk that the reader may suffer from some visual impairment. If proportional type is used, single line spacing is acceptable. Justification provides a neater report, but is not essential. Pages should be numbered.

Table 8.2 Outline of how to reference a book

Field	Example
Author(s) or editor's surname followed by initials	Kopperl, D.
Year of publication, in brackets	(1965)
Book title, in italics	*Manual of Document Microphotography*
City where published	Boston
Publisher name	Focal Press

(*Source:* Elsevier author guidelines with adaptation)

Example: Kopperl, D. (1965) *Manual of Document Microphotography*, Boston, Focal Press

Table 8.3: Outline of how to reference a journal

Field	Example
Author(s) surname and initials	Kopperl, D.
Year of publication of journal, in brackets	(1965)
Paper title, in inverted commas	'Techniques of Photography'
Journal title, in italics (abbreviations or acronyms are acceptable here)	*J. Appl. Photogr. Engn.*
Volume	2
Issue number	2
Part/section (if applicable)	1
Page numbers plus date article written if available	117–120

(*Source*: Elsevier author guidelines with adaptation

Example: Kopperl, D. (1965) 'Techniques of photography', *J. Appl. Photogr. Engng.*, 2, 2, 1, 117–120

Table 8.4: Outline of how to reference an Internet source

Field	Example
Author(s) surname and initial	Kopperl, D.
Year the website was constructed in brackets	(1965)
Title of the document (in italics) followed by [online]	*Techniques of photography [online]*
Website title plus complete URL	www.marketingonline.co.uk
Date you accessed the site in curved brackets	(03/07/04)

(*Source*: Elsevier author guidelines with adaptation

Example: Kopperl, D. (1965) Techniques of photography [online], *The Online Journal of Applied Photographic Engineering*, www.JAPE.co.uk/Kopp/TechPhot.html (03/07/04)

E-mails

Contrary to many people's expectations, e-mails are much more permanent than a paper letter. Once the hard copy (copies) of a letter is shredded, it is destroyed. E-mails go through systems with back-up security (in the sending organisation, in transmission and in the receiving organisation). There can be 'stray' copies around that you have no knowledge of and no control over. For this reason, and with the implications of data protection legislation, every care should be taken over e-mails just as you would with letters. That clever suggestion or lively joke could take on a different implication when examined in the cold light of day. Remember there is no such thing as a private communication in business (leaks and data protection legislation ensure this).

♦ **Computer header address block** – Gives all your addresses, your name and e-mail contact information. The 'To' block is for the target stakeholders (public/audience). The 'Cc' block is for people who may need to be kept informed. The 'Bcc' block allows you to circulate the e-mail to other people without the other recipients ('To' or 'Cc') knowing. The subject [title] block should give a one-line overview of the content. With busy inboxes, people often only display the 'From', 'Date' and 'Subject' fields. A meaningless subject (e.g. 'Re:' as default from the software setting) might only get you a quick click into the delete box. The date and time is automatically picked up. In most software, the heading block will also give the file names and type (e.g. PowerPoint, Word, etc.) of any attached files. Remember people with dial-up access and small-capacity inboxes do not appreciate large picture files.

♦ **The body of an e-mail** follows the rules of introduction, main body and conclusion. The introduction and conclusion may be very brief or omitted for a simple e-mail.

♦ **The signature block** is best set up by customising your software. This is much the same as for the signature block of a letter, but may also contain other contact information such as direct dial telephone number, website reference and so on.

♦ **Disclaimer block** – Normally this will be set up by the organisation and will be written by the legal department. It may cover such issues as to the non-disclosure of content if received in error, declaration of non-liability for virus damage, statement of organisation's communications policy (offensive content) and in some organisations (e.g. journalists working for TV, radio or press) that the individual's views are the individual's and do not necessarily represent the policy of the organisation.

For all their ease and speed, e-mails are part of the permanent record. The implications of data protection legislation are that only a fool will commit to an e-mail something that they would not like to defend in the media or in court. Some software allows tracking options that allows the sender to know when you have received the message, when you have read it and when you have deleted it. More like an instant 'recorded delivery' than an informal method of communication! Some organisations (sending, transmitting or receiving) may be monitoring content for offensive words.

E-mails should never be sent to large distribution lists, unless the list has been checked to ensure the recipients are all likely to be interested. Sending a 'circular' email runs the risk that many recipients will treat it as junk and bin it.

Memos

The e-mail format can be considered as an electronic format for a memo to be transmitted directly, rather than printed and sent by 'snail mail'. The heading is almost identical (clearly you cannot list 'blind' copies at the top of a memo!). The body follows the same rules. The signature block is usually simple and allows space for the handwritten signature, the sender's name and management position. Most memos are now composed within a word-processing package, and for convenience a note of the file name is often useful.

In some organisations, individuals may not file a hard copy of memos but maintain the file in a structured archive folder; attachments can be listed here too in this block. This way, duplicate copies of a document need not be held (in e-mails, attachments consume disk space, this way the memo block points to the original document file and this can save disk storage). Computer files take up no floor space and can be backed up systematically. Hard copy can get lost or destroyed (it only takes one coffee!).

Rather like the fax, the use of the memo in business is decreasing and being replaced with the quicker, cheaper, more environmentally friendly (no paper, no toner), more permanent, more secure (you can put an electronic track on an e-mail, and receive a 'read receipt', but you can never tell when a memo has been received or lost) and instant e-mail.

Effective communication

What makes communication effective?

When speaking with customers, whether face-to-face or on the telephone, it is important that what you say is perceived as helpful, welcoming and appropriate. In a face-to-face situation, the chart on the next page demonstrates that it is not just what we say that is important, but more about *how* we say it and our *body language* being consistent with the message being sent. Obviously, body language will not take an active part in telephone communication but that will put additional emphasis on the tone of voice used and other non-verbal cues such as speed of answering and ability to gain the required response.

It is sometimes ironic that the people who interact most frequently with the group of greatest importance to every organisation – *customers* – are sometimes the least well trained and lowest paid. Having spent a great deal of time and money on promotional messages and persuading the customer to purchase, the actual transaction will take place only if the customer is dealt with in a welcoming way and the interaction leaves them feeling valued.

Non-verbal communications (including kinetics)

Non-verbal communication consists of:

◆ The body language you use, such as eye contact, facial expression, posture, gesture and physical space. This is also known as 'kinetics' or sometimes 'kinesics'.

◆ The impression/atmosphere you create by your punctuality, hospitality, manners and personal appearance.

Non-verbal communication conveys messages without words or adds meaning to whatever words are being used. Although each body movement probably does not have its own unique meaning, several body movements tend to convey similar meaning. For instance, the cues of casual smiling, light laughter, forward body lean, open body posture, and frequent eye contact are perceived as conveying intimacy and non-dominance – the characteristics commonly associated with friendliness and courtesy. On the other hand, kinesics such as stoic facial expressions, either staring or avoiding eye contact, backward lean of body, and closed body posture are perceived as conveying dominance, unfriendliness, and emotional distance.

Eye contact

The look in someone's eyes can have a variety of meanings. In a romantic scene, the way an actor looks into the leading lady's eyes conveys a very different meaning to the way a person can stare in defiance or in a challenging way. In a business context, avoiding eye contact can convey disinterest or shiftiness but making positive eye contact while you are delivering a presentation shows that you are relating to and connecting with your audience. Therefore, in order for the message you are conveying to be taken as 'trustful', it is important that eye contact be maintained. In two-way communication, the fact that someone cannot meet your gaze may mean they are uncomfortable with what you are saying and you may wish to change the message content in light of this.

Facial expression

Your facial expression and coloration can convey various meanings. A flushed face can indicate embarrassment or shyness, while the colour draining out of your face can indicate shock. Pursed lips can reveal your irritation at something, a frown can show disapproval and a smile can indicate happiness, approval or a welcome.

The expression must be appropriate to the situation. People working closely with customers are often told to 'keep smiling'. However, if the customer is in the process of making a serious complaint, a fixed smile will only infuriate them further.

Posture

If you adopt an upright posture, it can show that you are attentive and the opposite can show that you are disinterested. If you were lounging in your seat when your managing director walks past, it could indicate that you do not respect the individual and you are probably not working that hard either.

It is important to adopt an open posture when dealing with customers, folded arms will put people off whereas leaning towards them will indicate listening. Other postures/gestures can be used to send out non-verbal messages – consider how you would feel if the person you are speaking to started drumming their fingers.

We now know from a series of studies on human and animal behaviour that we tend to mirror the body language of the person we are communicating with if we feel empathy with that person and their point of view.

Physical space

Physical space also refers to the invisible line that surrounds people and is referred to as *personal space*. By breaching someone's personal space you can intimidate him or her and be perceived as overbearing and insensitive.

An accepted move into someone's physical space in Britain is the friendly handshake. In Europe and other countries, kissing on the cheek may be acceptable. Different countries and cultures have different norms. In China, the size of acceptable physical space is much smaller than in Britain because their population density is much greater.

Physical space can also be about how people are seated whilst communicating. Sitting on a big chair behind a big desk so that people who enter your office have to sit on a lower chair opposite you, with the desk as a barrier, can communicate your authority and the level of formality you expect from others. Alternatively, you can achieve informality in meetings by using a horseshoe-shape layout.

The impression/atmosphere

You can create a favourable impression in a business situation with a smart appearance in terms of your clothes and personal grooming. If you are punctual and use the appropriate greeting, for example a formal handshake, particularly when meeting new business contacts, this can influence whether you are seen to be acceptable by conforming to the norms of business behaviour.

It is important in order that the person you are interacting with feels comfortable in the situation they find themselves and so feels able to communicate with you effectively. Much of what is covered here is basic in its approach and you may feel it is stating the obvious – however, consider how many of the issues raised here have happened to you when visiting other organisations, and how communication was affected.

In professional services situations (e.g. interactions between attorneys and clients), it is both appropriate and wise for customers to be welcomed with a firm handshake and eye contact. If the service situation involves considerable interpersonal conversation or discussion (e.g. physician, attorney, and therapist visits), service providers can effectively employ nodding and frequent eye contact to indicate understanding and empathy. In such situations, nodding is likely to enhance customers' perceptions of trust and courtesy. In all service situations, the use of frequent eye contact accompanied by other complementary nonverbal cues will help enhance perceptions of trust, believability, and sincerity. On the other hand, service employees should never use nonverbal cues that communicate dominance, unconcern, and superiority, such as scant or piercing eye contact, finger pointing, and closed body posture.

Think about recent sales/service encounters you have had, and how body language might have affected the outcome.

Paralanguage

This is not 'what is said', but 'the way that it is said'. For example, the speaker's tone of voice (is he angry or relaxed) or the way emphasis is placed on particular words or parts of a statement.

Interpersonal communication studies indicate that the noncontent or nonverbal aspects of a message are at least as important as the actual content. While verbal statements can convey states of being, listeners use paralinguistic cues, such as vocal pitch, loudness or amplitude, pitch variation, pauses, and fluency, to perceive the exact state of being. For example, a communicator might use a verbal statement to convey confidence (e.g. 'I am positively sure that...'), but listeners will consciously and unconsciously interpret the paralanguage to assess the communicator's degree of confidence. It is also known that, in any situation where people meet for the first time, listeners pay more attention to the paralanguage of a conversation, than they do to the actual content.

In service situations where it is appropriate (and perhaps even expected) for service providers to be particularly kind, warm, and friendly (e.g. in health and beauty care, hotel, restaurant, transportation, and counselling services), service providers need to use more paralinguistic cues associated with a conversational style. Such cues are likely to facilitate employees to portray an image that they are people-oriented rather than task-oriented. On the other hand, in service situation where consumers are likely to expect the provider to be more business- or task-oriented, (e.g. in the financial, legal, and advertising fields), service providers might place more weight on using a public speaking style. For example, an attorney who wants to present a competent and yet friendly image might use a public speaking style to portray competence and dynamism – but also the kinesic nonverbal cues of nodding, frequent eye contact, and occasional smiling to convey warmth and friendliness.

Meta-communications

This is 'communications about communications', or the feelings and emotions exchanged between participants to a conversation about how well (or badly) that communication is going. According to Shimojima et al. (1997):

> There are two different kinds of communications going on in a human conversation: (a) base-communications, namely, exchanges of information about the topic situation of a dialogue, and (b) meta-communications, namely, exchanges of information about the progress of the conversation itself. Meta-communications can be done by verbal means (texts, rhythms, pitches, powers, and speeds of speech) and non-verbal means (gestures, gesticulations, gaze directions, and inhalations), and they are often unintentional. Nevertheless, meta-communications play crucial roles in our joint-managements of conversation, for, without them, we cannot share the information about the progress of base-communications, problems occurring in them, turn exchanges, topic changes, and background knowledge of each participant.

Activity 8.3

If you have access to video recording, perhaps by means of a mobile telephone, record a conversation between two of your friends. Analyse the conversation for evidence of kinesics, paralanguage and meta-communications.

Promotional activities

Having identified the various segments that 'customers' can fall into, we have to consider the best methods of communicating with those groups. We must also realise that as ICT developments, such as e-mail and mobile phones, have made communication cheaper, faster and more frequent, customers are expecting to establish a dialogue as part of the buying decision-making process, to ensure the planned purchase will meet their needs.

To communicate with external customers, organisations use a range of activities that can be described as the *external communications mix*. These activities range from advertising, direct marketing and selling to public relations and the creation of a strong corporate identity. These activities are used to create brands, to inform customers about product improvements and to promote sales, and because most organisations are not interested in a one-off sale, communications are used to build an ongoing relationship with the customer.

Advertising

When combining the promotional tools to produce a customised communications package which meets the needs of our own organisation, it is important to consider how each of the tools used will complement and support each other in achieving the organisation's promotional objectives. Some methods more naturally slot into the role of *primary* media, enabling mass communication and building awareness on a large scale. These tend to be *above-the-line* media. The promotional toolbox contains the following above-the-line media.

◆ Television

◆ Press

◆ Radio

◆ Outdoor

◆ Cinema

◆ Internet

◆ Branding.

Much of the inter-media decisions taken will depend not only on the budget available but also the media characteristics that the brand/service requires in order that it be communicated in the best possible way. In looking at each of the following media we must also consider their ability to communicate:

◆ At a visual level

◆ At an audio level, and

◆ At the right level of detail.

While advertising is commonly used, it is relatively ineffective in the context of relationship management. Advertising tends to be an impersonal tool, whereas relationships are individual. While advertising has the potential to reach very large target markets, relationship management concentrates on one-to-one communication.

Sales promotions

Sales promotion is another communications tool that marketers use. It can be defined as:

> **Sales promotion** – a short-term tactical marketing tool that gives customers additional reasons or incentives to purchase. (CIM)

The incentive will be linked directly to the promotional objective. With an entirely new product the promotional objective will be to build awareness and the sales promotion objective will be to induce trial of the new product to turn trialists into *end-users*. With products in the maturity stage of the product life cycle (PLC) the promotional objective will be to remind people of the product benefits, the sales promotion objectives will be to get them to buy more (3 for 2) and render them less able to switch brands.

Sales promotions can be used as a dual-purpose tool by targeting two different customer groups. Consumer promotions to encourage consumers to go and buy, these are referred to as *pull* strategies because the customer by demanding the product is *pulling* it through the distribution chain. Trade promotions targeting the intermediaries in the distribution chain are used to encourage the intermediaries (often wholesalers or retailers) to stock or recommend the product. This is known as a *push* strategy as the organisation seeks to *push* the product through the chain towards the end-user. By using a combination of *push* and *pull* it should be possible to have the product in store at the precise moment the customer demands it.

So the objectives of a sales promotion can be expressed in any (or all) of these ways:

◆ **Encourage trial of product** – to overcome any negative perceptions, encourage brand switching.

◆ **Extend existing customer base** – by reducing the cost of brand switching.

◆ **Prompt customers to change brand**.

◆ **Generate bulk buying** – your consumers will not brand switch if they have residual stock of your product.

◆ **Overcome seasonal dips in sales** – which may result in peaks and troughs smoothing out in time.

◆ **Encourage trade to stock product** – as they know customers are to be incentivised.

Consumer sales promotions usually offer temporary added value to the customer at the point of purchase. There are many different versions of these:

◆ Price reductions

◆ Coupons/money-off vouchers

◆ Entry to competitions/free prize draws

◆ Free goods

◆ x per cent free

◆ 3 for the price of 2 (or Buy one get one free – BOGOF)

◆ Free samples or gifts

◆ Guarantees or extended warranties

◆ £x goes to y charity if you purchase

◆ Reward points/tokens against a free gift (e.g. air miles)

◆ Refunds or free gifts on a mail-in basis.

Sales promotions aimed at the trade include:

◆ Discount on bulk orders

◆ Free supplies

◆ Incentives (e.g. shopping vouchers for Marks & Spencer or a free alarm clock)

◆ Free prize draw competitions

◆ Deferred invoicing

◆ Merchandising and display material.

Sales promotions have great value in relationship management, if used wisely. Consumer promotions may trigger the first step in the relationship – a customer switching to 'our' brand. Many of the sales promotion tools also concentrate on encouraging loyalty – a key component of relationship management.

Similarly, trade promotions are used at every stage of the supplier–customer relationship. Once again, they can encourage switching or loyalty. Sales promotions are used widely in modern supply-chain management approaches, where organisations form long-term relationships for mutual benefit.

Public relations

The Institute of Public Relations has defined public relations as:

> **Public relations** – the planned and sustained effort to establish and maintain goodwill and mutual understanding between an organisation and its publics (IPR)

Public relations are essentially concerned with developing a corporate personality that communicates the general philosophies of that organisation to its publics. The PR activities therefore fall into three main categories:

1   Development of the corporate image – the face of the company.

2   Communication of that image and all that falls within it.

3   Specific related activities where the image is used.

The spectrum of public relations is increasing all the time in an era where there is little discernible difference between products and services. It is often the customer's perception of the *corporate personality* which PR seeks to create that offers the differentiation point.

Public relations can convey greater *credibility* than an advertising message as it is perceived to have originated from a more independent source. The credibility of the newspaper that is reporting on the organisation will be considered rather than the organisation itself.

Cost is relatively low in comparison to advertising. The cost of a press conference is relatively of good value when you consider the amount of press reporting and TV coverage you can achieve with a good PR message.

Communication to the correct target audience is reliant on the PR agency ensuring all the relevant press attend the conference, or that the vehicle to be sponsored is one that has links to the target audience.

Control can be an issue. Although you can make sure the press have all the information to pass on a positive perception to the stakeholders, if a particular journalist is looking for a more sensational story that day, then he/she can re-position the information to give a negative slant.

Public relations cover the following activities:

◆   Corporate image and corporate social responsibility

◆   Exhibitions, conferences and special events

◆   Press conferences

- ◆ Press releases
- ◆ Sponsorship.

Public relations often suffers the same drawbacks in relationship management as advertising – much PR activity is aimed at a broad market, rather than individual customers.

Digital technologies

Technological developments in communications are making massive changes to our personal and working lives. They are changing the way we shop, find out information, communicate with others inside and outside our organisation; they are affecting the way organisations promote their products/services and how they do business with suppliers and distributors.

The introduction of computers has transformed the way information is handled and communicated. Data in a digital format means that when a document is typed any mistakes can be quickly corrected before it is printed out and information such as invoices, forms and previous letters can be indexed and retrieved easily.

Electronic point of sale (EPOS) systems allow retailers to record and monitor sales data. Linked to 'smart' card purchases, EPOS data provides organisations with detailed profiles of customer preferences and purchasing habits. Databases can be used to store information about customer purchase history so that mail-merged documents can be sent to customers with offers tailored to their needs.

Even the way you use the telephone has changed. Mobile telephones mean you can be constantly in touch with colleagues and customers even when you are away from the office. People can leave voice mail and fax messages at any time, without having to rely on others to take the information down correctly. Businesses can deal speedily with massive telephone response through voice mail and automated processes.

We are now seeing the general use of videophone technology combined with mobile phones, which will change the way you communicate on the telephone, because your body language and facial expressions can be observed.

Laptop computers mean that you can work away from your desk or while on the move and still access or send information to your colleagues at the office. Wireless technology has removed the need for a docking station or physical connection to access the Internet.

The advent of electronic communication has probably had the most impact, and e-mail in particular has become so popular that for many people it is the main way they communicate with others. However, it is also true to say that new ways of working still have to develop acceptable ways of working and a sense of business etiquette guiding their use.

The ability to use the Internet has had a massive impact on the speed and cost of communicating, especially accessing information on websites or transacting business online.

You can also produce vast quantities of text, sound and picture information and store it on CD-ROM or in Digital Versatile Disc (DVD) format, which is an extremely interactive way for customers to access information. ISDN, and more recently broadband, lines have led to complex downloadable information being transmitted quickly and without the need for the now almost-redundant motorcycle courier.

Insight: The impact of broadband

The development of broadband technology demonstrates the impact that the digital evolution can have in terms of channel structure and the strategic shift that organisations need to make in order to remain competitive.

Films are traditionally marketed first through cinemas, then through video releases and finally through television (as video on demand, then pay-for channels and then terrestrial services). The full financial potential is realised through this channel structure. The development of digital technologies and Internet facilities offer certain advantages to film studios but it is not necessarily to their advantage to cut out these intermediaries. For example, not all films are successful and some go 'straight to video' in which case the video rental store plays a significant part in the marketing channel.

Broadband services enable people to see films online, whenever and wherever they want. For organisations such as Blockbuster video rental stores, this development posed a major threat. With 65 million cardholders and 6300 stores worldwide (Oliver, 2000), the company needed to anticipate the changes in supply and demand. Blockbuster's response was to change the fundamental purpose or mission of the organisation to be an overall entertainment provider for the home. The development of e-commerce facilities has been a key part of their strategy.

Central to this strategy was the non-exclusive digital download and video streaming rights agreement with the studio MGM and independent film operator AtomFilms. This enables Blockbuster to showcase selected films on its website (www.blockbuster.com). (This first step may lead to agreements with other studios and may well prove attractive to other entertainment-based companies that might enter into partnership deals.)

The website also enables people to purchase CDs, DVDs and games as well as the core product, videos. In addition, Blockbuster has used interactive technologies to provide a higher level of customer personalisation in the services they offer. For example, its 'Blockbuster Recommends' facility suggests films to customers based upon their previous selections or a list of films rated *I hate it* or *I like it*. Another example of the personalisation approach is the facility to suggest films to match the mood of the viewer. For example, if someone is feeling depressed then it may suggest a Gene Wilder film to cheer them up. All of these changes have been supported with a substantial off-line advertising campaign to inform current customers of the changes and to remind them of the Blockbuster proposition and values, to attract and persuade potential new customers to visit the site or a local store, and finally to reposition the brand by differentiating it from its previous position and its main competitors.

Effectively, the company has revised its strategy to accommodate changes in the environment, implemented the necessary changes to its offering, and then rebranded itself to be repositioned in the home entertainment business.

Source: Fill, C. (2002) *Marketing Communications – Contexts, Strategies and Applications,* 3rd edition.

Intranet/extranet

An intranet is an information system that is used to communicate internally within an organisation. This allows all employees within an organisation, regardless of how many sites they are located at or the geographical location of those sites, to communicate almost instantaneously. This effectively negates the need for memos as we highlighted earlier, but also allows for electronic transfer of any electronically held information such as reports, letters and data to be transmitted as attachments. The organisational address book allows users to select by name without putting in the whole e-mail address.

An extranet extends the intranet capacity to suppliers and distributors. Along with other approaches detailed in this chapter, this can replace time-consuming and costly invoice raising and sending out cheques, by fully automating these processes alongside many others. Different media forms can be accommodated with photographs, videos and artwork being transferable.

Insight

It is particularly important for a customer service organisation to develop good communication channels with its stakeholders, especially its customers and employees. The Inland Revenue operates in a fast changing environment with its culture changing to become more customer-focused. It has assumed responsibility for new areas of work and developed modern internal and external systems to enhance multi-channel 'Hints and Tips'.

It is vital that responsive, informed, employees identify and meet their customers' needs as quickly as possible. In order to meet this challenge, the Inland Revenue has embraced a range of communications methods that take full advantage of the latest technology.

Core to these communications systems are online communications. Internal e-mails are as part of the internal communications push to ensure all staff are fully briefed on all aspects of their workload.

Online communications also allow consumers to complete their tax return, claim tax credits and transact a variety of business with the Inland Revenue directly online, thereby saving a lot of time. An important advantage to this method is that ongoing 'help' is provided by pop-up help facilities. This is a cheap, quick and efficient method of communication.

Intranets and extranets are powerful tools in relationship management, as they are only open to current relationship 'partners'. Like all digital media, the content viewed can be tailored or personalised by means of cookies (packets of data identifying the user) so each viewer receives a personal communication.

Internet

Internet access is available in over 60 per cent of homes in the United Kingdom. Although the profile of users is becoming closer to the national profile, it is still heavily utilised by younger more affluent people. Over 50 per cent of e-mail usage emanates from people under 25 years of age.

Internet advertising allows varying levels of visual, audio and interactive messages to be developed dependent upon the budget and creativity of the designer. A great deal of information can be transmitted, with the level of interaction being determined by the 'viewer'. Usage will fall into two broad categories: those who require a specific piece of information to act upon, or those who are 'browsing' – any advertising must fulfil the needs of both.

All *offline* communications must feature the website address to build awareness of the site and its offerings. *Online* advertising is also used to drive traffic through to the website using the following methods:

◆ **Links with other sites** – these can be general sites with a similar profile of users to whom you are targeting, for example the *Sunday Times*, Amazon. Special interest sites, such as the Formula 1 website, will provide more targeted opportunities.

◆ **Advertising on ISP portals** (Internet service provider) such as Wanadoo and Yahoo! These can also be targeted as they have the demographic details of their subscribers and have details of their high traffic sites.

◆ **E-mail advertising** – using information gained from customer details or purchased as lists from many organisations.

◆ **SMS messaging** (using mobile phones) is not strictly an Internet medium but is often used in the same way, targeting people by sending text messages. Airtime providers use this a great deal to market their own services but are now providing lists of numbers to other organisations, specifically for targeting hard to reach groups such as young adults.

The type of advertisement used will depend on the target audience, media chosen and the degree of information/creativity needed and possible. The advertisements are created in one of the following ways:

◆ **Banner advertising** – The most common form of advertising, banner advertisements appear on linked sites and offer the ability for the viewer to click through into the advertising organisation's website. There are also e-banners that allow e-transactions to take place.

◆ **Pop-up ads** – Often used not to advertise but to arouse interest via use of a game or clip of a film. Encourages the viewer to leave contact details to allow contact at a later stage.

◆ **Superstitals** – These appear whilst pages are being downloaded and provide entertainment whilst that is taking place. British Airways inserted one on the download to *The Times* newspaper website. However, with the improved penetration of broadband, opportunities may be limited in the future.

◆ **E-mail and SMS** as detailed above, where a very specific message can be sent directly to the recipient.

The Internet, like other web-based media, is a powerful relationship management tool. All methods and media allow us to be very targeted or quite general in our target, dependent upon the linked site or portal chosen to carry the advertising. Content can be personalised, so each user receives information and messages that are relevant to them specifically. All uses are very measurable in that we are able to monitor the degree of 'click through'. A high level of interaction can also be built in to engage the viewer, and the content is flexible and can be updated regularly – at a cost.

Case study: The C3 launch

Launching the C3 family car, Citroen realised it would have to branch out beyond traditional media channels to target women with young children. It worked with media agency OMD to tie up an ad partnership with AOL Time Warner, which enabled it to use two formidable ad platforms – AOL and IPC media – to target its audience.

America Online launched a branded micro-site offering ideas and tips on getting the best day out to support the creative idea, 'Family Days Out'. IPC magazines also ran advertorials and produced its own guides for mums, which supported the micro-site.

The campaign was a huge success – 110,000 AOL members visited the Citroen branded micro-site with AOL the primary driver of traffic.

Electronic data interchange (EDI)

For many organisations the Internet will enable them to source parts, reduce waiting times for stock, cut the storage area they need for stockholding, and will mean cheaper distribution costs. For example, a network of franchised garages had their purchasing organised centrally using the Internet. This now means that if a franchise operator uses an exhaust from stock, this information is automatically communicated to the exhaust manufacturer, who can then re-stock the garage automatically. Whilst EDI is strictly a communications protocol, which is largely being replaced by tools such as Extensible Markup Language (XML), it is still often applied to other forms of data interchange. Business process and business communication are also transformed so that there are fewer telephone calls and less paperwork, which has a great impact on the efficiency of the organisation.

EDI is also used to keep track of inventory. For example, FedEx have opened up the 'back room' to business customers so that they can order courier service and track a package. This adds real value to their business relationship with customers. It also means that staff are not tied up with routine queries about the whereabouts of a package but have more time to spend dealing with orders and more complex forms of enquiry.

In organisations with a large number of transactions such as grocery supermarkets the EPOS systems which record the quantity and price of what the customer has purchased on their individual account till receipt can also then feed the same information into the EDI system to keep a check on stock control. If EPOS tells the stock control system that 58 of the 60 tins of beans have been sold, the EDI system can then activate an order for more beans. This results in the large grocery organisations such as Tesco and Sainsbury's having to dedicate less storage space to warehousing, freeing up more space to sell customers more products.

EDI can, therefore, improve a company's ability to work with others in terms of sharing documents and other information, which improves strategic partnerships on a worldwide basis. This has great value in relationship management terms.

Point of sale

Point of sale display and merchandising refers to the in-store display that can influence consumers to purchase products in shops. It involves the layout and design of the shop and the way the goods or merchandise are presented. Manufacturers can have in-store display material produced to remind customers of their products at the point of purchase. For example, manufacturers of chocolates and confectionery might arrange with shops to display special branded stands, mobiles or life-size cardboard cut-outs of characters used to advertise the chocolate brand.

This has now been extended to actually branding the whole shop facia – a technique used with newsagents by Cadbury and Mars confectionery.

Similarly, cosmetics manufacturers might supply shops with hanging signs or revolving display stands. This is another tool for marketers to communicate brand imagery and act as a reminder at the point of purchase.

Powerful manufacturers who spend vast amounts on advertising tend to have more influence on retailers in terms of where their products are displayed. The most effective display areas are at 'eye level', where products are easy to see and reach for. Powerful retailers will use this tool, often charging manufacturers to move their products to more visible and high-traffic sites.

Insight: POP displays

A point-of-purchase (POP) display is the final chance for a cosmetics company to convince the consumer to choose its brand over the competitors. Almost one-third of the sales of cosmetics can be linked to being noticed and attracted to a display. Many are also, in part, impulse buys. Consequently, the design and placement of POP displays represent a key element of the promotional efforts of cosmetics and manufacturers.

Colours are one key ingredient. Colours can create sophistication, fun and various emotions. Colours are often linked with individual companies. The colours of the display should match the packaging of the product and the integrated marketing communications theme that the cosmetics firm presents in other places.

The POP displays should lead the consumer to touch or pick up the product. Once a consumer has touched a product, a purchase almost always follows. Teenagers are more likely to pick up items with bold and bright colours and designs. Global Beauty Concepts targets 12- to 15-year-old girls with its brightly designed Petunia range of cosmetics. On the other hand, Fine Fragrances uses simple lines and colours in the attempt to reach key 'high street' retailers and their customers.

Males prefer more neutral colours than females. Products such as razors and colognes are more likely to sell with more minimalistic POPs. Unisex products also sell better with a more subdued approach. Calvin Klein cosmetics has led the way in promoting unisex products in its displays for CK fragrances.

A more recent trend in POP displays is to make them interactive. Clairol Cosmetics pioneered the use of interactive displays. Customers use a keypad or touch screen to select more information about the company's products.

Beyond a sturdy display rack, many factors go into the design of an effective cosmetics POP display. Colour, shape, size, positioning of 'testers' and other elements of design are key ingredients in the sale of these highly profitable items.

Source: Clow and Baack (2001) *Integrated Advertising, Promotion and Marketing Communications.*

Case study: Cadbury

Cadbury is one of the best-known brands in the United Kingdom and is synonymous with chocolate. In order to communicate and develop its brand with customers and other stakeholders, it uses a variety of communications methods. Some of the main ones are as follows:

◆ Advertising
◆ Point of purchase
◆ Public relations
◆ Direct marketing
◆ Website
◆ Personal selling
◆ Exhibitions and events
◆ Packaging
◆ Sales promotions
◆ Café Cadbury
◆ Sponsorship (*Coronation Street*)
◆ Trade promotions
◆ Product placements
◆ Cadbury World – associated merchandise
◆ Field marketing
◆ Vending machines.

One recent addition to this impressive list has been the development of Café Cadbury and its entry into the expanding coffee house market. Positioned as a 'Chocolate Experience', the Cadbury cafés seek to extend the Cadbury brand even though direct sales through these outlets will be small. The objective, as reported by Mason (2000), is to keep the Cadbury brand high in the minds of the public and to maintain the quality and trust that the brand has evoked. Cadbury refers to this brand extension as part of its present marketing programme.

Source: Fill, C. (2002) *Marketing Communications – Contexts and Strategies and Applications*, 3rd edition.

Personal selling

When one visualises the 'salesperson' many people will call to mind some negative images of either an unhelpful and impolite sales assistant in their local supermarket or a brash and unrelenting hard-sell salesman, usually connected with cars or double-glazing. Both of these scenarios communicate to the customer – in these cases, very badly.

The most important feature of personal selling as a tool of communication is that it involves two-way interactions. This makes it the single most valuable tool in relationship management. Personal selling can be used in different ways dependent upon who the customer is.

In consumer communications, personal selling can provide the confused consumer with additional information at the point of sale. Customer objections can be investigated, discussed and hopefully dispelled. The salesperson can help the customer to evaluate the alternatives and choose the product or service that is best for them. If this is carried out in an unpressured professional manner the customer will feel empowered to decide, and valued as a customer.

In a B2B situation, the success of an organisation can depend upon the relationships that its sales people have within the industry. This salesperson has more of a differentiating role to play, highlighting the benefits of his products/services across those in the competition. Objections will still need to be overcome, probably with accompanying guarantees as the customer seeks foolproof solutions, which will reflect well upon him in a pressured business environment. More emphasis will be placed on the terms and conditions of the relationship and the level of after-sales service and support on offer.

Direct marketing

Direct marketing is a medium that is changing rapidly and could become a more strategic tool in the future. At present most of the uses are tactical in their nature and are methods of generating short-term sales leads. Direct marketing allows us to send a personalised message to a consumer, generating a one-on-one communication. It is possibly the most targeted method of communication available to us marketers, yet the one that is least welcomed by the recipient.

Technology is enabling many changes within the direct marketing arena. We need to ensure that those changes allow us to use direct marketing techniques more sensitively in order to try to reduce negative perceptions of the medium in the minds of the consumer.

Technological advances mostly generate the changes that are occurring within direct marketing. With direct marketing, the changes have been primarily concerned with the collection, and manipulation of data – namely customer data and databases. We can now collect much more data than ever before from many different sources. Digital technology and the ability to establish more two-way methods of communication mean we can now access and process many more pieces of information into intelligent useable data. We can buy lists of customers of certain demographic profiles and product usage that are of a higher quality in terms of their accuracy than ever before. We now need to use these advances to become more targeted in our approach.

The customers have also evolved and are using their power. More customers are using services to opt out of receiving direct mail by a variety of services that have evolved to rid them of this intrusion into their lives. It is now possible to remove your name from mailing lists, express your wish not to receive direct marketing telephone calls and to bin direct mail communications.

E-mail and e-newsletters

E-mail can be used in the same way as direct mail with the communication adapted to be screen size and easy to print off. Attachments or hyperlinks to websites can further enhance the message although after many virus scares concerning unsolicited attachments, consumers are choosing to delete 'Spam' in droves without even opening the e-mail. However, the significant cost and time benefits of e-mail over postal methods especially on a global scale will continue to secure its future use.

Web pages

Other methods are not personalised and rely on the message recipient responding to the initial communication. Technology has widened the scope of the messages that can be sent. Mail order used to be totally dependent upon the postal and telephone system, now mail order is changing significantly with the use of websites and online ordering (e-commerce). The inclusion of website addresses on all forms of communication is encouraging people to contact the organisation for either more information or to order the product. For these methods to work, websites must be kept up to date and relevant. Ease of use and navigation is also important online. Security and speed of fulfilment are important when ordering online.

Interactive TV

Direct response TV gives the customer two ways of communicating with the organisation. Digital viewers can use the 'Red Button' option if advertisers in-build this function into their television advertising. Renault used this with the launch of the re-styled Megane. The red button led the viewer to more detailed information, lists of local dealers and an invitation to test drive. Non-digital viewers are offered a telephone hotline number to gain more information.

Leaflets and direct marketing

Direct mail can be a powerful communication tool but where it is sent indiscriminately it can irritate people and be judged as 'junk mail'. Wastage can be reduced if the mail shots are targeted at the right people. For example, it is very annoying for existing customers to be sent details of an 'introductory' offer that they cannot take up because they are not a new customer.

Activiy 8.4

Re-read the section in Unit 6 on pages 86–87 about the importance of managing a customer database to ensure the data is 'clean'.

Although the style of a letter is personal there are some techniques that you can use when writing direct mail letters:

◆ **Say what you mean clearly** – be clear what your key message is.

◆ **Sound enthusiastic** – if you are writing with an offer, make it sound worth taking up.

◆ **Write personally** – where possible use computer software that enables you to personalise letters with names and even inserting the address or a reference to the customer's current product package in the text of the letter. So, for example, a breakdown recovery service could write to its existing customers and in the text of the letter say, 'Now Mrs Wood, if your car wouldn't start outside 10 Acacia Avenue, wouldn't it be convenient if you had the "home start" service added to your current breakdown cover?'

◆ **Questions** can be used to good effect when you are trying to get your recipients to desire or want your product/service.

◆   **You can go into detail** in a direct mail letter in a way that you cannot in an advertisement.

◆   In most circumstances you should **use a friendly tone** – but it does depend on the situation. So, if you were writing about a critical illness cover, your tone would be more serious.

If you want a response or some form of action from the recipient, make it very clear what it is; perhaps mention it more than once. The P.S. at the end of a direct mail letter can be used to good effect to remind the customer what they need to do and by when. For example, you could say 'P.S. Don't forget that if you want the two free books when you join our book club you need to complete the attached post card and return it before 31 May...'

Case study: Tesco's loyalty card

As we noted in Unit 1, Tesco's club card loyalty device is perhaps the most successful sales promotion of its day. The club card device was instrumental in Tesco overtaking Sainsbury's to go into the Number 1 Grocery Retailer slot, and going on to build a gap that Sainsbury's have never been able to bridge.

However, the club card continues to reap rewards even now in the arena of direct marketing. By monitoring the volume, frequency and brand choice of shoppers, Tesco are able to target direct mail to their customers. This means they can promote not only goods in store, but also other Tesco products such as insurance, credit cards, telephone networks and savings. It is now possible to leave your home, insured by Tesco, drive to the store in your car, insured by Tesco, pay for your shopping with a Tesco Credit card, collecting reward points on your club card for family days out that you can ring people up on your Tesco network to tell people about!

Tele-messaging

Telemarketing is becoming a less acceptable way of communicating with customers, as the misuse of this medium by certain product categories (e.g. double-glazing) has led to customers feeling intruded upon and response rates are minimal. Legislation has led to this practice being illegal during certain times of the day. The continued misuse can only mean that reputable organisations should avoid this method and use others such as e-mail or mail shots.

Digital messaging

Text messaging is most widely used by airtime providers to try to get their customers to utilise more-paid-for services (such as latest football scores). It is probably the most immediate personalised method of direct mail, especially to the ever-evasive youth market. The issue at present is that this form of communication is seen as intrusive, and more creative ways of producing tailor-made messages are required for the consumer to see the benefit.

Customer databases and tactical marketing

In the last section we looked at the range of direct marketing tools that we can use to communicate with customers and other stakeholders. As we saw in Unit 7, customers can be internal (i.e. elsewhere in the organisation) or external (i.e. outside it). We need to briefly consider how databases can help us to target communications at these different customers, and other stakeholders. To communicate with customers effectively, we need to know who they are, what needs the products or services are required to meet, where they are located and the most cost-effective methods of communicating with them. In the next unit we will look at the detailed content and use of customer databases.

Internal market

We all keep a database of internal customers, whether we intend to or not. Most e-mail systems (such as Microsoft's Outlook) allow us to access address books or contact lists, and these can be used to build mailing lists for internal direct marketing. Most users, however, do not use these tools to their full capabilities. A typical address book function will store details of name, job title, physical address, e-mail address, department, location and much more. This information can be used to build distribution lists of potential e-mail recipients that share common characteristics, such as 'all managers', 'all head office staff' and so on.

A corporate intranet can also be used to target direct marketing in the same way as any website. Staff can be sent RSS feeds, summaries of information with links should they wish to find out more, based on their stated interests or even on their historic viewing profiles. In this way, recipients should only be mailed about things they are interested in, and should receive less internal junk mail.

External market

Communicating with external customers and prospects is more important, and more complex, than with internal customers. We need to know who these individuals or organisations are, and much more. A database of external customers is not something that should be trusted to an individual employee in any but the smallest organisation. It would be too easy, for example, for two employees to send the same customer conflicting or confusing communications, or even to overload them with direct marketing messages. As we shall see in the next Chapter, an organisation needs a structured and controlled approach to the management of both a customer database and customer communications.

Connected stakeholders

There are big ethical and legal issues related to passing customer data to third parties, as we shall see in the next unit. However, an organisation can extract certain data, or summarise it, and pass this anonymous data to other interested parties. For example, a retailer might analyse the buying patterns of customers and pass this data to its suppliers so they can make changes or improvements to their products. Similarly, an organisation supplying financial services might realise that customers need a particular service that is outside the organisation's area of expertise. This information could be 'sold' to a third party organisation in return for commission on any resultant sales to the target market.

Managing a communications budget

Establishing a budget

In general terms, there are two ways to establish a budget for any functional expenditure:

- **Incremental budgeting** – where we take last year's budget for the same function (in this case, customer communications) and adjust it for any known differences between last year and this. We then add on an 'uplift' to take account of any cost inflation, and we have our budget.

- **Zero-based budgeting** – where we make a list of the communication activities we would like to carry out, prioritise the list, eliminate any planned activities that do not seem to make financial and business sense, and decide what level of resource and how much money we need to carry out the remaining activities. This then becomes the budget for next year.

Obviously incremental budgeting is much quicker and easier, but often leads to poor cost control (as expenditures are not understood) and a high level of 'budget slack (where managers 'pad out' a budget to make it easier to achieve). Most organisations now recognise that zero-based budgeting, while expensive and time-consuming, leads to better financial planning and budgetary control.

Identifying costs

The costs of any communications activity can be broken down into two distinct types:

- **Direct costs** – which are those incurred as a direct consequence of the activity. These would typically include the cost of any sub-contracted services (such as agency work), any direct labour costs (that could be avoided if the activity were not undertaken, and any materials and other costs such as printing and postage.

- **Indirect costs** – such as overheads (heat, light, rent, depreciation etc.) that are incurred in supporting the general activity of the organisation but must be recovered from the organisation's revenues. Many of these costs will be incurred whether a particular communications activity is undertaken or not, but a share of such costs should be apportioned to the activity to reflect the true cost of carrying it out.

Allocating costs

As seen above, there is a clear difference between direct and indirect costs. It is much easier to identify which communications activity has given rise to which direct costs. Individual invoices from sub-contractors can be allocated to the activity to which they relate, or split according to some pre-agreed formula if they relate to more than one activity.

Indirect costs are more difficult to allocate, and most organisations use a simple system of *cost recovery* to ensure that all indirect costs are allocated fairly to different activities. The total budgeted indirect cost for the function is calculated (say, £50,000), as is the total budgeted direct cost (say £100,000). The relationship between the two levels of budgeted expenditure (1:2) is then used as a basis for cost recovery. If a communications activity incurs direct costs of £30,000 it is charged with £15,000 of indirect costs.

Working to budget

It is useful to pause for a moment, to consider why organisations budget for their activities. A budget has five key roles (Figure 8.3) in organisational management:

1   The budget is a **target** for the level of expenditure the organisation expects will not be exceeded in the period, provided the level of activity is in line with the budget assumptions.

2   The budget is a **communications** tool, to allow the organisation to let all relevant parties know what is expected of them.

3   The budget is a **co-ordination** tool, to ensure that each part of the organisation understands how their activity relates to that of other parts.

4   The budget is a **control** tool, so managers can tell whether activity (and the associated costs) is happening in line with the targets set.

5   The budget is an **evaluation** tool, so the performance of individuals and departments can be appraised to see how well (or badly) they are doing.

Figure 8.3: The roles of a budget

Working to budget is therefore important, as long as the underlying assumptions used to establish the budget are still valid. Such assumptions would include activity levels, the organisation's strategy, and external factors such as inflation or competition. Many organisations now use 'flexible budgeting', to allow the budget to be adjusted (or 'flexed') to take into account the impact of any changes from the original assumptions (such as, for example, a major customer going out of business).

Using spreadsheets

The most common software tool for budgetary control is the spreadsheet. A budgetary control spreadsheet can be prepared for an individual communications activity, a department, or the whole of the marketing function.

Typically, budgetary control spreadsheets divide the year into accounting periods, and spread the budget across these time periods against the different direct and indirect cost headings. Actual expenditure can then be shown alongside the budget for each time period (as the year progresses), and any differences or 'variances' between actual and budget highlighted. Such variances are often identified, by colour, or simply by 'sign' (i.e. positive or negative) as 'favourable' or 'adverse'. A favourable variance is where expenditure is less than budget, or income is higher than budget. An adverse variance is obviously the opposite.

Measuring the success of communications campaigns

How can success be measured?

In considering which media to use within a communications campaign one of the factors that influences our choice is 'what has worked well in the past', so it is important that we can effectively evaluate what each medium has contributed towards the overall campaign results.

Accountants and marketers have long argued about the measurability and accountability of spending what is probably the single biggest expenditure that the organisation makes.

Television is perhaps the most audited of the above-the-line tools. Day-by-day, minute-by-minute audience figures tell us who is watching at any time during the 24-hour day. Digital television has introduced two-way communication, so for the first time we can actually measure the audience's response by the number of 'red buttons' clicked. The inclusion of website addresses and direct response telephone numbers has also introduced a measurable aspect into television advertising.

But, in real terms, the role of advertising is to develop long-term brand values and the benefit of the expenditure can only be measured by a shift in customer attitudes over time. This is also true of all other above-the-line media in that although they all have a short-term measurable aspect to their use, their real value is as a strategic tool used consistently over time. It is not coincidence that some of the world's icon brands such as Coca-Cola, IBM and Kellogg's are also those that have consistently appeared in the top-ten-advertising spend tables over the last 10 years.

Is it the role of marketing research to measure these shifts over time on both a brand/service level and within the marketplace. It is really the only way we get a complete picture of how customers perceive our offering.

There will always be significant debate about the validity and effectiveness of the advertising pound. We now have to communicate to compete and we are now in possession of more information than ever before. We now have to learn how that information can be used effectively.

Inquiry/response levels

To measure the response to a sales promotion campaign that used a '20p off' coupon you could set up a system with retailers to count the number of redeemed vouchers. By media coding the coupon you will know which magazine produced the most responses.

Similarly, the response rates from direct marketing campaigns should be evaluated and, if appropriate, a further check made to calculate how much response is actually converted to sales. This way the cost of a campaign can be measured against the monetary gain from sales.

Sales increases

It is not appropriate to only look at sales when you are measuring the success of an advertisement or a campaign because other factors in the marketing mix or the external environment could affect sales (in either a negative or a positive way). For example, if there was media coverage of a research report suggesting that chocolate improved your IQ and reduced stress at the same time as the 'Chocco' advertising campaign, then this could be the reason for a sales increase and not the effect of the advertising campaign. Or, perhaps weather conditions could affect cocoa production adversely, which could cause price rises and reduce demand for 'Chocco', no matter how effective the advertising campaign.

Media evaluation

Within the promotional message the evaluation has two elements to consider, the content of the message itself and how well that worked at communicating, and the efficiency of the media chosen in transmitting the message.

The message content can be evaluated either by commissioning marketing research or by looking at the accuracy in the feedback we are getting from the consumer. If they are entering retail stores asking for the product or lots of people are walking round singing our jingle, we can assume the message is getting through.

The effectiveness of the media can also be measured by marketing research but although we may be aware that awareness has risen to 80 per cent how can we judge which media helped to achieve that the most.

Satisfaction surveys

Good customer service is the lifeblood of any business. Although new customers are important, good customer service will help generate customer loyalty and repeat business. With each satisfied customer a business is likely to win many more customers through recommendations. Remember, if you are not taking care of your customers, your competition will.

A customer satisfaction survey will help an organisation not only to see how effective its efforts have been, but also to identify problem areas for further action. It will also demonstrate to customers that the organisation cares and is proactively looking for ways to improve the service that it provides.

As well as obtaining valuable market research data, customer surveys are also a good way to publicise aspects of an organisation's service that its customers may not be aware of. It is important to read through a survey from a market research view point, to check that it asks the right questions in the right way and that the feedback information will make informed decisions possible. Then, read through the survey from a marketing viewpoint, checking that each question is phrased in such a way that every opportunity has been taken to promote the business.

To benefit most from a customer survey, the organisation needs to be prepared to accept the worst. A customer satisfaction survey should be designed to highlight problems so that they can be addressed; undertaken regularly, such surveys will prevent complacency and will also give early warning on where competitors' initiatives may be losing the organisation business.

Case study: Nielsen's

Arthur C. Nielsen Sr. founded his namesake company in 1923 to perform surveys of the production of industrial equipment. Over time, however, he saw a larger opportunity in helping companies take the mystery out of their marketing. As the retail pioneer John Wanamaker once famously mused: 'I know I waste half my money on advertising. I just don't know which half.' Nielsen set out to solve that riddle by counting, measuring, and analyzing what people buy, eat, read, watch, listen to, and otherwise consume. In the process he fathered one of the most powerful business concepts of the 20th century: market share. Today, as it happens, Nielsen is headquartered in the refurbished Wanamaker's department store building in Manhattan.

Having popularized the idea of market share, Nielsen Sr. and son Arthur Nielsen Jr. made sure over the years to seize as much of it as possible. Nowhere were they more successful than with the television ratings system, launched in 1950, that made Nielsen a household name. Almost six decades later the service still functions as a near-monopoly. Nielsen has honed its methods over the years, but some ad buyers and media executives are still critical that Nielsen derives its national TV ratings from a mere 14,000 'Nielsen families' who have meters hooked up to their TVs. Nielsen also rates local and cable viewership, among other things. Altogether, Nielsen Media Research makes up roughly one-third of the company's $4.5 billion in sales.

Another third of the company's revenues is generated by A.C. Nielsen, which commands more than 60 per cent of the retail research market globally. Overall, the company gathers data by employing two separate armies. One comprises some 31,000 people worldwide who do nothing but organize and retrieve retail sales figures from stores. The other includes more than 700,000 people who participate in ongoing research panels in which, for modest sums, they anonymously lay their consumption patterns bare to Nielsen's statisticians.

How do companies use Nielsen's data? Say Nestlé wants to introduce a new flavour of Häagen-Dazs ice cream. For starters, Nielsen can tell them that Pittsburgh is the ice cream buying capital of America. (Who knew?) One Nielsen business, BASES, can forecast how the flavour will do before a single pint is produced. Another can determine the best addresses to locate a new Häagen-Dazs shop. The main A.C. Nielsen figures can parse by market how the flavour is doing against rivals. And the media side of Nielsen can help figure out how and where ads are sold, and even monitor passing mentions of it on TV shows and blogs.

Source: Siklos, R. (2008, Made to Measure [online] in *'Fortune'* at http://money. cnn.com/2008/02/18/news/newsmakers/siklos_calhoun.fortune/index2.htm (28 February 2008))

Practice work-based tasks

Role

In your role as a communications assistant with a major marketing consultancy, you have been asked to review the article reproduced opposite, which profiles five new product or service ideas. Using this material, address the following tasks.

Task 1: Customer communications (40% weighting)

You are required by your manager to produce an informal report for circulation to relevant colleagues to demonstrate how a range of different communications methods might be used to assist the launch of new products and services.

Using the information from the article provided, prepare a report that covers the following tasks, using examples from other organisations with which you are familiar to illustrate your points:

◆   Explain how different media and messages can be used at the various stages of the AIDA model.

◆   For each of the *five* new product/service ideas outlined in the attached article, identify and discuss *three* different communication methods that might be used to inform potential customers of the features and benefits of the product or service, or persuade those potential customers to purchase. For each method chosen, demonstrate which stage or stages of the AIDA model it might fulfil.

◆   For *any one* of the communications activities (that is, a communication method for a product or service) you have identified in the previous task, explain how knowledge of the Schramm 'communications cycle' model can be used to ensure that the communication is effective.

◆   For the communications activity chosen in the previous task, discuss three different ways of measuring the success of that communications activity.

Word count 1000 words, excluding relevant appendices

Comments on practice work-based tasks

A case study approach has been adopted for this assignment. Material provided refers to particular industries/sectors and a range of organisations. The intention is to offer candidates a wealth of examples, so that they can contextualise their answers, even if they are not working within a marketing department.

It is envisaged that the material provided will form the basis of group discussion and candidates should be encouraged to use other material and information sources in addition to what is provided. The case study material can be used to reinforce the theoretical concepts and encourage the candidates to be more analytical in their approach.

Group analysis and discussion of the case material is acceptable, although it is very important that the assignment tasks are undertaken individually, and not as part of a group. The examiners will be expecting to see originality of thought in the interpretation and application of the assessment tasks.

Meet the wellderly – they're the future of banking

Forget golden oldies, OAPs and seniors. We need a new word for the retired who can look forward to 20-plus years of good health, a reasonable income and a productive life – meet the wellderly. There are millions of them in Europe and the US and they could be the future of financial services. A report from HSBC says that the over-55s have about 70 per cent of global wealth, so it's not surprising that some banks are beginning to target them. US bank Wells Fargo has set up an Elder Services Group, targeting people over 55 with more than $1m (£490,000) to invest. As well as banking services they will pick up Grandma's prescriptions and dry cleaning and even help her select a nursing home.

(Sources: *The New York Times*, *The Economist*)

Smart clothes

Forgotten to wash your gym kit and left it mouldering in the bottom of your sports bag? It may no longer be a problem. Scientists in the US have developed self-cleaning clothing that can be worn for weeks without washing. Originally developed for the US military, the technology is expected to be used by sportswear brands soon.

(Source: Nowandnext.com)

Brand space for the very young

Airports and babies don't usually mix. But Numico baby-food brand Nutricia has its HQ in Amsterdam's Schiphol airport and has come up with an airport "Babycare lounge". Seven quiet, private cubicles with cots for babies are available free of charge. There are also microwaves for heating food, changing facilities and baby baths. It's a brand space where consumers can try things out without being expected to buy. And when it comes to building brand loyalty, empathy can play a big role.

(Source: Springwise.com)

Driving on air?

As concern about climate change increases, could car manufacturers face a similar advertising ban to tobacco firms? Some futurologists think so. But in the meantime, Peugeot thinks that lighter cars may be the answer, while Moteur Development International is working on a car that runs on air.

(Source: *Red Herring*)

FIVE TO WATCH

1 2 3 4 5

Sweets to improve skin tone? Self-cleaning clothes? Meet the trends we're all going to be talking about

IMAGES: ISTOCK

Eat yourself beautiful

Want beautiful, glowing skin? The solution is improbable – try snacking on a handful of gummy bears. US beauty company Borba's chewy sweets contain antioxidants, vitamins and plant extracts that claim to improve skin tone. It's just one of a range of "cosmeceuticals" created by the company, which also sells fortified "beauty" water. Even big corporations are getting into this market: Coca-Cola and L'Oréal have joined forces to create the new health and beauty drink Lumae, due next year.

(Sources: *Montreal Gazette*, *Brandweek*)

Source: The Marketer, September 2007

Task 1

This task is designed to allow the candidate to identify and discuss different methods of communicating the features and benefits of a new product or service to customers. It would also be interesting to put this in context by looking at initiatives adopted by other organisations in similar situations. It would also be useful to explore how very different the communications might be, rather than just modifying a 'standard set' of basic communications methods.

A level of justification with regard to why certain initiatives would or would not be possible, alongside a brief consideration of the benefits delivered, would be expected for the higher grades.

Candidates should be encouraged to pick a more challenging and innovative example to develop through the second and third tasks. Applying knowledge of the communications cycle, and how to measure success, to a straightforward direct mail campaign, for example, might not give candidates the opportunity to demonstrate the depth and breadth of their knowledge relating to these areas of the syllabus.

The wording used within this task is designed to allow the candidates a degree of flexibility in their approach and to allow them to demonstrate their ability to understand how customer communications works. Any answer is in theory as valid as another, as long as the thinking is supported by valid argument.

Candidates should be encouraged to think about the report format and how this could be presented and communicated to colleagues who are, in effect, internal customers.

Customer care and customer service

Customer care and service

Customers want to feel valued by the employees they encounter. They want their questions answered in a confident and courteous way, not using jargon, and not assuming they have a high level of subject knowledge. How many times have you gone into your local electrical retailer to make a relatively simple purchase to be blinded by jargon and science when you get in there, leaving fairly hastily because you are frightened to reveal your ignorance? What you really wanted was someone to listen to your needs and then advise you on which one of the plethora of products available will meet those needs.

Customer service

Ultimately, all systems will impact on the customer and so should be evaluated in order to establish how these can add to the customer experience rather than become a source of complaints.

Figure 9.1: Customer service systems

The five key areas where systems exist (Figure 9.1) are as follows:

1   **Sales and ordering** – consider the speed of processing orders. Is the customer updated regularly?

2   **Accounts and invoicing** – accuracy and a variety of payment methods are key here. Is affordable credit required?

3   **Delivery** – is delivery time specific, when the customer wants? Are the goods delivered intact?

4   **After sales** – dealing with customer questions. How easy is it for customers to contact you?

5   **Complaints** – how easy is it to complain? Do complaints get resolved?

Case study

For many years Marks & Spencer held a unique position within the Christmas gift buying season. It was well recognised that as the M&S 'offering' was the same countrywide, it was possible to buy gifts from the store confident in the knowledge that if it didn't fit the recipient, or was a duplication, they could pop along to a local M&S and change the present for something more suitable.

However, in more recent times, with sales starting on 26th December, customers were taking gifts back to be replaced, often finding sizes now out of stock and only being allowed the 'sale price' as a refund or as part-payment to another item.

Customers felt cheated that goods that had been charged out at full price were now seemingly worth a fraction of the cost through no fault of their own or of the gift purchaser.

This belligerence on behalf of M&S led to a decline in sales, alongside a lot of other contributing factors. The response was actually an idea of other retailers in the sector who provided the purchaser with a special 'Gift Receipt', which although it bore no price enabled the price paid to be tracked back to the day of purchase. Therefore, full refunds were able to be issued.

Unfortunately, by this stage M&S had upset a great many of customers with their inflexibility in this area, and no longer has the same position in the minds of the gift-buying consumer.

Care and service in different sectors

The level of customer service that a customer expects will depend upon their past experiences and the type of organisation which they are dealing with. However, in each of these different examples from across different market sectors, the same basic criteria are responsible for delivering good customer service. They are:

◆   Friendly and knowledgeable staff

◆   Appropriate procedures and processes

◆   Product/service reliability.

Insight: Consumer (FMCG) markets

The organisational culture will also affect the level of service determined to be appropriate and how the staff carry out that service. Tesco's can-do attitude is evidenced in the store when you ask a staff member where a certain product is in the store. The Tesco worker will ask you to follow them, take you to where it is, and ask if you need any further help. In contrast, some other stores have a more detached attitude and will respond to the same question by pointing (often impatiently), if you inform them that you cannot find the item then the response will probably be 'If it's not on the rails it's not in stock. You can order it downstairs.' It helps to clarify why Tesco are so successful and others have so many problems. Walking the floor is also a practice undertaken by the Tesco Chairman Terry Leary in a concerted attempt to keep a finger on what is happening on the shop floor and to seek out employee opinion.

Activity 9.1

Why do supermarkets have express checkouts?

Why did Argos move their tills to the side of the store, from in front of the collection point where they used to be?

Why is there always a queue to pay in IKEA?

Business-to-business markets

Within a B2B environment, the organisations within the supply chain expect all parties to be focused on the needs of the consumer at the end of the chain. They will expect empathy between parties with a recognition that by pulling together the consumer will benefit. There may not be so many documented processes to enable this as in a B2C environment but the end aim is the same.

Not-for-profit markets

The not-for-profit sector also needs to keep in mind customers' perception of their role and how customer service staff communicate. It is unlikely that you will ask for a refund in a charity shop, but will feel more aggrieved if the assistant is rude to you. Customer service in these sectors is about building long-term relationships.

Public sector markets

In the public sector it has been difficult to implement a customer service type culture in organisations that are typically very process orientated and are usually in a non-competitive situation. We all have a mind's eye picture of 'the man from the council' and probably go into a problem situation not expecting too much sympathy. It is also important that the service is maintained and that the customer service ethos is not just a thin veneer. With the growth of the MRSA bug in hospitals, more patients are concerned with the level of hygiene than whether the nurse says 'Hello' in the morning.

Customer care and relationship marketing

Customer satisfaction as an objective

Satisfying customers is at the heart of marketing. Who then assumes responsibility for this important function? Possibly the marketing department or the sales force? True, such personnel can have an influence on customer satisfaction, but marketing as a philosophy is wider than this narrow group of employees. Employees outside the marketing department or sales force can also play an important role in determining customer satisfaction.

Marketing is more than just a range of techniques that enables the company to determine customer requirements; rather it is a shared business ethos. The marketing concept is a philosophy that places customers central to all organisational activities. The long-term strategies of an organisation might be centred on profit maximisation, market share growth, or growth in real terms but none of this can be achieved without satisfying customers. Without customers there would be no business.

Customer service in the marketing mix

An organisation's people come into contact with customers and can have a massive impact on customer satisfaction levels. In the customers' eyes, staff are generally inseparable from the total service. This implies the need for well trained, motivated staff mindful of the adage 'the customer is always right'. It is important therefore that every member of staff contributes to the marketing philosophy and support sthe firm's external marketing activities.

As organisations introduce streamlined hierarchies and more flexible working practices, marketing offers the opportunity for their employees to operate in interdisciplinary teams furthering an overall marketing philosophy. Corporate investment in their most valuable asset, employees, through training and development supports the processes of creating and defending competitive advantages gained from successful marketing.

A customer focus implies that the company focuses its activities and products on customer needs. In the customer-driven approach, customer needs are the drivers of all strategic marketing decisions. No strategy is pursued until it passes the test of customer research. Every aspect of a market offering, including the nature of the product itself, is driven by the needs of potential customers.

The three 'additional' Ps of the marketing mix were added to reflect the service content of a purchase. Re-read the first few sections of Unit 3, to remind yourself.

An alternative formal approach to this customer-focused marketing is known as SIVA (Solution, Information, Value, Access). This system is basically the four original Ps renamed and reworded to provide a customer focus.

Product	=	**Solution**
Promotion	=	**Information**
Price	=	**Value**
Place	=	**Access**

The four elements of the SIVA model are:

◆   **Solution** – How appropriate is the solution to the customer's need?

◆ **Information** – Does the customer know about the solution, and if so how and from whom? Do they know enough to let them make a buying decision?

◆ **Value** – Does the customer know the value of the transaction, what it will cost, what are the benefits, what might they have to sacrifice, what will be their reward?

◆ **Access** – Where can the customer find the solution? How easily/locally/remotely can they buy it and take delivery?

This model was proposed by Chekitan Dev and Don Schultz in the *Marketing Management Journal* of the American Marketing Association, and presented by them in *Market Leader* - the journal of the Marketing Society in the UK.

Relationship marketing

Relationship marketing is the devoting of marketing resources to maintaining and exploiting the firm's existing customer base rather than using the resources solely to attract new customers. During the 1980s, relationship marketing attracted increasing attention from practitioners, consultants and academics. This was in response to a number of factors:

1 The increased willingness of buyers to switch suppliers, and to break long-standing market relationships.

2 The increased costs of attracting customers such as promotional expenditures and initially low prices.

3 The strategy of increasing the breadth of products being offered by the supplier could only be justified if the customer could be retained.

4 The realisation that in mature markets the most likely source of future earnings was through retaining and increasing the value of the firm's existing customers.

The differences between relationship marketing and conventional transactional marketing are summarised in Table 9.1.

Table 9.1: Relationship marketing versus transactional marketing

Transactional marketing	Relationship marketing
A focus on single sales or transactions	A focus on customer retention and building customer loyalty
An emphasis on product features	An emphasis on product benefits that are meaningful to the customer
Short timescales	Long timescales, recognising that short-term costs may be higher, but so will long-term profits
Little emphasis on customer retention	An emphasis on high levels of customer service which are possibly tailored to the individual customer
Limited customer commitment	High customer commitment
Moderate customer contact	High customer contact, with each contact being used to gain information and build the relationship
Quality is essentially the concern of production and one else	Quality is the concern of all, and it is the failure to recognise this that creates minor mistakes which lead to major problems

Designing a customer care programme

Stages in the process

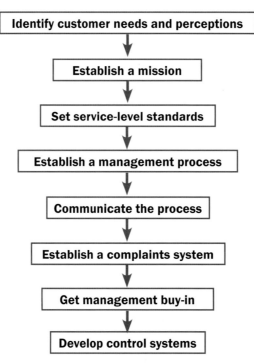

Figure 9.2 Designing a customer care programme

Identifying customer needs and perceptions

The work carried out in establishing the level of customer service required will feed into this start point. The aim of the customer care programme will be to continue the provision of what we have established as a base level standard. This area will, as shown earlier, focus not just on the product/services provided but also the systems used and staff skills available. Research will be needed to ensure this base standard is current and this could include an element of 'benchmarking' against not just competitive products but also other industries that are considered best in their provision of customer service. UPS parcel systems and Singapore Airlines have excellent service standards, which are recognised across the world. Some of the elements of the service could be transferred into other industry sectors.

Establishing a mission

Obviously, the organisation's approach to customer service must be echoed within this mission statement, as essentially it is the means of communication to both the customer and the employees of the organisation. The mission statement gives direction and purpose, also expressing the cultural glue that determines how the organisation will interact with their customers. The provision of a mission statement also implies top-level commitment within the organisation, which is essential to the success and ease of implementation of the programme.

Setting service-level standards

Standards covering all aspects of the service in terms of staff behaviour, appearance and courtesy and responsiveness are required. These should be prescriptive where necessary, that is answer the phone within four rings, but also be sufficiently flexible for the staff member to feel empowered to deal with the situation. Situations which should be referred to a senior person should clearly be highlighted.

The complaints procedure should be clearly documented with time scales and supporting paperwork necessary for the smooth running of the system. There should also be a customer-friendly version for communicating in store, on website, or within a telephone conversation. Follow-up procedures also need to be put in place to follow up complaints and to ensure they are all resolved.

Service standards for systems and processes also need to be considered and deadlines set. 'Delivery within 24 hours' or 'You won't find it cheaper anywhere else' are statements that systems need to monitor and highlight where corrective action may be required.

Establishing a management process

This is the area which should define who does what, by what and when! Responsibility needs to be allocated and timescales set. Information flow needs to be enabling rather than disabling for the system to work well.

Communicating the process

Internal communication, in terms of training and objective setting, should be done to ensure everyone knows how they should be completing tasks and how they will be measured.

Feedback from staff should be encouraged to ensure procedures that are unworkable are not imposed on the very people who have most experience.

Communication systems may need to be implemented, these could include team meetings, intranet systems and training away days.

Establishing a complaints system

The customer needs to be able to complain. Those 44 per cent of people who did not complain, but wanted to, are still remembering and repeating their negative experience, but without giving us the chance to put it right. Therefore, we need to ensure the process of complaining is not a painful one. This can be achieved in several ways:

◆ Ensure staff are trained and have empathy with the cause of complaint.

◆ Ensure there are systems and procedures in place to record reoccurring faults/bad service to ensure rectifying action can be taken.

◆ Ensure the complaints procedure is fully documented and the essence communicated to the customer, for example, refunds on faulty goods are only given on production of a receipt.

◆ Ensure that the customer knows what action is to be taken and the timescales that are appropriate to the situation, for example 'We will write to you with a response in the next 7 days.'

◆ Make it easy – a customer service desk, a 'contact us' section on the website, a helpline number.

It is important to remember that complaints are emotive issues that have many causes. Sometimes the staff member may be at a loss to see why a certain aspect is such a problem. But there are always opportunities – to rectify faults for the future and to demonstrate how well we as an organisation deal with them because we care.

Satisfied customers take up less time, cause less stress and deliver job satisfaction. Word of mouth is the most effective promotional tool. Customer service is essential for survival and growth.

Having management commitment

This is necessary to gain access to the resources in terms of recruitment, skills and systems that may need to be put in place for the system to work. It is also necessary to echo the cultural push towards delighting the consumer. Consumers quickly pick up on insincere messages and empty promises.

Developing control systems

The programme must be developed in such a way that measurable objectives can be developed and performance measured against those objectives. Systems need to have defaults that highlight reoccurring problem areas and upcoming deadlines.

Performance towards objectives should be communicated and hopefully celebrated. A system of continuous improvement needs to be maintained in order that the service received by the customer continues to evolve and change to meet their needs.

Obtaining customer feedback

The importance of feedback

Customer satisfaction surveys are often regarded as the most accurate barometers for predicting the success of a company. Because they directly ask about the critical success factors of a business, when done effectively, customer satisfaction surveys can deliver powerful, incisive information and provide ways to gain a competitive edge.

By implementing customer satisfaction surveys into a customer relationship management (CRM) strategy, enterprises are able to gather, measure, and analyse valuable information to gather critical feedback about questions similar to the following:

◆ How satisfied are you with the purchase you made?

◆ How satisfied are you with the service you received?

◆ How likely are you to buy from us again?

◆ How likely are you to recommend our company to others?

Obtaining customer feedback in a timely and useable format helps ensure that a business is meeting and exceeding customer expectations, and gives insight on where changes should be made to increase satisfaction and overall success. High quality customer service is a key factor for retaining customers.

Methods of collecting feedback

Mail surveys

The mail survey has to do everything you would do if you were with the customer. It has to the visually appealing, have a pleasant tone, and be clear. The survey instrument is under the direct control of the customer. Its physical look will affect the customer's willingness to respond; the clarity of the instructions and questions will affect the customer's ability to interpret their meaning correctly.

Single-page questionnaires and comment cards should be attractive and easy to read. Longer questionnaires should be printed in booklet form, on A4 paper that is folded in half and stapled in the middle to produce a standard A5 page. The cover should be visually appealing to interest the customer, and no questions should appear on the cover. The cover should give the title of the survey activity and indicate who is conducting the work.

Survey questions should be presented in a logical sequence. Many survey experts believe that the first question on the survey, more than any other, will determine whether your customer completes or discards the questionnaire. Starting with a fairly simple question is a good idea because it suggests to the customer that completing the survey will be neither difficult nor time-consuming. It is also advisable to ask a fairly interesting question to gain the customer's interest.

The next set of questions should focus on matters that the customer is most likely to consider useful or salient. This continues the process of attracting the customer's attention so that he or she becomes engaged with thinking about the questions being asked and becomes interested in completing the survey.

Grouping questions together that share common themes makes sense because the customer then focuses on that particular area of enquiry. To the extent practical, you should group questions that have similar types of response options. For example, questions that have yes/no responses should be together and questions that have scale responses should be together.

Telephone surveys

As customers have no questionnaire in front of them during a telephone survey, concerns about visual appeal are not applicable. Issues regarding ordering and clarity of questions are important, and the same principles apply as with mail surveys.

In-person and telephone surveys involve spoken language, which can be very different from written language, and customers must be able to respond to questions based only on the information they hear. So it is critical that your interviewers be well trained and speak clearly. Also, the interviewers act as an intermediary between the customer and the questions posed.

The following principles apply to telephone surveys:

◆ The introduction the customer hears will probably determine whether the interview is conducted or the customer hangs up. The introduction should be concise, state the purpose of the call, estimate the length of the call, and assure confidentiality.

◆ Because customers will rely on verbal cues and instructions, rather than written ones, questions should have a limited number of responses (about three or four).

◆ Each question should be relatively short.

◆ Avoid questions that ask customers to look up information or check with others.

◆ In constructing the questionnaire, be sure to read the questions aloud to others to see if they sound clear and understandable. Remember, what works for the written word does not always work for the spoken word.

◆ When changing subjects, telephone surveys should cue the customer with transitional statements such as, 'Now, I'd like to turn to your experiences with...'

◆ Instructions for the interviewer must be perfectly clear, and the same format should be used throughout the survey. For example, interviewer instructions are typically written inside brackets, in all capital letters.

Suggestion boxes

High tech isn't always the way to go. The original customer feedback device, the suggestion box, is still effective and easily administered. Check it daily and regularly replenish pencils and forms. The normal customer follow-up procedures apply.

Online surveys

Internet surveys use a web-based form that the user completes online at a designated web address. You should only consider this method of data collection if the potential respondents have access to the Internet.

To administer an Internet survey, you must have a method of contacting the people selected for the sample. After compiling the sample list, send an e-mail alert that will lead potential respondents to the survey website. Upon entering the website, respondents can then log in and take the survey. Internet surveys have several advantages:

◆ They are interactive, like telephone surveys, allowing programmed skip patterns and links to more detailed survey instructions. Unlike a telephone survey, respondents can see the questions.

◆ Respondents can complete the questionnaire at a time convenient to them.

◆ There are no calling or mailing costs.

◆ E-mail surveys are one of the fastest and least intrusive means for gathering customer feedback. Up to 50 per cent of the responses are received within 24 hours.

◆ They are also cheaper to conduct since you pay no interviewers or printing and distribution costs.

◆ In addition, the survey will definitely get to the right individual; they will usually not be intercepted and routed to another person.

However, there are also some disadvantages. For example, it is likely that respondents will have no perception of anonymity. Also, as e-mail use increases, people are becoming less patient with the many unsolicited messages they receive.

Focus groups

The focus group is a popular technique in marketing circles, and one that is frequently used in the early stages of product design or specification. Typically a group of between six and ten people are invited to discuss potential products or services, usually prompted by

174

a series of carefully worded questions or statements. In this way a group enables potential users to voice their wants and discuss the features that they might like to see in new products or services.

The disadvantage of the focus group is that it depends entirely on what potential users say about their preferences and wants, rather than what they actually need in reality. These two things are often not the same at all, and if the group becomes dominated by one or two people it is possible to find that many stated opinions are merely the results of group dynamics rather than the real needs and wants of users.

In some instances this might be appropriate. These effects can be used to predict the response of the public at large to image changes, for example.

Online focus group research offers exciting new possibilities for on-line conferencing. Traditional focus groups require:

◆ The rental of a physical facility, transportation for participants, refreshments, recording facilities for transcription purposes, and time set-up and cleanup

◆ The recruitment of participants from the immediate local area

◆ Travel costs for moderators who must be located at the same site as the participants.

Online focus groups overcome many of these limitations.

Features of online focus groups include:

◆ The ability to restrict access to pre-authorised participants

◆ Automatic production of instant word-for-word transcripts

◆ Use of online survey forms without leaving the focus group

◆ Use of online participant profiles filled out in advance (reducing the need for 'get acquainted' activities)

◆ Elaborate electronic moderator discussion controls

◆ Display (with no action needed by participants) of discussion materials such as PowerPoint slides, Excel charts and spreadsheets and other text materials, photographs and other visuals, live web sites and their contents, live pictures from web cameras, and even streaming audio and video

◆ The ability to continue discussion on a split screen while viewing materials such as those described above.

Informal methods

If your business relies on customers coming to you, dedicate a percentage of your day to mingling with them.

◆ Treat each customer exchange individually.

◆ Avoid the generic: 'Is everything okay?' Instead try 'If you were to suggest one thing we could improve, what would it be?'

◆ Carry a notebook to capture customers comments, logging them in their presence.

Monitoring the success of customer service

Why monitor success?

Continuous improvement, through the adoption of such initiatives as total quality management (TQM), business process re-engineering (BPR) and Kaisen, has been one of the core themes of business management during the past decade.

The goal of modern business is no longer just 'to be good' but 'to be better than our competitors'. Organisations cannot stand still, or they run the risk of being overtaken by competitors that change and improve their products and service standards.

Regardless of the product or service that an organisation supplies, that product or service is surrounded or 'augmented' by an overall service package, which the customer experiences from the first moment they come into contact with the organisation. In a world where the core products and services offered by competitors are very similar, it is often only the customer service package that differentiates one organisation from another.

Number of complaints

Is it the case that a fall in the number of customer complaints means that our customer service levels are improving? Or are our customers no longer complaining *to us* (because they realise it does no good) and are now complaining to each other (or, even worse, to our competitors)?

While the number of customer complaints can give an indication of how they perceive our service levels, we cannot rely on it as an accurate measure. Perhaps more customers are complaining because we have changed our systems to make it easier for them to do so. Or maybe the level of customer complaints has fallen because they are now using an open forum on the Internet rather than coming to us.

In a 'steady state', or in the short term, customer complaints can give us an indication whether service levels are improving or worsening. In the longer term, however, we must supplement data about complaints with other measures.

Measuring service standards

The only people who can accurately judge our service levels are our customers. In the previous section we looked at ways to gather customer feedback, and all of these can give us data about how our service levels are perceived. This data, together with that relating to complaint levels, must be combined with data from other sources if we are to really understand our service level performance.

Sales records

The 'bottom line' of customer service is the level of revenues we earn. If sales are rising, we must be doing something right. The problem with using sales data as an indicator of customer service levels is that it is affected by so many other variables. Have we just launched a new advertising or promotional campaign? Has one of our competitors done the same? What about changes in the global environment? Are customer disposable incomes up? What is happening to the rest of our industry?

Customer retention

It is very true that 'a happy customer comes back for more'. Looking at the conversion rate from 'new customer' to 'repeat purchase' can give us an indication of how customers perceive our service levels, but no more than that. Once again, this data is dependent on a wide variety of variables from elsewhere in the marketing mix (product quality, pricing strategy, brand perception, promotional activity) and the business environment (competition, economy, social factors) that it is almost impossible to identify what component part of any change is due to service levels.

Existing customer data

If a happy customer comes back for more, then a very happy customer probably comes back more frequently, and for ever-greater quantities. Once again, data relating to purchase frequency and volumes can be affected by myriad influences, but it may be possible to identify some impact of service levels. Of course, the best way to find out how customers feel about our service levels is still to ask them!

Mystery shoppers

The point-of-sale is the critical moment of truth in determining whether a customer is satisfied, the sale is made, or if a customer ever buys from you again. Evaluation of this interaction is important in understanding the type of service your customer is receiving and whether sales associates or team members are following your prescribed procedures and protocols. In essence, on-site mystery shoppers look at sales and service efforts from two perspectives – the customer's as well as the company's. It doesn't matter if the evaluation is for a retail store, restaurant, car dealership, apartment development, or fun park.

On-site mystery shoppers also have the advantage of being able to assess the physical aspects of the location including: the cleanliness and upkeep of the facility, the proper use of merchandising and marketing materials, the appearance of the staff and their attire (including uniforms), product presentation and demonstration, etc.

Provided the identity of mystery shoppers is kept confidential, this is one of the best ways of getting direct feedback about service levels, from three perspectives:

1   At a point in time – how are we doing?

2   Over time – are we improving?

3   In comparison to our competitors – are we better than them?

Using IT in customer service activities

The range of IT systems

Relationship marketing requires the storage and manipulation and analysis of huge amounts of customer information in order that the relationship can deliver added value to the customer. The use of customer databases to store and manipulate this data has led to the term 'database marketing'.

Loyalty schemes work on a similar principle: the large supermarkets can use their EPOS not only for stock control purposes but also to target offers that are relevant to customers.

For example, a customer who regularly buys dog food would not be sent money-off vouchers to keep the customer 'loyal' for cat food.

Customer relationship management systems work on a similar principle. The key idea is that each customer is treated as an individual, and in particular, organisations can use computer software to identify the customers with the highest customer lifetime value (CLV). For example, basic current account holders are not particularly profitable customers for banks compared to those with (or wanting) loans, mortgages, insurance business and pensions are much more profitable. The idea behind CLV is to spend marketing time and effort on those customers who are likely to be the most valuable over their lifetime.

The length of 'lifetime' will vary by industry. Manufacturers of baby products will know that families will probably be in that market sector for about 8 years – the average time between the oldest and the youngest child moving into the 5 years plus bracket. However, these organisations will also have products in other sectors such as household cleaning materials and hair care, where the positive experiences gained from the baby care products will result in the customer entering a relationship for a longer lifetime with different products. Hence, it is possible to have a relationship and retain loyalty for a 'lifetime'.

Insight: Data mining

Data mining is when sophisticated systems are used to track customer/client files to identify products/services that could be targeted in the future. The high-street retailer Next uses this technique with their mail order catalogue noting when customers make key life-cycle purchases. A sudden change in purchasing, for example homewares, will mean the customer may have just purchased their first home, so Next will send more information concerning their range of furniture or someone ordering maternity wear will shortly be interested in baby wear. Being first to communicate with the customer is a widely accepted mission statement for the approach to customer care itself.

Database applications

Database marketing involves using computers to capture and store data relating to customers' past purchase history. For instance, if a mail order company sells clothing in its catalogue, each customer file is computerised so that contact (name, address, postcode) and purchase details (type of item, size, colour preference, price, etc.) are stored. All the departments in the firm can access this information quickly and cheaply. For example, the accounts department may need to access it to chase payment and the marketing department could use it to target offers to customers. So customers who buy clothes for people under a certain height would only be sent information relating to the 'petite' range of clothing based on their past purchase behaviour.

Data components

The type of data held in a typical customer database might include the following:

◆ **Geographic** – Where do our customers live? How far do they travel (if at all, they might buy from home)?

◆ **Demographic** – What socio-economic group do our customers belong to? How old are they? What occupations or professions are represented? What life stage are our customers at?

◆ **Psychographic** - Attributes relating to personality, values, attitudes, interests, or lifestyles. They are also called IAO variables (for Interests, Attitudes, and Opinions).

◆ **Buying pattern** – How frequently do our customers buy? What do they buy, and in what quantities?

◆ **Other** – The basic data such as name, address, telephone number, loyalty scheme membership.

Ensuring the data is up-to-date

One of the major issues in managing any database application is that of 'data redundancy' – what proportion of the data is no longer fulfilling the purpose for which it was collected and held? Data can be redundant for three reasons:

1 **It is obsolete.** Much of the data in any customer database relates to ex-customers – those that used to purchase from us, but no longer do. This may be because we have lost the customer to a rival, or simply because they have moved from the area.

2 **It is duplicated.** This is a very common issue with customer data. How many organisations send you multiple copies of their direct mail or catalogue, because you appear more than once on their database? Do you have two or more loyalty cards for the same retailer?

3 **It should have changed.** Data that is not updated rapidly becomes of little value. If you have used direct mail, you will know just how many items are 'returned to sender'. How many of you get direct mail items addressed to people who lived at your address many years ago?

On-line application processing (OLAP) information systems can improve data redundancy levels by automatically capturing data, but the sheer volume of data held on a typical customer database means that a level of data redundancy of 10 to 20 per cent is not uncommon.

Meeting legal and ethical requirements

The Data Protection Act 1998 (DPA) defines a legal basis for the handling in the UK of information relating to living people. It is the main piece of legislation that governs protection of personal data in the UK. Although the Act does not mention privacy, in practice it provides a way in which individuals can enforce the control of information about them.

The Act covers any data that can be used to identify a living person, and thus applies to all customer databases. This includes names, birthday and anniversary dates, addresses, telephone numbers, fax numbers, e-mail addresses etc. It only applies to that data which is held, or intended to be held, on computers ('equipment operating automatically in response to instructions given for that purpose'), or held in a 'relevant filing system'.

The Act defines eight principles of information-handling practice:

1 Personal data shall be processed fairly and lawfully.

2 Personal data shall be obtained only for one or more specified and lawful purposes, and shall not be further processed in any manner incompatible with that purpose or those purposes.

3　　Personal data shall be adequate, relevant and not excessive in relation to the purpose or purposes for which they are processed.

4　　Personal data shall be accurate and, where necessary, kept up to date.

5　　Personal data processed for any purpose or purposes shall not be kept for longer than is necessary for that purpose or those purposes.

6　　Personal data shall be processed in accordance with the rights of data subjects under this Act.

7　　Appropriate technical and organisational measures shall be taken against unauthorised or unlawful processing of personal data and against accidental loss or destruction of, or damage to, personal data.

8　　Personal data shall not be transferred to a country or territory outside the European Economic Area unless that country or territory ensures an adequate level of protection for the rights and freedoms of data subjects in relation to the processing of personal data.

It is clear, therefore, that organisations have a legal duty to comply with the DPA, in addition to any ethical 'duty of care' to their customers. This makes the management of customer databases a professional issue, and it should not therefore be trusted to any and every individual within the organisation.

Managing yourself

The performance management cycle is a simple process by which your personal performance is managed within an organisation. It consists of a series of appraisal meetings (which may be formal or informal) at which past performance is reviewed and future performance is planned. Work is then carried out, and a further meeting held to review performance, and so on.

A typical appraisal meeting will therefore have three component parts:

1　　Reviewing past performance

2　　Setting objectives for the coming period

3　　Planning personal development activities, and any other support the organisation can give to ensure the individual performs as required.

Setting personal objectives

Everyone should know what the organisation expects of them. Some objectives may be set by managers during the appraisal process, and others may be set by the individual themselves.

Personal objectives generally fall into two categories:

◆　　Objectives related to value, such as improving processes, reducing costs, or increasing customer service levels.

◆　　Objectives related to outputs, such as sales levels or quantities produced.

SMART objectives

Objectives should be 'SMART' (Figure 9.3):

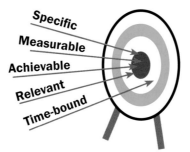

Figure 9.3: SMART objectives

◆ **Specific** – The objective should be expressed in terms that are clearly defined and understood. This is easy with quantitative objectives (such as 'increase sales by 5%') but less straightforward with qualitative objectives (such as 'increase customer satisfaction levels'). Making the objective measurable can help in the latter case.

◆ **Measurable** – For an objective to be valid, you have to know when you have achieved it. This may be a quantified level of performance, or may be a specific deliverable (a report, for example).

◆ **Achievable** – This aspect of the objective is about ownership. The individual to whom the objective is applied must perceive achievement as being attainable. Good objectives are in the form of 'stretch targets' – only achievable with a high degree of effort. This not only improves performance significantly, but also motivates the individual.

◆ **Relevant** – The variable being measured must be within the sphere of influence of the individual to which it applies. There is no point, for example, asking a member of the accounts department to improve the time taken for customers to pay, if the only person who can influence this is the sales representative who visits the customer.

◆ **Time-bound** – By when? If performance is to be reviewed on, for example, a six-monthly basis, then an objective should be set at such a level that it could be achieved in that timescale. If the objective is long term, then progress measures must be identified so regular reviews can be held.

Activity 9.2

Identify three objectives that relate to your personal performance, either at work or at college. Put each into 'SMART' form.

Working to achieve objectives

Once your personal objectives have been agreed, you need to work out how to achieve them. This involves a series of steps, as shown in Figure 9.4:

1 Break each objective down into a series of achievable and time-bound short-term goals. Not only will this allow you to measure your progress towards achieving your objectives, it will motivate you as you 'tick off' the goals.

2   Identify the tasks that need to be performed in order to achieve each goal. These tasks might be such things as processes to perform, documents to create, or meetings to attend.

3   Identify the time required for each task. In summation, these times will allow you to check that all your objectives really are achievable within the constraint of the total time you have available.

4   Identify the resources you need in order to achieve each goal within the time specified. These resources may be financial, material (such as a PC), or human (such as the help of colleagues).

5   Prioritise your objectives and goals, so you can recognise the relative urgency of each and work out which should take precedence over the others.

6   Produce a detailed time and resource plan for the period between now and your next review meeting. Show which tasks you will perform, what resources are required, and when you expect to achieve each goal and objective.

7   Perform the tasks, and compare performance to the plan.

8   Revise the plan as you go, and don't be afraid to recognise that some goals and objectives might become unachievable due to your own poor performance or external influences. Report such instances to your manager, so they are aware in advance.

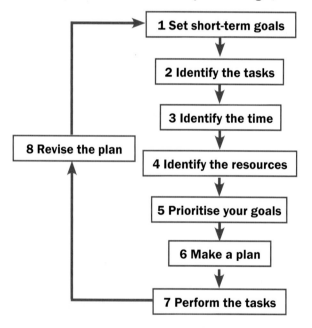

Figure 9.4: Working through objectives

For any one of the objectives you identified in the previous activity, produce a detailed progress plan in line with the first six steps outlined above.

Effective resource utilisation

In step 4 of the process outlined in Figure 9.4 above, we looked at identifying the resources needed to perform each task. In all organisations, resources are scarce, and demand often exceeds supply. It is therefore essential that resource utilisation is planned in such a way that the organisation's objectives are achieved. If it is not possible to achieve all the objectives, resources must be allocated to those tasks that support the objectives that are perceived as higher priority.

Mediating in discussion relating to resource allocation between conflicting objectives is a key role of managers.

Completing tasks on time

Most objectives, and therefore the tasks performed in moving towards their achievement, have three dimensions (as shown in Figure 9.5):

◆ The scope and quality of the task. That is, what needs to be done, and what level of achievement or quality of output is expected.

◆ The cost of the task. How much resource is required, and how much that resource costs the organisation.

◆ The time taken to perform the task, and the deadline for completion.

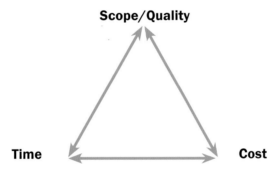

Figure 9.5: Constraints on tasks and objectives

These three dimensions are in conflict, each with the other. If, for example, we need to re-duce the cost of a task, this can often be achieved by using less resource (and quality falls) or by working only when 'spare' time is available (and the task takes longer to complete). Similarly, a task can be performed more quickly by allocating more resources (increasing cost) or by sacrificing quality.

In many instances, one of the three constraints is likely to be most important. Often, 'time is of the essence', and cost and quality must come second to meeting a deadline.

Activity 9.3

Identify three tasks that you regularly perform, one where each of the three constraints (cost, quality and time) is more important.

Closing out customer enquiries

Right back at the beginning of this coursebook, we looked at the idea that marketing is the responsibility of everyone in the organisation, not just marketing staff. The same is true of customer service, particularly if you include internal customers. Even if you are not in a customer-facing role, there will be many occasions when you, or one of your colleagues, makes a promise to a customer that you have a hand in meeting. If you 'buy into' the idea that business is about satisfying customer needs, any task or objective with a customer service aspect must, necessarily, be accorded high priority. In terms of which customer promises should take preference, obviously external customers should take precedence over internal customers.

Monitoring achievement and success

In order to get the greatest benefit from any performance review process, it is essential that you record and monitor all progress that you make towards the achievement of your objectives. This will allow you, in conjunction with your manager, to review your effectiveness. Keeping a record of your achievements is not just important for performance review, but also adds value to your curriculum vitae (CV).

Practice work-based tasks

Role

Your manager is interested in developing a better understanding of the organisation's customers and wishes to know how standards of customer care can be improved and assessed.

During a meeting with the marketing team, it was felt that it would be useful to review different approaches that a range of other organisations use to develop their customer care initiatives.

In your role as a marketing assistant, you have been asked to review the article provided on pages 178-9, which profiles different organisations and their individual approaches to managing customer care. Using the supporting material, and your knowledge of other organisations gained from research, address the following tasks:

Task 1: Improving Customer Care (25% weighting)

Using the article reproduced on pages 186-7, produce a presentation consisting of 10 slides with supporting notes, suitable for presentation to the marketing team.

The presentation should:

◆ Briefly explain, on the basis of the information provided in the appendix and your research, how the Internet can be used to gather feedback from customers.

◆ Explain the process of designing a customer care programme, and discuss the possible role(s) of the Internet and associated technologies (intranet, etc.) in that process (with the exception of gathering feedback, which was covered in the first section of the presentation).

◆ Identify how the Internet and associated technologies might be used by your organisation, or one with which you are familiar, to improve standards of customer care.

Word count 750 words, excluding relevant appendices

Task 2: Planning and measuring performance (15% weighting)

Having completed the previous tasks given and, in preparation for your appraisal with your manager, you have been asked to obtain feedback about your skills, attributes and performance from a range of people that you know well. These may include fellow students, tutors, friends, family, colleagues and/or supervisors. You should interview a maximum of four people.

Produce a discussion document for use at your appraisal that:

◆ Summarises the feedback received on your skills, attributes and performance.

◆ Briefly analyses the feedback received, identifying your strengths and areas for development.

◆ Identifies a set of personal objectives for the next 12 months that addresses your areas for development.

◆ Outlines how your performance against these objectives would be measured.

Word count 500 words, excluding relevant appendices

Comments on practice work-based tasks

A case study approach has been adopted for this assignment. The material provided refers to particular industries/sectors and a range of organisations. The intention is to offer candidates a wealth of examples, so that they can contextualise their answers, even if they are not working within a marketing department.

It is envisaged that the material provided will form the basis of group discussion and candidates should be encouraged to use other material and information sources in addition to what is provided. The case study material can be used to reinforce the theoretical concepts and encourage the candidates to be more analytical in their approach.

Group analysis and discussion of the case material is acceptable, although it is very important that the assignment tasks are undertaken individually, and not as part of a group. The examiners will be expecting to see originality of thought in the interpretation and application of the assessment tasks.

Task 1

This task is designed to allow the candidate to identify different ways that the Internet and associated technologies can be used in customer care programmes. It would also be interesting to put this in context by looking at initiatives adopted by other organisations.

Determining which initiatives could be used successfully in another organisation could either be related to the candidate's own organisation, or another organisation that they are familiar with if they are not currently in a suitable role. A level of justification with regard to why certain initiatives would or would not be possible, alongside a brief consideration of the benefits delivered, would be expected for the higher grades.

The wording used within this task is designed to allow the candidates a degree of flexibility in their approach and to allow them to demonstrate their ability to understand what motivates customers to purchase. Any answer is in theory as valid as another, as long as the thinking is supported by valid argument.

Supporting material: Blogging

To Blog Or Not To Blog?

Marketers are not short of advice about how to incorporate blogs, discussion forums and other online communities in their marketing communications. Indeed, there is plenty even within the pages of this magazine. But is there really a business model that brands can utilise when it comes to these peer-to-peer networks, and how does the technology fit into tried and tested marketing practice?

Buyer behaviour, reference groups, opinion leaders and opinion formers are all well-understood concepts in the marketing fraternity. Online communities are simply informal, electronic reference groups made up of individuals with similar interests or needs. Indeed, many consumers search out websites and forums that provide a community of like-minded individuals.

As with all reference groups, online communities include opinion leaders and opinion formers. These are the bloggers and long-standing members of discussion forums who make credible and robust recommendations that encourage purchase. The power of the internet makes it very easy to become an opinion former if you can engage and maintain an audience.

Anyone with access to the internet can tell anyone in the world who is prepared to listen exactly what they think of our products. And people are listening. Brands' target markets are becoming both marketing and technology savvy. A writer with a sharp wit and an insatiable appetite for products has a platform and can build a loyal fan base.

But the extent to which brands themselves should use blogs and discussion forums is debatable. Authenticity is still paramount in marketing communications, and encouraging marketers to pose as happy customers in online discussions and expecting real consumers to trust and absorb these messages – an all-too-common practice – is asking for trouble.

Nike's experiment with blogs garnered a mixed response from marketing academics, although it generated positive buzz among consumers. In partnership with blog giant Gawker, the youth brand commissioned 15 short films from digital film makers, who each presented their interpretation of 'speed'. Nike admitted that beyond winning 'cool' points, it was difficult to gauge the success of the campaign. But it maintains it learned a valuable lesson on what blog readers will permit, and even welcome, in terms of marketer involvement, and it will be fascinating to see what it comes up with next.

Some marketers are using online communities to generate buzz by wooing so-called 'e-fluentials' with free product samples. This might be an effective way to create new opinion leaders, but there is no guarantee that they will like the product or write glowing reviews. Negative publicity may undo any positive sentiment in a reference group.

Most supporters of discussion forums as a communications tool are technology and engineering companies, who believe that online communities facilitate the meaningful, thought-provoking, peer-to-peer interaction needed to drive innovation and new product development. Microsoft, for example, often provides development blogs during the NPD process of a new product. These blogs serve to humanise the company in the minds of software developers, a key target market, who feel involved in the process and are, therefore, very interested in the final product they helped design and de-bug.

However, the benefits are less obvious in the consumer marketing arena. One analyst recently commented: "There are a lot of companies trying to find out whether there is a business here, and most of them are finding it difficult." As he points out, marketers are used to engaging with consumers, but less used to consumers talking right back. Some commentators suggest that organisations have to accept that content democracy is key and that they must give their consumers a voice. The power of word-of-mouth at online communities should not be underestimated and the most effective way to learn about your consumer is to strike up a dialogue.

But while engaging with such communities might work well for youth brands, such as Coca-Cola's extreme sports energy drink 'Relentless', it is less appropriate for, say, a financial services brand, which might find its blog quickly degenerating into a public complaints forum.

There is no shortage of research telling us that consumers are more likely to share negative experiences with each other than they are positive experiences – and this effect is magnified on the internet, where you can publish your bad experience once, and it is available to read by the entire World Wide Web.

Marketers should not underestimate the commercial importance of digital media for procuring new customers and for developing and maintaining brand loyalty. The problem for brands is that the 'voice' of the online word-of-mouth revolution is not coming from the brand bourgeoisie, but the consumer proletariat, and their manifestos are not pamphlets, but blogs – anywhere between several hundred thousand and several million of them. What's more, they are read by between 14 million and 20 million people every week.

Online communities are certainly the future for consumers, but marketers who believe they are the future for brands could be misguided. tm

Source: To blog or not to blog?, Thorne J., *The Marketer*, July/August 2007

The Dos and Don'ts of blogging

Don't throw money at bloggers. Traditional ad placements will not work: the majority of bloggers have no direct control over banner ad placement anyway, or prefer to provide their blogs ad-free.

Do present humorous, engaging adverts that may turn into viral campaigns – postmodern consumers are intelligent and respond to clever, wry and sarcastic humour.

Don't pretend to be a consumer to plug your product. Source credibility is still key in communications and members of online communities will not be fooled.

Do engage in a dialogue and be prepared to respond to positive and negative feedback. Marketers are used to sending messages one way and then measuring performance against communications objectives, but online responses, reactions and opinions are shared immediately and among a wider audience.

Don't talk to blog users using the typical messaging strategies. See them as gatekeepers to a wider audience and be prepared for an ongoing relationship.

Source: K. Oser, More marketers test blogs to build buzz, *Advertising Age* Vol. 75 Issue 37

Candidates should be encouraged to think about the presentation format and how this could be presented. In their job role they may be expected to have PowerPoint skills and to be able to produce speaker's notes to accompany the slides.

Task 2

This task is designed to get the candidates to reflect on both the learning that has taken place and their own efficiency and effectiveness within their organisational role.

The final task in the assessment will always be based on aspects of syllabus reference 4.7, and will encourage candidates to consider precisely what has been achieved and how this will benefit them in their career progression and through the period of their CIM study.

Candidates therefore need to know that this aspect of the syllabus will be part of the assessment, and should prepare for this by developing a view on their own personal development during the course.

Further work

For your organisation, or one with which you are familiar, investigate whether the relationship marketing concept is being applied. If it is, identify ways in which relationship marketing activities might be improved. If not, identify the benefits to the organisation of adopting such an approach.

For your organisation, or one with which you are familiar, investigate how customer feedback is collected and recommend improvements.

For your organisation, or one with which you are familiar, identify ways in which the performance appraisal process might be improved, particularly from the point of view of the individual whose performance is being appraised.

Unit 10 Review: Understanding customer relationships

Using this unit

This unit is a summary of chapters 6 to 9, for revision purposes. It has two key component parts:

◆ Revision notes, for you to revise before the assessment, and to give you clues and hints while practising assessments.

◆ Overview diagrams showing the key points. These can be used as the basis for your own final revision tools. You should supplement them, not with notes based on this text, but with additional material found by looking at other sources, or at relevant organisations.

Customers and needs

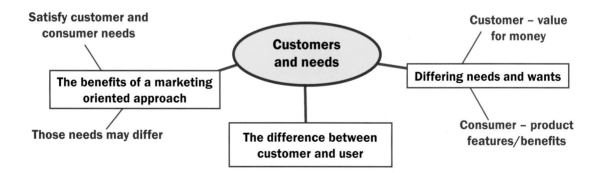

- The difference between customer and user
  - Customers
    - Purchase goods
    - For themselves, or their family (B2C)
    - For an organisation (B2B)
  - The consumer/user
    - The end user
    - May not purchase
    - Family DMU for durables
- Differing needs and wants
  - Customer – value for money
  - Consumer – product features/benefits
- The benefits of a marketing oriented approach
  - Identify, anticipate and satisfy customer and consumer needs.
  - Those needs may differ

Collecting information about customer needs

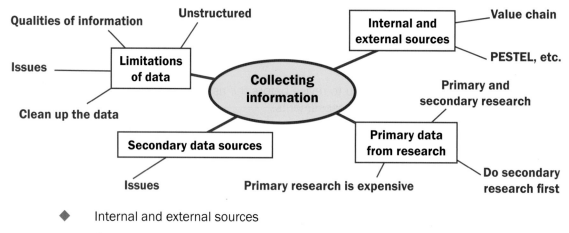

- Internal and external sources
  - Value chain
  - PESTEL, etc.
- Primary data from research
  - Two types:
    - Primary research (e.g. questionnaire)
    - Secondary research (e.g. government statistics)
  - Do secondary research first
  - Primary research is expensive
- Secondary data sources
  - Issues
    - Date

- How was the data collected?
- 'Political' research
- The limitations of data
  - Data is unstructured
  - Qualities of information:
    - Timely
    - Accurate
    - Complete
    - Concise
    - Understandable
    - Relevant
    - Economical.
  - Issues
    - May be out of date
    - May contain errors
    - Purpose may have been different
  - Clean up the data
    - Issues of date
    - Issues of number

Creating a customer database

- Creating a database
  - Typical contents
    - Name
    - Contact Information
    - Role/occupation
    - Profile information
    - Purchase records
    - Media profile
  - Get clean data
  - Or clean it up
- Controlling access
  - Security
  - Legal issues

The value of customer information

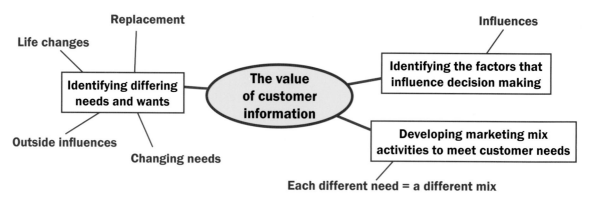

- ◆ Identifying the factors that influence decision-making
    - ◆ Influences
        - • External (e.g. economy)
        - • Internal (e.g. family)
- ◆ Identifying differing needs and wants
    - ◆ Replacement
    - ◆ Life changes
    - ◆ Outside influences
    - ◆ Changing needs
- ◆ Developing marketing mix activities to meet customer needs
    - ◆ Each different need = a different mix

Internal and external customers

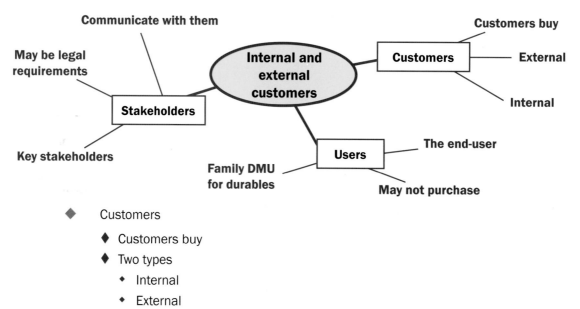

- ◆ Customers
    - ◆ Customers buy
    - ◆ Two types
        - • Internal
        - • External

- External customers
  - B2C
  - B2B
  - C2C
- Internal customers
  - Other departments
  - Line manager
  - C olleagues
- Users
  - The end user
  - May not purchase
  - Family DMU for durables
- Stakeholders
  - Internal and external individuals or groups, who come into contact with an organisation or who affect or are affected by its activities
  - Communicate with them
  - May be legal requirements
  - Key stakeholders may include
    - Customers
    - Financial supporters
    - Suppliers and distributors
    - Local community
    - Employees

Marketing and customer relationships

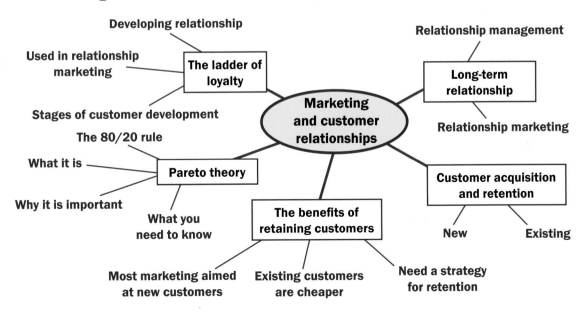

- Long-term relationship
  - Relationship management
  - Relationship marketing
    - Network of relationships
    - Create and sustain win–win outcomes
- Customer acquisition and customer retention
  - Two types of customer
    - Existing customers
    - New customers
- The benefits of retaining customers
  - Most marketing aimed at new customers
  - Need a strategy for retention
  - Existing customers are cheaper
- Pareto theory
  - The 80/20 rule
  - What it is
    - Customers
    - Channels
    - Markets
  - Why it is important
    - Identify most profitable
    - Look after them
    - Find more
    - Concentrate on them
  - What you need to know
    - How productive is marketing?
    - What generates revenue or profit?
    - How can we target them?
- The ladder of loyalty
  - Developing relationship
  - Used in relationship marketing
  - Stages of customer development
    - Prospect
    - Customer
    - Client
    - Supporter
    - Advocate
    - Partner

Marketing and customer loyalty

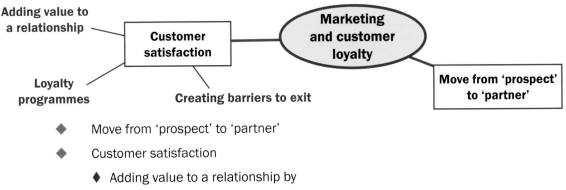

- Move from 'prospect' to 'partner'
- Customer satisfaction
  - Adding value to a relationship by
    - Making reordering easier
    - Offering add-ons
    - Solving problems jointly
  - Loyalty programmes
  - Creating barriers to exit

Supply chain marketing

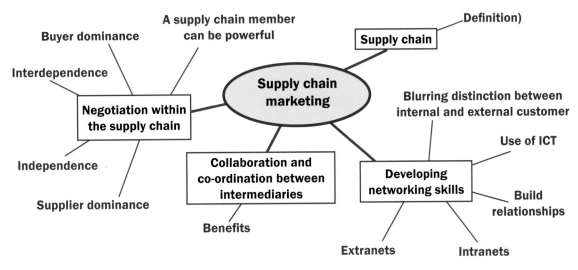

- Supply chain
  - The network of suppliers, manufacturers and distributors involved in the production and delivery of a product (CIM)
- Developing networking skills
  - Blurring distinction between internal and external customer
  - Use of ICT
  - Build relationships
  - Intranets
  - Extranets

- ◆ Collaboration and co-ordination between intermediaries
  - ◆ Benefits
    - ◆ Innovation
    - ◆ Improved performance
    - ◆ Lower costs
    - ◆ More holistic solutions to problems
    - ◆ Better understanding of the needs of all parties
    - ◆ New ways of working together
    - ◆ More co-operation
- ◆ Negotiation within the supply chain
  - ◆ A supply chain member can be said to be powerful if:
    - ◆ Other members are dependent upon them for essential components
    - ◆ They have control over significant financial resource
    - ◆ They play a central part in the network
    - ◆ What they supply is not substitutable, or
    - ◆ They have the ability to reduce uncertainty for the other players.
  - ◆ Buyer dominance – few buyers, many suppliers
  - ◆ Interdependence – few buyers and sellers and both have high switching costs
  - ◆ Independence – many buyers and sellers and both buyer and seller have low switching costs
  - ◆ Supplier dominance – few suppliers and the buyer has high switching costs

Building and developing relationships

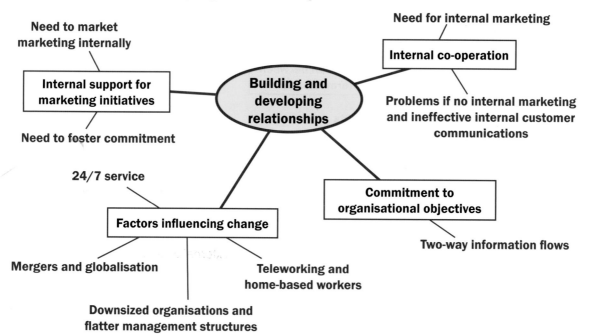

196

- Internal co-operation
  - Need for internal marketing
  - Without internal marketing and effective internal customer communications:
    - Communication problems
    - Frustration and non-cooperation
    - Time-wasting and inefficiency
    - Stress and lack of job satisfaction
    - Poor quality of work
- Commitment to organisational objectives
  - Two-way information flows
- Internal support for marketing initiatives
  - Need to market marketing internally
  - Need to foster commitment
- Factors influencing change
  - Downsized organisations and flatter management structures
  - Teleworking and home-based workers
  - 24/7 service
  - Mergers and globalisation

Sources of conflict

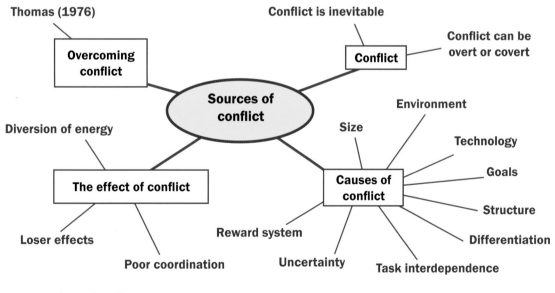

- Conflict
  - Conflict is inevitable
  - Conflict can be:
    - Overt
    - Covert

- ◆ Causes of conflict
  - ◆ Environment
  - ◆ Size
  - ◆ Technology
  - ◆ Goals
  - ◆ Structure
  - ◆ Differentiation
  - ◆ Task interdependence
  - ◆ Uncertainty
  - ◆ Reward system
- ◆ The effect of conflict
  - ◆ Diversion of energy
  - ◆ Loser effects
  - ◆ Poor coordination
- ◆ Overcoming conflict
  - ◆ Thomas (1976)
    - ◆ Based on
      - ◆ The degree of assertiveness in pursuit of one's interests, and
      - ◆ The level of cooperation in attempting to satisfy others' interests
    - ◆ Solutions
      - ◆ Avoidance
      - ◆ Accommodation
      - ◆ Compromise
      - ◆ Competition
      - ◆ Collaboration

Co-operation and collaboration

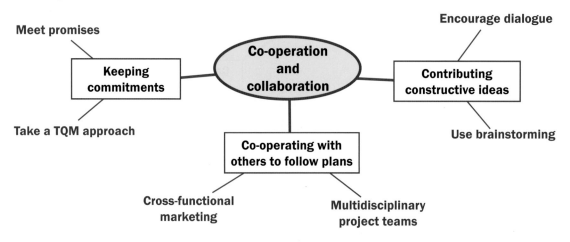

◆ Contributing constructive ideas

♦ Encourage dialogue

♦ Use brainstorming

◆ Co-operating with others to follow plans

♦ Cross-functional marketing

♦ Multidisciplinary project teams

◆ Keeping commitments

♦ Meet promises

♦ Take a TQM approach

The importance of communication

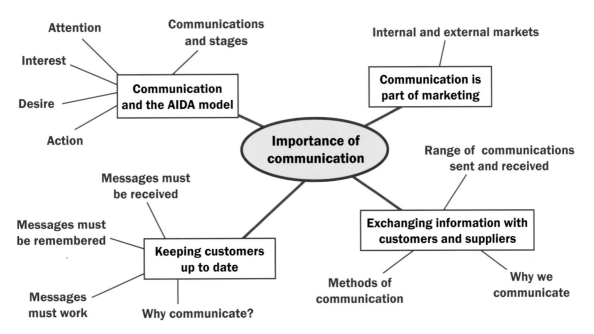

◆ Communication is part of marketing

♦ Internal and external markets

• Internal and external communication

◆ Exchanging information with customers and suppliers

♦ View all communications as part of:

• The range of communications sent by the organisation

• The range of communications received by the stakeholder

♦ We communicate

• To build relationships

• To give specific instructions

• To disseminate information

- To share ideas and values
- To negotiate
- To discuss
- To motivate, interest and stimulate
- To create an awareness
- To establish a two-way communication process
- Methods
  - Post
  - Telephone
  - E-mail
  - Fax
  - Letters
  - Direct mail
  - Meeting
  - Report
  - Presentation
  - Informal
- Keeping customers up to date
  - Messages must be received
  - Messages must be remembered
  - Messages must work
  - Why communicate?
    - Differentiate
    - Remind
    - Inform
    - Persuade
- Communication and the AIDA model
  - Attention
    - Must gain impact
  - Interest
    - Sell the benefits
  - Desire
    - Specific benefits to the individual
  - Action
    - What next?
  - Communications and stages
    - Different communications for each stage

The communications cycle

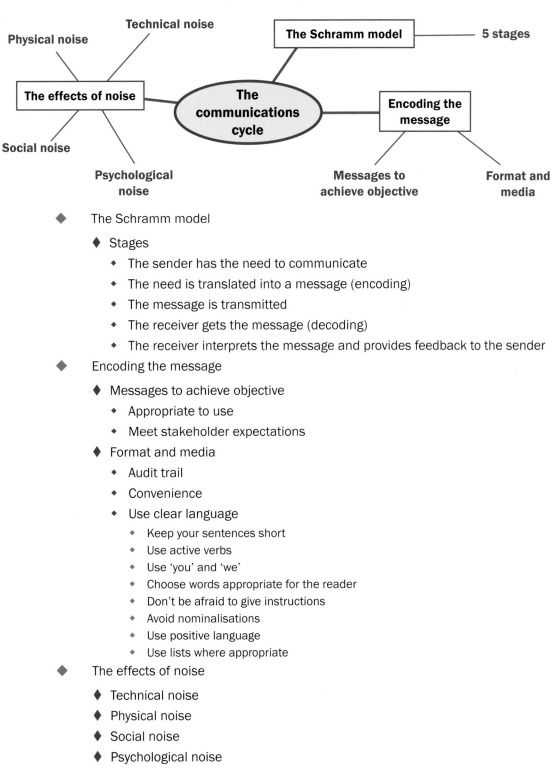

- ◆ The Schramm model
  - ◆ Stages
    - ◆ The sender has the need to communicate
    - ◆ The need is translated into a message (encoding)
    - ◆ The message is transmitted
    - ◆ The receiver gets the message (decoding)
    - ◆ The receiver interprets the message and provides feedback to the sender
- ◆ Encoding the message
  - ◆ Messages to achieve objective
    - ◆ Appropriate to use
    - ◆ Meet stakeholder expectations
  - ◆ Format and media
    - ◆ Audit trail
    - ◆ Convenience
    - ◆ Use clear language
      - ◆ Keep your sentences short
      - ◆ Use active verbs
      - ◆ Use 'you' and 'we'
      - ◆ Choose words appropriate for the reader
      - ◆ Don't be afraid to give instructions
      - ◆ Avoid nominalisations
      - ◆ Use positive language
      - ◆ Use lists where appropriate
- ◆ The effects of noise
  - ◆ Technical noise
  - ◆ Physical noise
  - ◆ Social noise
  - ◆ Psychological noise

Business communication formats

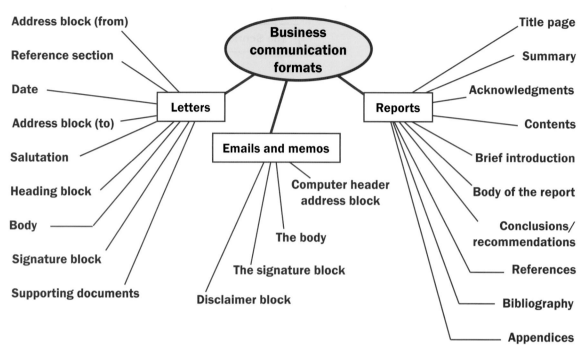

- ◆ Letters
  - ◆ The address block (from)
  - ◆ The reference section
  - ◆ The date
  - ◆ The address block (to)
  - ◆ The salutation
  - ◆ The heading block
  - ◆ The body
  - ◆ The signature block
  - ◆ Supporting documents
- ◆ Reports
  - ◆ Title page
  - ◆ Summary
  - ◆ Acknowledgments
  - ◆ Contents
  - ◆ Brief introduction
  - ◆ Body of the report
  - ◆ Conclusions and recommendations
  - ◆ References
  - ◆ Bibliography
  - ◆ Appendices

- E-mails
  - ◆ Computer header address block
  - ◆ The body
  - ◆ The signature block
  - ◆ Disclaimer block
- Memos
  - ◆ As email

Effective communication

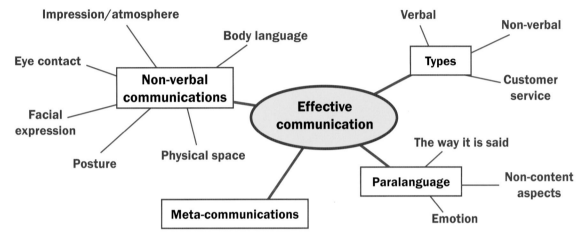

- What makes communication effective?
  - ◆ Verbal
  - ◆ Non-verbal
  - ◆ Customer service
- Non-verbal communications
  - ◆ Body language
  - ◆ Impression/atmosphere
  - ◆ Eye contact
  - ◆ Facial expression
  - ◆ Posture
  - ◆ Physical space
- Paralanguage
  - ◆ The way it is said
  - ◆ Non-content aspects
  - ◆ Emotion
- Meta-communications
  - ◆ Communications about communications
- Advertising

Promotional activities (1)

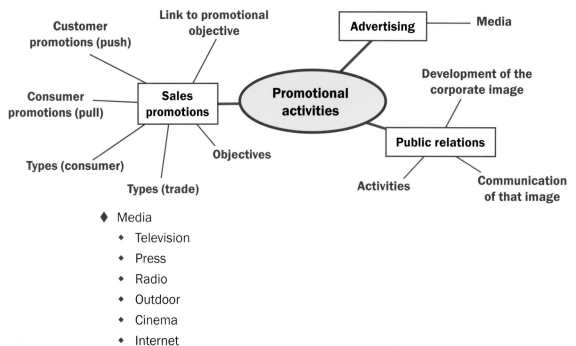

- ◆ Media
  - • Television
  - • Press
  - • Radio
  - • Outdoor
  - • Cinema
  - • Internet
  - • Branding
- ◆ Sales promotions
  - ◆ A short-term tactical marketing tool that gives customers additional reasons or incentives to purchase. (CIM)
  - ◆ Link to promotional objective
    - • Buy once (first or switch)
    - • Buy more
      - • Buy more frequently
  - ◆ Customer promotions (push)
  - ◆ Consumer promotions (pull)
  - ◆ Objectives
    - • Encourage trial
    - • Extend existing customer base
    - • Generate bulk buying
    - • Overcome seasonal dips in sales
    - • Encourage trade to stock product
  - ◆ Types (consumer)
    - • Price reductions
    - • Coupons/money-off vouchers
    - • Entry to competitions/free prize draws
    - • Free goods
    - • x per cent free

- ◆ 3 for the price of 2 (BOGOF)
- ◆ Free samples or gifts
- ◆ Guarantees or extended warranties
- ◆ £x goes to y charity if you purchase
- ◆ Reward points/tokens
- ◆ Refunds or free gifts on a mail-in basis
- ◆ Types (trade)
  - ◆ Discount on bulk orders
  - ◆ Free supplies
  - ◆ Incentives (e.g. shopping vouchers)
  - ◆ Free prize draw competitions
  - ◆ Deferred invoicing
  - ◆ Merchandising and display material
- ◆ Public relations
  - ◆ The planned and sustained effort to establish and maintain goodwill and mutual understanding between an organisation and its publics (IPR)
  - ◆ Development of the corporate image
  - ◆ Communication of that image
  - ◆ Activities:
    - ◆ Corporate image and corporate social responsibility
    - ◆ Exhibitions, conferences and special events
    - ◆ Press conferences
    - ◆ Press releases
    - ◆ Sponsorship

Promotional activities (2)

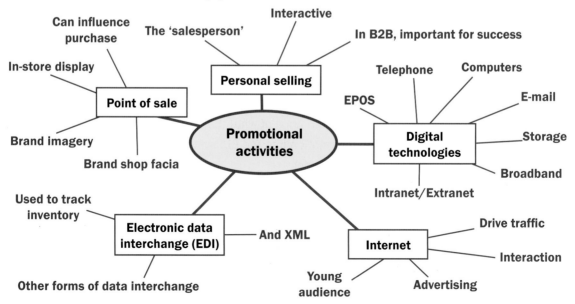

- Digital technologies
  - EPOS
  - Telephone
  - Computers
  - Wireless
  - E-mail
  - Internet
  - Storage
  - Broadband
- Intranet/extranet
  - Intranet = internal
  - Extranet = external
- Internet
  - Young audience
  - Internet advertising
  - Interaction
  - Drive traffic
    - Links with other sites
    - Advertising on ISP portals
    - E-mail advertising
    - SMS messaging
  - Types of advertisement
    - Banner advertising
    - Pop-up ads
    - Superstitals
    - E-mail and SMS
- Electronic data interchange (EDI)
  - A communications protocol
  - Being replaced by Extensible Markup Language (XML)
  - Often applied to other forms of data interchange
  - Also used to keep track of inventory
    - Record the quantity and price of what the customer has bought
    - Feed the same information into the EDI system
    - Can then activate an order
- Point of sale
  - In-store display
  - Can influence consumers to purchase
  - Manufacturers can have in-store display material produced
  - Extended to branding the whole shop facia
  - Tool for marketers to communicate brand imagery

◆ Personal selling

 ♦ The 'salesperson'

 ♦ Involves two-way interactive communications

 ♦ Can provide with additional information at the point of sale

 ♦ In B2B, success can depend upon relationships

Direct marketing

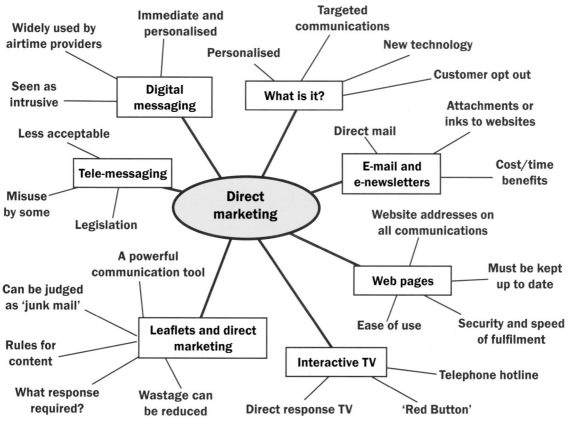

◆ What is it?

 ♦ Allows us to send a personalised message to a consumer

 ♦ The most targeted method of communication

 ♦ Technology is enabling many changes: collection, and manipulation of customer data

 ♦ Customers are using their power to opt out

◆ E-mail and e-newsletters

 ♦ Direct mail

 ♦ Attachments or hyperlinks to websites

 ♦ Cost and time benefits

◆ Web pages

 ♦ Inclusion of website addresses on all forms of communication

- ◆ Websites must be kept up to date and relevant
- ◆ Ease of use and navigation
- ◆ Security and speed of fulfilment
- ◆ Interactive TV
  - ◆ Direct response TV
  - ◆ The 'Red Button'
  - ◆ Telephone hotline
- ◆ Leaflets and direct marketing
  - ◆ A powerful communication tool
  - ◆ Can irritate people and be judged as 'junk mail'
  - ◆ Wastage can be reduced
  - ◆ Rules:
    - ◆ Say what you mean
    - ◆ Sound enthusiastic
    - ◆ Personalise letters
    - ◆ Questions can be used
    - ◆ Go into detail
    - ◆ Use a friendly tone
  - ◆ If you want a response, make it very clear what it is
- ◆ Tele-messaging
  - ◆ Becoming less acceptable
  - ◆ Misuse by certain product categories
  - ◆ Legislation
- ◆ Digital messaging
  - ◆ Widely used by airtime providers
  - ◆ The most immediate personalised method of direct mail
  - ◆ Seen as intrusive

Customer databases and tactical marketing

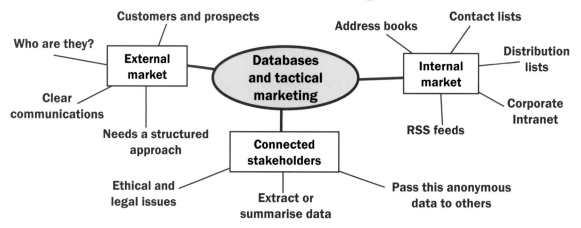

- Internal market
  - Address books
  - Contact lists
  - Build distribution lists
  - Corporate Intranet
  - RSS feeds
- External market
  - Customers and prospects
  - Need to know who they are
  - Avoid conflicting or confusing communications
  - Needs a structured and controlled approach
- Connected stakeholders
  - Ethical and legal issues
  - Extract or summarise data
  - Pass this anonymous data to others

Managing a communications budget

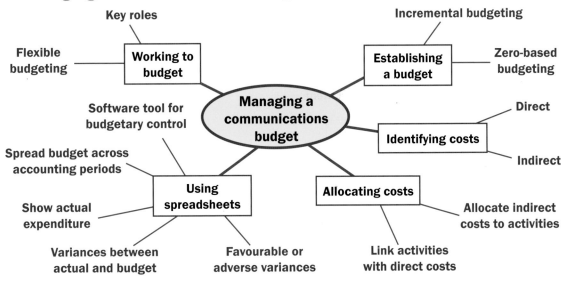

- Establishing a budget
  - Two ways to establish a budget:
    - Incremental budgeting
    - Zero-based budgeting
- Identifying costs
  - Two types:
    - Direct costs
    - Indirect costs

- Allocating costs
  - Identify which communications activity has given rise to which direct costs
  - Use a system of cost recovery to allocate indirect costs to activities
- Working to budget
  - Key roles
    - The budget is a target
    - The budget is a communications tool, to allow the organisation to let all relevant parties know what is expected of them
    - The budget is a co-ordination tool
    - The budget is a control tool
    - The budget is an evaluation tool
  - Many organisations now use 'flexible budgeting'
- Using spreadsheets
  - The most common software tool for budgetary control
  - Divide the year into accounting periods
  - Spread the budget across these time periods
  - Actual expenditure shown alongside the budget
  - 'Variances' between actual and budget highlighted
  - 'Favourable' or 'adverse' variances

Measuring the success of communications campaigns

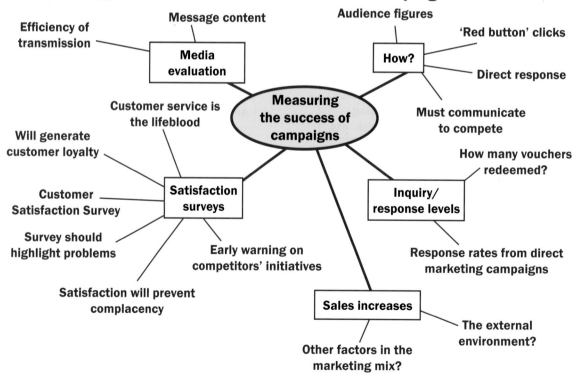

- How?
  - Audience figures
  - The number of 'Red Buttons' clicked
  - Direct response
  - Have to communicate to compete
- Inquiry/response levels
  - Count the number of redeemed vouchers
  - Response rates from direct marketing campaigns
- Sales increases
  - Other factors in the marketing mix?
  - The external environment?
- Media evaluation
  - Two elements
    - The content of the message itself
    - The efficiency of the media in transmitting the message
- Satisfaction surveys
  - Customer service is the lifeblood of any business
  - Will generate customer loyalty and repeat business
  - Customer satisfaction survey
    - See how effective efforts have been
    - Identify problem areas for further action
    - Demonstrate to customers that the organisation cares
    - Publicise an organisation's service offering
  - Survey should be designed to highlight problems
  - Customer satisfaction will prevent complacency
  - Early warning on competitors' initiatives

Customer care and service (1)

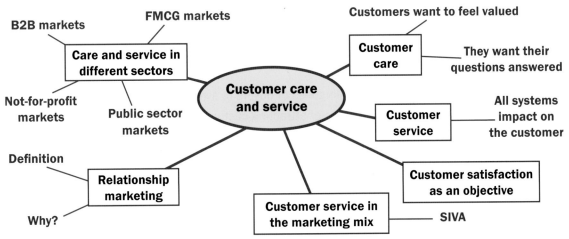

- Customer care
  - Customers want to feel valued
  - They want their questions answered
- Customer service
  - All systems impact on the customer
    - Sales and ordering
    - Accounts and invoicing
    - Delivery systems
    - After sales
    - Complaints
- Care and service in different sectors
  - Consumer (FMCG) markets
  - Business-to-business markets
  - Not-for-profit markets
  - Public sector markets
- Customer satisfaction as an objective
  - Satisfying customers is at the heart of marketing
  - Employees outside the marketing department or sales force play an important role
  - Marketing is a shared business ethos
  - Places customers central to all organisational activities
  - Without customers there would be no business
- Customer service in the marketing mix
  - SIVA (Solution, Information, Value, Access)
    - Product = Solution
    - Promotion = Information
    - Price = Value
    - Place =Access
- Relationship marketing
  - The devoting of marketing resources to maintaining and exploiting the firm's existing customer base
  - Why?
    - The increased willingness of buyers to switch
    - The increased costs of attracting customers
    - Increasing the breadth of products being offered could only be justified if the customer could be retained
    - In mature markets future earnings come from retaining and increasing the value of existing customers

Customer care and service (2)

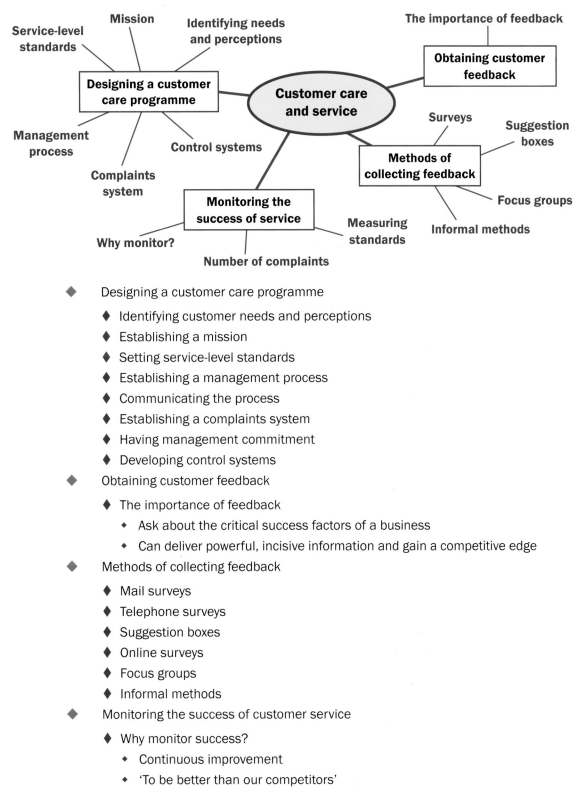

- ◆ Designing a customer care programme
  - ◆ Identifying customer needs and perceptions
  - ◆ Establishing a mission
  - ◆ Setting service-level standards
  - ◆ Establishing a management process
  - ◆ Communicating the process
  - ◆ Establishing a complaints system
  - ◆ Having management commitment
  - ◆ Developing control systems
- ◆ Obtaining customer feedback
  - ◆ The importance of feedback
    - ◆ Ask about the critical success factors of a business
    - ◆ Can deliver powerful, incisive information and gain a competitive edge
- ◆ Methods of collecting feedback
  - ◆ Mail surveys
  - ◆ Telephone surveys
  - ◆ Suggestion boxes
  - ◆ Online surveys
  - ◆ Focus groups
  - ◆ Informal methods
- ◆ Monitoring the success of customer service
  - ◆ Why monitor success?
    - ◆ Continuous improvement
    - ◆ 'To be better than our competitors'

- Number of complaints
  - Can give an indication of how they perceive our service levels
  - We cannot rely on it as an accurate measure
- Measuring service standards
  - Sales records
  - Customer retention
  - Existing customer data
  - Mystery shoppers

Using IT in customer service activities

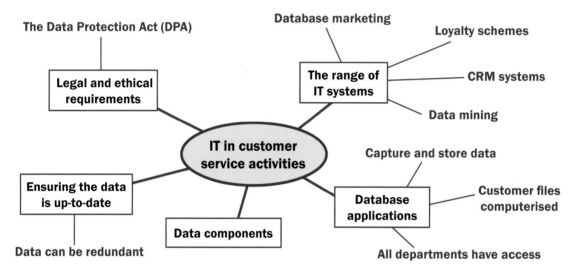

- The range of IT systems
  - Database marketing
  - Loyalty schemes
  - Customer relationship management systems
  - Data mining
- Database applications
  - Capture and store data
  - Each customer file is computerised
  - All the departments in the firm can access this information quickly and cheaply
- Data components

Geographic

  - Demographic
  - Psychographic
  - Buying pattern
  - Other
- Ensuring the data is up-to-date

- ◆ Data can be redundant for three reasons:
  - ◆ It is obsolete
  - ◆ It is duplicated
  - ◆ It should have changed
- ◆ Meeting legal and ethical requirements
  - ◆ The Data Protection Act (DPA)
    - ◆ UK Act of Parliament
    - ◆ Information relating to living people
    - ◆ Eight principles
      - ◆ Fairly and lawfully
      - ◆ Specified and lawful purposes
      - ◆ Adequate, relevant and not excessive
      - ◆ Accurate and, where necessary, kept up to date
      - ◆ Not be kept for longer than is necessary
      - ◆ Processed in accordance with the rights of data subjects
      - ◆ Technical and organisational measures
      - ◆ Personal data shall not be transferred

Managing yourself

- ◆ Setting personal objectives
  - ◆ Objectives related to value
  - ◆ Objectives related to outputs
- ◆ SMART objectives
  - ◆ Specific
  - ◆ Measurable
  - ◆ Achievable
  - ◆ Relevant
  - ◆ Time-bound
- ◆ Working to achieve objectives
  - ◆ Set short-term goals

- ◆ Identify the tasks
- ◆ Identify the time
- ◆ Identify the resources
- ◆ Prioritise your objectives and goals
- ◆ Produce a time and resource plan
- ◆ Perform tasks, compare performance to plan
- ◆ Revise the plan
- ◆ Effective resource utilisation
  - ◆ Resources are scarce
  - ◆ Demand often exceeds supply
  - ◆ Resources must be allocated to higher priority tasks
  - ◆ Mediating is a key role of managers
- ◆ Completing tasks on time
  - ◆ Most objectives have three dimensions
    - ◆ The scope and quality of the task
    - ◆ The cost of the task
    - ◆ The time taken to perform the task
  - ◆ These are in conflict
  - ◆ One is likely to be most important
- ◆ Closing out customer enquiries
  - ◆ Marketing is the responsibility of everyone
  - ◆ The same is true of customer service
  - ◆ Customer service tasks must be accorded high priority
  - ◆ External customers should take precedence over internal customers
- ◆ Monitoring achievement and success
  - ◆ Record and monitor all progress
  - ◆ Review your effectiveness
  - ◆ Keep a record of your achievements

Assessment information

Both units will have their own assessment and be as follows:

Unit 1 – What is Marketing? – A 1 hour online test, consisting of objective format questions

Unit 2 – Understanding Customer Relationships – A written project made up of a number of short work-based tasks

Success in an assessment associated with each unit will lead to the award of that unit. Students who wish to be awarded the CIM Introductory Certificate will have to successfully complete the assessments associated with both units.

Practice work-based assessments

Role

Your manager is interested in developing a better understanding of the organisation's internal and external customers and wishes to know how this can assist in designing appropriate marketing activities that will engage and support customers, and in this way achieve long-term customer loyalty.

During a meeting with the marketing team, it was felt that it would be useful to review different approaches that a range of other organisations use to develop their internal and external customer relationships.

In your role as a marketing assistant, you have been asked to review the case studies provided in the article on pages 101 to 104, which profile different organisations and their individual approaches to managing customer relationships. Using the case studies as supporting material, address the following tasks:

Task 1: Meeting differing customer needs (25% weighting)

Using the resources provided on British Airways, produce a presentation consisting of *ten* slides with supporting notes, suitable for presentation to the marketing team.

The presentation should:

◆　Briefly describe the specific initiatives adopted by British Airways to more closely meet customer needs.

◆　Compare these initiatives with those adopted by *one* of British Airways' competitors.

◆　Identify the strengths and weaknesses of *two* of these initiatives.

◆　Explain what other organisations can learn from these approaches.

Word count 750 words, excluding relevant appendices

Task 2: The customer facing role (25% weighting)

With reference to the B&Q case study, your manager has asked you to produce an e-mail for circulation internally to all customer facing personnel that:

◆　Identifies the qualities and interpersonal skills needed by customer facing staff as representatives of an organisation

◆　Explains the importance of good verbal and non-verbal communication when dealing with customers, using illustrative examples.

Word count 750 words, excluding relevant appendices

Task 3: Information for marketing decisions (35% weighting)

You are required by your manager to produce an informal report for circulation to relevant departments to demonstrate how a better understanding of customer needs can benefit organisations.

For your organisation, or one of your choice, prepare a report that covers the following tasks, using examples to illustrate your points:

◆ Provide a background to your chosen organisation, its customer base and product/ service range (two sides of A4 maximum).

◆ Identify the needs of *two* different customer groups.

◆ Describe how internal and external information sources can help the organisation to understand the buying behaviour of these *two* customer groups.

◆ Outline the different methods that are used by the organisation to obtain feedback from these *two* customer groups.

◆ Recommend *two* promotional tools that could be used to develop and maintain relationships with these groups, giving reasons for your choice.

◆ Identify the internal departments to which your report should be circulated, giving reasons for your choice.

Word count 1,000 words, excluding relevant appendices

Task 4: Planning and measuring personal performance (15% weighting)

Having completed the previous tasks given and, in preparation for your appraisal with your manager, you have been asked to obtain feedback about your skills, attributes and performance from a range of people that you know well. These may include fellow students, tutors, friends, family, colleagues and/or supervisors. You should interview a maximum of *four* people.

Produce a discussion document for use at your appraisal that:

◆ Summarises the feedback received on your skills, attributes and performance.

◆ Briefly analyses the feedback received, identifying your strengths and areas for development.

◆ Identifies a set of personal objectives for the next *12* months that addresses your areas for development.

◆ Outlines how your performance against these objectives would be measured.

Word count 500 words, excluding relevant appendices

Feedback and answers

Unit 1

Question 1.1

Where demand far exceeds supply and the consumer is not discerning due to the shortage of this product or service. Twenty years or so ago this was particularly true within the former Eastern bloc countries where queues formed to buy food and goods irrespective of quality. In some cases those queuing did not know the precise goods they were queuing for!

Question 1.2

Customers were loyal to these stores because of the recognition and personal attention they received. These small stores have been virtually wiped out through the advent of supermarkets.

♦ Supermarkets have a much wider variety of goods: The average grocery store had 800 SKUs on its shelves. Supermarkets today have 30,000 or more SKUs.

♦ Mass marketing took over.

♦ Prices came down.

♦ Variety increased.

Food purchases fell from 31% of the average family budget in 1950 to about 10% today, yet the food we buy with that 10% is better in quality and quantity to that bought with 31% in 1950. We have all gained.

At the same time, we have lost something valuable. Companies today have tens of thousands, in some cases millions, of customers. We do not know who they are. We cannot recognise them and talk to them as the old corner grocers did. Loyalty has disappeared. Customers are loyal until tomorrow's newspaper, or until they click the next item in an Internet search engine, or until they see a promotion for something at another store and they are gone. What is true of grocery stores is also true of department stores, chemists, hardware stores, office supply stores, banks, cinemas – virtually every sales organisation today.

Answers to objective test questions

A: 2

B: 3

C: 1

D: 3

E: 2

F: 1

Unit 2

Activity 2.4

Some selected issues are shown below:

♦   **Political** – Fast food; its source, manufacture and consumption have become politicised.

♦   **Economic**– Shifts in disposable income, changes in amounts people are prepared to spend when eating out.

♦   **Social** – Move to healthy eating, Atkins diet and concerns over food production.

♦   **Technological** – Evidence regarding addictive foods.

♦   **Environmental** – Customers' lack of care in disposing of containers.

♦   **Legal** – Raft of food laws, potential liability cases from overweight people.

Note that the skill is not to produce a generalised list but to develop a focused analysis relevant to the marketing context being considered.

Answers to objective test questions

A: 2

B: 1

C: 1

D: 3

E: 2

F: 3

G: 2

H: 2

Unit 3

Activity 3.3

Only selected issues are given below. You may well have considered additional aspects.

♦ Weekly supermarket run replaced by Internet ordering and home delivery.

♦ High-street travel agents are on the decline as more people 'e'-book travel and hotels directly.

♦ Pirate (illegal) radio stations broadcasting alternative music can now become legal and reach a global audience by pod casting over the Internet.

♦ New groups can distribute their music by a similar mechanism. They do not have to hope for a big record company to back them. Minority interest music can become freely available.

♦ How long will the high-street video hire shop last with video on demand over broadband and a large selection of recent films available on a 'pay-per-view' basis?

♦ Already music charts have a 'download' chart. This may ultimately be the death of the high-street 'record' shop. Moreover, it may change the way artists release material. Now if you only want four tracks from an album, you can choose to download only these tracks rather than buy the whole album.

♦ Portable sensors monitoring key health parameters (e.g. blood pressure) can communicate to and from a domestic home base using wireless technology (e.g. Bluetooth) and link the patient to the surgery for remote diagnosis.

♦ Specialist surgery is difficult to provide in lightly populated areas. Experiments are under way with medical robotics. A specialist surgeon in a major city may be able to complete a procedure remotely in a regional small hospital many hundreds of miles away. In part, the 'digital doctor' might replace the 'flying doctor'.

♦ E-banking is popular with customers (the bank that is always open) and with the banks (vastly reduced costs when compared with services at a high-street branch).

Activity 3.5

♦ Speed
♦ Flexibility
♦ Convenience
♦ Attractive use of time
♦ Potential for lower prices
♦ Potential for shopping around easily
♦ Potential for databases.

Answers to objective test questions

A: 2

B: 1

C: 3

D: 3

E: 1

F: 3

G: 1

H: 2

I: 2

J: 1

K: 2

L: 3

M:2

Unit 4

Activity 4.1

Economic/task factors (price, delivery, location, quality, reliability, customer care, after care)

Non-task factors (personal risk or gain, previous decisions, politics, those influencing the purchaser, perception)

Or, probably, some combination of both.

Significant B2B marketing mix features include quality assurance, reliability, delivery, price and after sales service.

Activity 4.2

The consumer is a participant in the service process. Environmental surroundings of the service operation need attention, for example, the decor of a hairdressers, the cleanliness of the hospital ward, etc.

Services are perishable therefore consideration might be given to differential pricing, for example, seats left unsold on airplanes one hour before flight might have to be heavily discounted.

Services are intangible, communication might recognise that feelings and emotions are important (e.g. 'sleep safely with house cover from Royal Life').

Services are people-orientated and the characteristics of the workforce determine the effectiveness of the service. The implication is that attention must be paid to key human resourcing issues such as recruitment and training.

Output measurement is less easy to evidence, therefore multiple indicators might be stressed, for example, length of hospital stay, cost of operation, post-operation support, etc.

Answers to objective test questions

A: 1

B: 2

C: 3

D: 2

E: 2

F: 3

Unit 5

Answers to objective test questions

A: 2

B: 3

C: 2

D: 2

E: 2

F: 2

G: 1

H: 1

I: 3

Unit 8

Activity 8.1

Differentiate – can be used in two ways, first to bring attention to a unique attribute that the product/service can offer such as the Dyson bagless vacuum system, and secondlto try to provide a point of difference between products where very little difference actually exists. For example, Daz washes whiter, Persil cares and Ariel digests stains but they all get clothes clean.

Remind – is often used for products in the maturity stage of the product life cycle. Well known and probably used by all at some time, people need to be reminded to use again or to use more frequently, for example Kellogg's cereals, Lemsips, Horlicks, After Eight mints and so on.

Inform – is often used where the potential customers need to make an informed decision about the product service choice they are about to make, because their personal circumstances will mean they need a slightly different product to the next person. Financial products such as pensions, insurance and mortgages fall into this category as well as mobile phones and related airtime packages.

Persuade – often used for luxury items or again products that have very little real difference between them. Think of the strapline attached to the L'Oreal range 'Because you're worth it'. Often used for chocolate and other nice things to eat, for example Mr Kipling's 'exceedingly good' cakes.

Index